StarGates

Squares, oppositions, destiny
& Karma 7, 116

StarGates

*Essays on Astrology, Symbolism and
the Synchronistic Universe*

Ray Grasse

Inner Eye Publications/Chicago, Illinois 2020

Also by Ray Grasse:

The Waking Dream: Unlocking the Symbolic Language of Our Lives

Signs of the Times: Unlocking the Symbolic Language of World Events

Under a Sacred Sky: Essays on the Philosophy and Practice of Astrology

An Infinity of Gods: Conversations with an Unconventional Mystic

Urban Mystic: Recollections of Goswami Kriyananda

Cover photo courtesy of NASA (photographed by astronaut Scott Kelly)

Typeset by Amnet Systems

Inner Eye Publications | Chicago, Illinois

ISBN-13: 9798682515103

For Tem Tarriktar and Kate Sholly, whose friendship and support over the years I'll always be grateful for

What you do is what the whole universe is doing, at the place you call here and now.

— Alan Watts

TABLE OF CONTENTS

ACKNOWLEDGEMENTS

I want to express my gratitude to all those who offered feedback, support or friendship during the writing of this book, including Judith Wiker, Laurence Hillman, Bill and Sharon Hogan, Barbara Keller, Linda Puffer, Colleen Mauro, Greg Bogart, Normandi Ellis, Dave Gunning, Jon Parks, Elizabeth Avedon, Kirk Baldwin, Gale Ahrens, Paula Finnegan, Maureen Cleary, Goswami Kriyananda, Shelly Trimmer, Debby Sher, Victoria Martin, Nan Geary, Allison Gawor, Dany Petrova, Ronnie Grishman, Gary Lachman, Bess Demopolous, Jane Wodening, Mary Plumb, Tony Howard, Richard Tarnas, John David Ebert, Sharon Steffensen, Maureen Cleary, Richard Smoley, Karin Hoffman, and of course my parents, Raymond and Catherine. I also want to extend a special thanks to The Urania Trust for their support, without whom this book wouldn't have been possible. My deepest appreciation to you all!

PREFACE

During the more than four decades I've been actively involved with astrology, my sense of wonder about this art has only deepened. Time and again, it's revealed itself to be a seemingly bottomless well of knowledge concerning not only human psychology but the cosmos itself. It was that original spirit of wonder which drove me to continue my explorations into this discipline through the years, and led me to share my thoughts about its myriad insights with others.

What follows is a collection of my essays on many different aspects of astrology, ranging from the down-to-earth and practical to the philosophical and abstract. I begin with the simplest and move from there into the more complex. Many of these have been published previously, quite a few not, but even those which appeared in print before have undergone considerable tweaking to reflect my changing views. While there is a general thematic unity underlying all the chapters, each essay is intended to work as a standalone discussion unto itself, so each can be read without having to really know what comes before or after it (though that helps).

While I hope this work stimulates your own thinking about the deeper implications of the astrological art, I also hope it provides working astrologers with a variety of practical, hands-on methods they find useful in their work with clients, family members or friends. That's because, in the end, astrology isn't simply about wonder, inspiration, and philosophical stimulation—important and enjoyable as these may be—but about how we can use the knowledge of the heavens to improve and enrich our lives, while helping others navigate the challenging straights of their own daily experiences. I hope this book provides a good deal of both.

—Ray Grasse, August 2020

CHAPTER 1

MUSINGS ON MUSIC,
MAGIC, AND ASTROLOGY

Some of my earliest memories are those of music—listening to my mother play the piano, hearing songs on the radio or the family record player, or memorizing theme songs from TV shows or movies. My mother noticed this early fascination and arranged for me to have weekly lessons with a very stern, strictly-by-the-book German piano teacher down the street from us.

I took those lessons for five years—and they felt like dog years. That's because she taught music much the same way that many other instructors teach music, I've since learned: by focusing entirely on practice, memorization, and reading sheet music, with little or no emphasis on composing or improvising. Little or no emphasis on *creating*, in other words. I've likened the situation to a child finally being allowed to go out onto the playground only to be told he had to spend the entire time just doing calisthenics. That definitely wasn't for me. When I finally told my mother I just couldn't take it any longer, she was heartbroken.

It was three years later that I wandered back to the piano, shortly followed by the guitar. This time, though, I focused my energies mainly on improvising and composing, and it felt like an entirely different world. I came alive whenever I played music, making things up in the moment or composing rough little songs and instrumentals. I realized at that point that I didn't want to simply memorize or perform other people's music, like Timmy the trumpet player one block over, who eventually wound up performing with big symphony orchestras around the world. All power to Timmy, I thought, but I wanted to hear what was inside of *me*, however clumsy and imperfect that might prove to be.

I was a shy, seriously uptight kid and didn't date at all through high school, and while I had a few good friends I always preferred to spend my time at home working on my creative projects, including music. I followed the popular music scene closely, which throughout the 1960s and early 70s offered up an extraordinary buffet of new and exciting recordings on a constant basis. Every week, it seemed as though some great new album would be released. One week, it might be something by the Beatles, the next week, Bob Dylan or the Rolling Stones, the Four Tops, Burt Bacharach, the Moody Blues, Jimi Hendrix, Joni Mitchell, Stevie Wonder—and on and on it went, a virtual tsunami of sonic riches. In a different vein, I was also discovering the music of Debussy, whose compositions held a nearly transcendental power for me, like hearing music streaming in from other worlds or dimensions. It still feels that way to me sometimes.

But things started changing in my 20s, when I began turning my attention more to reading, writing, and thinking about philosophical matters. Up to that point, I'd practically shunned academic interests, believing (arrogantly) that the arts were far superior to mere intellectual pursuits. But the more I began looking into philosophy, literature, science, and history, the more I not only came to appreciate those fields, I also began to realize I didn't seem to *think* in quite the same way as many others around me did, at least those more academically trained than myself.

For example, rather than follow lines of thought in relatively linear, logical ways, I tended to think about subjects *laterally*, focusing more on cross-associations and analogies, free-associating between disciplines and subjects in ways that didn't always make sense in conventional contexts. (While I was ruminating to a friend about a curious synchronicity I noticed in the news one day, he remarked to me, "You have a strange way of thinking about things, Ray." By his standards, I'm sure he was right.)

It was then that I began to wonder if all this might have something to do with music. I read an article discussing research that suggested musical education in childhood appeared to wire the brain differently than more conventional studies and learning, creating different kinds of neural pathways through the brain. That made sense to me. I'd always been fascinated by harmony in music, but I was now becoming fascinated by "harmonies" between events, phenomena, historical episodes, and subjects. I began to suspect that maybe my brain had been wired by music to search out those kinds of connections. Sometimes those connections were silly and meaningless, while at other times they seemed more substantial—like noticing similarities between ancient Rome and modern America, or noticing how certain themes seemed to pop up in different movies or books around the exact same time, despite there being no obvious connection between them. Things like that.

My eye for analogies and correspondences came in especially handy when I began delving into subjects like astrology and synchronicity, since those were based heavily on analogies and correspondences. How could a prominent Neptune in someone's horoscope relate to their love for sailing, or even a propensity for alcohol? Or how could a strong activation of Uranus in the sky possibly explain a sudden rash of aviation accidents in the news? Those were the sorts of connections that made no sense at all to my literal-minded friends, but for anyone with a brain tuned to harmonies and correspondences, they seem quite natural.

My love of music stimulated my thinking in other ways as well. For instance, whenever I've had the good fortune of attending a musical performance that moved me deeply, I'd be reminded of the close resonance between our English words for "music" and "magic." Music is the close sister of magic, and there's deep

3

mystery in its ability to transform consciousness, with its proportions and ratios stirring chords in the depths of the soul. Both of those arts—music and magic—employ intricately arranged elements that act on the unconscious in ways the rational mind can't truly fathom.

But how is it that patterns of sounds can affect our awareness and emotions so profoundly? It has nothing at all to do with logic, and instead operates deep down in subterranean caverns of the psyche, far below the brightly lit plateaus of consciousness and rationality. This is something we take for granted whenever we tap our foot or sing to some piece of music in the shower, but we really shouldn't, because it's truly profound and mysterious.

In turn, that led me to contemplate another aspect of music, what we call "beat." There are many factors that go to make up any piece of music—melody, instrumentation, tonal scale, etc. But the framework of any composition is its *rhythm*, or *beat*. When you look at a musical score, there is generally a time signature indicated, such as 4/4, 3/4, or 2/4, which establishes the rhythm. Time signature is to music what a skeleton is to a body; it's the structure on which the flesh and the muscles of music hang.

But this had me wondering whether a person's *life* doesn't also have a "time signature." For instance, some of us live according to the rhythmic beat of hours (like a radio announcer who delivers the news at the top of each hour), while some of us live according to the rhythm of days and weeks (like your average five-day-a-week worker), and still others live more according to the seasons (like a farmer).

But astrology suggests it's considerably more complex than that, since each person's horoscope embodies a *rich network* of cycles and rhythms, from those of the Sun and Moon to those of all the planets. Each planetary orbit establishes a kind of "beat," not just in the way these bodies circle back around to their starting points but also in the ways they interact with one another to create a complex weave of celestial frequencies. Our personality and emotions are an expression of our own symphony of rhythms, notes, and harmonies, all unfolding through time.

There is one other way music influenced my way of thinking about astrology. I'm sometimes asked by students how much we are limited by our horoscopes, and whether we have any real free will to act differently from what our planetary patterns describe. My answer has always been that a horoscope is like a piece of sheet music in some ways, in that it presents certain boundaries and structures but allows for enormous leeway in how we interpret those notes.

For example, think of how differently a musical composition such as Beethoven's "Moonlight Sonata" would be played by a classical pianist, a rock-and-roller, a jazz musician, or even as programmed by a robot. Our horoscope is a bit like that, in that the patterns may appear to be set in concrete, yet the performance of them doesn't have to be. We might even choose to improvise wildly around those basic themes, if we wanted to. That may help to explain why two people born around the same time, like twins, can seem so different from one another.

But that difference in musical styles likely holds another secret of interest to astrologers, which I'd convey through a strange question: *What style of music is most beautiful?* Would it be soft, pastoral music? Complex baroque compositions? Sad orchestral works? Happy pop tunes? Rock music? Country? Gospel? Jazz?

As even a moment's reflection should reveal, it's a meaningless query, since "beauty" isn't so much a function of a particular style as it is of *the quality of talent brought to it.* Pick any particular musical style, and you'll likely find a wide range of quality in works composed in that style—some brilliant and beautiful, others badly written or even unlistenable.

Take the category of "sad orchestral" music, for instance. There are pieces of music that are sad but are also beautiful, like Samuel Barber's "Adagio for Strings," Mozart's "Requiem," or even Hank Williams' "I'm So Lonesome I Could Cry." Or, consider music in a more discordant vein, like Stravinsky's "Rite of Spring." While it shocked audiences at its premiere in 1913, it has a unique beauty all its own. Or take rock music. There are some truly awful pieces of rock, and then there are works like Neil Young's "Heart of Gold," the Beatles' "A Day in the Life," or Marvin Gaye's "I Heard It Through the Grapevine."

What am I getting at here? Just this: Some horoscopes have a more intrinsically "sad" quality or style (due, say, to a Saturn–Moon conjunction in the 1st house), while others display a rougher, more discordant" style (for example, lots of Aries or Scorpio, with a couple squares to Mars thrown in for good measure); while still others have a "happier" or more inspiring style (for instance, Jupiter–Venus in Leo trine the Moon in Sagittarius). In short, there are many different horoscopic moods or "styles."

A couple of years ago, I heard someone complain about their difficult horoscope, and how they wished they'd been born with a happier, more "positive" chart. Okay, I get that. But I also believe in playing the hand you're dealt, and toward that end *any* horoscope can give rise to great things, if played right. Helen Keller didn't have an easy horoscope, but she certainly made great "music" with it.

Which leaves us with the question: What "music" are you composing with *your* horoscope?

This essay first appeared in the August/September 2019 issue of The Mountain Astrologer magazine.

CHAPTER 2

STARGATES: PLANETARY PORTALS AND WINDOWS IN TIME

I n his book *The Invention of Air: A Story of Science, Faith, Revolution, and The Birth of America,* writer Steven Johnson explores the life and mind of famed scientist Joseph Priestley (1733-1804). As part of his study, Johnson points out the extraordinary streak of research and pioneering work Priestley undertook between the years 1767 and 1775. Besides the discovery of oxygen, that streak included publishing major papers on electricity, inventing new apparatuses for the creation of electrical charge, making a breakthrough in our understanding of photosynthesis, and writing more than fifty books and pamphlets on politics, education, and faith.

And if that wasn't enough, he also invented soda water.

Reflecting on that extraordinary run of achievements, Johnson then asks the reader to consider the question of not just *what* happened, but *why:*

"Intellectual historians have long wrestled with the strangeness of this kind of streak. The thinker plods along, publishing erratically making incremental progress, and then, suddenly—the floodgates open and a thousand interesting ideas seem to pour out. It's no mystery that there are geniuses in the world, who come into life with innate cognitive skills that are nurtured and provoked by cultural environments over time. It's not hard to understand that these people are smarter than the rest of us, and thus tend to come up with a disproportionate share of the Big Ideas. *The mystery is why, every now and again, one of these people seems to get a hot hand."* (Emphasis mine) [1]

"Hot hand," indeed. What explains why certain historical periods are times when important new ideas burst onto the scene in profusion, not just for single individuals but for society as a whole, almost as if a dam had burst and creative works in various fields flooded into and transformed the culture?

Not too surprisingly, astrology offers some possible answers to that question. As even a cursory study of history shows, the movements of the heavens coincide in a variety of striking ways with cultural developments down here on Earth.

But while there are any number of celestial patterns which appear to accompany significant developments in society, it's clear that configurations involving the outer, slower-moving planets—Uranus, Neptune, and Pluto—play an especially important role in opening up "portals," those periods when novel ideas, creative works, and inventions flow more readily and frequently into global consciousness.

One of the advantages of having lived through a number of decades myself is the chance to witness, first-hand, a variety of significant planetary configurations involving those slow-movers. Among other things, it's allowed me to sense how there's definitely something "in the air" when these bodies join forces. Such periods seem "richer" somehow, more pregnant with possibility, for better or worse—not just creatively but scientifically, politically, even spiritually. It's almost as though the proverbial veil between worlds thins during such times and allow us access to the energies, ideas and feelings of non-ordinary states of consciousness, and perhaps even other dimensions.

In previous articles and books I've written about a number of these periods from history, including the epic conjunction of Uranus and Neptune that took place during the 1990s. Among other things, that was a time when global culture was turning its attention to more alternate forms of spirituality along with an assortment of unconventional subjects that included explorations of the paranormal and the possibility of extraterrestrial civilizations. TV shows like the "X-Files," "Sightings," and "Star Trek: Next Generation" became hugely popular during this time while, in the real world, the Hubble Telescope was literally giving us access to other previously unknown worlds beyond our own.

But I'd like to turn my attention to one event in particular from that period which struck me as an especially telling symbol for the development I'm describing here. I'm referring to the blockbuster Sci-Fi movie *Stargate*, which premiered in 1994 near the height of that planetary conjunction, and featured at its center a technology that operated as a portal through which individuals could travel through the cosmos—the so-called "stargate" of the movie's title.

© Lions Gate Home Entertainment

By stepping through this unusual device—highlighted by various celestial symbols along its metallic rim—individuals were transported to distant worlds instantaneously. The fact that this cinematic image emerged into popular culture exactly at the peak of this planetary configuration struck me as deeply synchronistic in the way it coincided with what was happening in the world according to astrology. Under the influence of those outer planetary forces, it really did seem as though a portal was opening up in the collective consciousness, enabling us to access other worlds of both thought and feeling.

(The synchronicities didn't end there, by the way. In the movie's narrative, the "other worlds" opened up by this device were distinctly Egyptian in nature. As it so happened, the early 90s was likewise a time when Egypt-related topics became hugely popular in both mainstream and alternative circles. Just one year earlier, John Anthony West's provocative TV special "Mystery of the Sphinx" drew blockbuster ratings for NBC, while books, magazines and TV shows on ancient Egypt sold like wildfire throughout the entire 90s. Among the more controversial books of the period was Adrian Gilbert and Robert Bauval's controversial tome *The Orion Mystery,* which suggested that the three main pyramids on the Giza Plateau were intentionally positioned to reflect the three main stars of the belt of Orion. [Adding to this synchronicity was the fact that same constellation occupied a key place along the rim of the aforementioned device featured in the movie *Stargate.*] Indeed, it seems as though Uranus/Neptune conjunctions are archetypally related to Egypt-related interests in a more general way. I say that because the previous time those two planets came together, during the early 1820s, was likewise a period when interest in ancient Egypt reached a fever pitch, climaxing in arguably the most important development in all of modern Egyptology: the deciphering of ancient Egyptian hieroglyphics by the French scholar Jean-François Champollion in 1821.)

To my mind, that cinematic image of the stargate not only seemed like an apt metaphor for what was happening throughout that period but for what happens during *any* period involving major configurations between the outer planets. During such times, it's as though a tear in the fabric between worlds opens up, to where we even see a notable surge of interest in spiritualism, mediumship and "channeling," where individuals attempt to communicate with disembodied spirits. This was a trend that flourished during both the 1890s and 1990s.

Now, the early 1990s involved an alignment of only two bodies, Uranus and Neptune, just as the alignment of the 1890s also involved only two bodies, Pluto and Neptune. So it's natural to wonder, what sort of effect would we expect to see if *all three* of the outer planets were to form a major configuration? What kind of "mega-portal" in consciousness would *that* create?

In fact, we have several examples of that from history to study—and they're dramatic indeed. As one example, consider the fact that Uranus, Neptune and Pluto moved into an extremely rare "Grand Trine" during the years 1769 and 1770. Did anything important happen during that period? Aside from that being the era which paved the way for the American and French Revolutions, those two years saw the birth of such towering cultural figures as Beethoven, Napoleon, Hegel, and Alexander von Humboldt.

As one way to think about the meaning of a period like this, consider how the outer planets carve out exceptionally broad orbits in space, far beyond the boundaries defined by the visible inner planets. This offers a helpful analogy for how the outer planets symbolize larger, more generational concerns beyond strictly personal domains of experience. With that in mind, note how each of the four individuals I cited born during that particular Grand Trine expressed uniquely broad visions in their work, with a predilection for especially "big ideas." In the case of Beethoven, those ideas were musical in nature; for Hegel, they were philosophical and historical; for Napoleon, they involved broad social reforms and military conquests (extremely bloody ones, alas); while for von Humboldt, that "bigness" manifested in the scope of his extraordinary travels and scientific speculations. It's also worth mentioning that 1769 and 1770 also saw the birth of poet William Wordsworth and the German writer Frederick Holderlin, while in 1770 Captain James Cook became the first European to set foot on the continent of Australia, thus inaugurating a turbulent new phase in the life of that continent and its peoples.

But it's also important to point out those two years happened to coincide precisely with the creative "portal" I opened up this article with, when Joseph Priestly experienced his astonishing run of scientific achievements. So when writer Steven Johnson pondered what might account for the "hot hand" Priestley experienced at that time, he might well have considered the role played by astrology!

Even comparatively modest configurations involving these three outer planets can pack a formidable punch of their own. For instance, in the early 1940s those bodies moved into a somewhat less dramatic configuration when Uranus formed a trine to Neptune, and those two bodies in turn formed a sextile to Pluto. Although this was a time of considerable turmoil, happening as it did in the midst of World War II, this was also a period of extraordinary cultural ferment in cinema, literature, and music. To cite just one area, consider some of the influential pop musical figures born during this outer planet trifecta: Joni Mitchell, Mick Jagger, George Harrison, Jimmy

Page, Barbara Streisand, Brian Wilson, Paul McCartney, Jimi Hendrix, and Keith Richards. In fact, Joseph Priestly was himself born during a configuration involving these three planets, albeit of a slightly different sort: at his birth on March 13, 1733, Neptune was opposing Uranus, while Pluto was in turn aspecting those two. In short, it's not necessarily just the so-called "harmonious" aspects between the three outers that give rise to influential time-windows or individuals, but any close contacts at all.

But if any configuration involving the three outer planets would seem to be important, that would be the conjunction, when the energies of planets join forces in especially close proximity. Have the three slow-moving outers ever joined up in that way?

As a matter of fact, there *was* one such period—indeed, it was the only time in all of recorded history that we know of, and it took place during the 6th century BCE. In the five decades between the 590s and the 550s BCE, Uranus, Neptune and Pluto came into close alignment, and it was an occurrence so rare it won't take place again until the year 3370 AD. This was a period that philosopher and astrologer Richard Tarnas refers to as "historically unprecedented and still unparalleled." He goes on to write:

"These decades constituted the very heart of the axial age that brought forth the birth of many of the world's principal religions and spiritual traditions. This was the age of Buddha, bringing the birth of Buddhism in India, of Mahavira and Jainism in India, of Lao-Tsu and the birth of Taoism in China, which was followed a decade later by the birth of Confucius, Lao-Tsu's younger contemporary. This same epoch coincided with that sudden wave of major prophets in ancient Israel, Jeremiah, Ezekiel, and the second Isaiah, through whom a deep transformation in the Judaic image of the divine and understanding of human history was forged, one that is still evolving. In this same era the Hebrew scriptures were first compiled and redacted. The traditional dating for the immensely influential Zoroaster and the birth of Zoroastrianism in Persia, though still elusive to historians, has long centered on the sixth century." [2]

Into that time frame we could also insert the names of such important figures as King Nebuchadnezzar of Babylon, the Greek philosophers Thales and Anaximander, the first great lyric poet of Western culture Sappho, and even Pythagoras, who was born during this era. This wasn't simply an important period in history, in other words, it may well be the *single most important period in all of recorded history*, in terms of seismic cultural developments that left a lasting imprint on world culture for centuries or even millennia to come.

The Personal and the Collective

As should be obvious, not every individual alive during such historically potent periods responds as fully or creatively to the energies they offer. What accounts for the way some individuals seem more attuned to their possibilities, while others are more oblivious to them?

Here again, astrology offers some useful answers. I've sometimes likened it to how elephants can hear certain frequencies inaudible to humans because of the longer wavelengths involved, which human ears can't detect. To my mind, that's analogous to the perception of subtle states associated with the outer planets, Uranus, Neptune and Pluto. These represent especially long "wavelengths of consciousness," as it were, which only certain individuals seem able to hear. What allows them to detect those subtle vibrations? Simply put, it has to do with how their horoscopes are attuned to those specific planets, whether through close aspects between personal planets and the outer bodies, or through the prominent placement of one or more of those slow-movers in the horoscope, such as conjunct the Ascendant or Midheaven.

For example, take Beethoven and the outer planet Grand Trine that was in effect at his birth. When we look at his horoscope (December 16, 1770), we see several points of contact between his personal planets and the outer planets, including the fact that his Moon formed a tight square to Neptune, while Venus was in a wide conjunction to Pluto—suggesting a strongly creative or spiritual connection with the cosmic forces in play. Or in the case of Napoleon, he was born under the influence of that same Grand Trine, but his *Mars* conjuncted the Neptune leg of that Grand Trine, suggesting his attunement to that generational energy was more militaristic in nature. Likewise, when we look at all of the influential pop music luminaries of the early 1940's I mentioned, such as Joni Mitchell, George Harrison, and Mick Jagger, we invariably find close contacts between personal planets and that outer planet triad.

In all these instances, in other words, we see that elephant-like ability to hear "broader wavelengths" of consciousness that concern larger swaths of humanity, rather than just the interests of isolated individuals. In and of itself, that ability is neither inherently positive or negative; after all, Napoleon and Hitler clearly had a capacity for "big ideas" with an attunement to global concerns, and both of them left a trail of death and destruction behind. Whenever these planetary portals of consciousness open, they can unleash either angels or demons. Likewise, it's worth remembering that the extraordinary energies of the late '60s not only gave us the Moon Landing and Woodstock but also Charles Manson and the tragic rock concert at Altamont.

In the end, only one thing seems certain: whenever these star-gates open wide, the world is never quite the same again.

This essay first appeared in the November/December 2019 issue of Dell Horoscope Magazine.

CHAPTER 3

DO THE PHYSICAL PLANETS HOLD CLUES INTO THEIR MEANING AS ASTROLOGICAL PRINCIPLES?

During a conversation in 1978 with the yogi and astrologer Shelly Trimmer, I was intrigued by a remark he made at one point about the significance of Jupiter in the horoscope, and how its qualities were reflected in that planet's astronomical features.

For astrologers, he said, Jupiter symbolizes a person's broader capacity for logic and their philosophical perspective on life (as opposed to Mercury, which concerns small perspectives and is more concerned with processing *data* or *information*). In terms of mythological symbolism, that's why Jupiter is associated by some esotericists with the figure of Moses, Shelly said, since he was the great *law-giver*, the arbiter of society's morality and values.

But that symbolic function was reflected in this planet's role in our solar system, he added. He explained how Jupiter is so large compared with the other planets that it establishes the plane of the ecliptic for the entire solar system; its gravitational presence is so great that all the other planets are forced to fall into line with its orbit, thus making it the *astronomical* "law-giver" of the solar system, as it were. In an analogous way, the astrological Jupiter establishes the framework of our *ideological* and *moral* perspectives throughout life.

I thought a great deal about that way of looking at things long after our conversation, and wondered just how far it could be applied it to the other bodies of our solar system. What I'd like to do here is expand on some thoughts I first touched on in my book *The Waking Dream* in this spirit, beginning with the two luminaries.

The Sun

The most obvious feature of our Sun in the simple but profound fact it's the only light-emitting body in our system. Whereas all the other planets and their moons shine by its reflected light, the Sun is completely self-illuminating. Symbolically, that speaks to the fact that the astrological Sun is the source of *consciousness,* the essential "ground zero" by which everything else in the chart draws meaning and significance. Although all the other bodies in the horoscope possess a certain meaning of their own, to some extent that's always in reference to the Sun. For that reason, any planetary aspects to the Sun are especially important to study as conduits for (or blockages of) that essential light and the expression of one's core identity.

The fact that the Sun is the central hub of our local system also sheds light on the role it's played in traditional tables of correspondence formulated by mystics through the centuries, based on the so-called "law of analogy." Hence, as the Sun is to the other bodies of our solar system, so gold is to all metals, a king is to his kingdom, honey is to all foods, the heart is to all one's bodily organs, and so on. In other words, the Sun embodies the principles of *centrality* and *preeminence,* and within the horoscope is the symbolic "king" around which everything else in the chart is essentially subordinate. When strongly emphasized in the horoscope, it can also indicate a certain "kingly" desire to stand out from the crowd, in ways indicated by the sign it's in and any aspects being formed to it.

Being the illuminator of the daytime, the Sun also holds a decidedly extravertive and public significance. As I wrote in *The Waking Dream*: "As the orb which illuminates the daytime world, this archetype governs the outer world in general, and thus one's public self-expression. In our lives, the Sun is linked symbolically to fathers and other prominent individuals—those we might call 'stars'—along with all creative or theatrical institutions and situations involving public exposure or recognition." [1]

But while the Sun represents the core awareness of our being, its fiery nature harbors potential dangers, too. Like the desert Sun at noon, where excessive heat can make nourishment or even survival impossible, the Sun in the chart can overpower or "dry up" whatever it comes into contact with, a condition astrologers refer to as *combust*. When overemphasized in a chart, the Sun's influence can give rise to an extreme focus on outer concerns like career or fame without the counterbalancing effects of reflectivity and the inner cultivation of soul—factors governed by our next body, the Moon.

The Moon

While the Sun is the great illuminator of our world, the Moon serves as the great mirror to that solar brilliance. "Radiant with the reflected light of the Sun," I remarked in *The Waking Dream*, "the Moon is associated with the principle of reflectivity and the archetypal feminine in all her aspects. In our lives the Moon governs water, mirrors, women, and the emotions."

Whereas the Sun is outgoing and dynamic in its assertive projection of self, the Moon is reactive, introvertive, and the indicator of our *emotional responses* to situations. In contrast with the Sun, the Moon archetypally rules the night side of life, that time when we retreat from the glare of the marketplace into our own private world. Thus it relates to our dreams, feelings, and the fluid realm of fantasies.

Which brings us to an especially important aspect of the Moon's astronomical features. Unlike the Sun, which is the central light for all the bodies in our solar system, the Moon is strictly a *local* body, and thus holds astrological relevance only for those of us on Earth. That reveals a great symbolic secret about its role in the chart, too. Whereas the Sun astrologically pertains to factors that are more objective and visible for the whole world to see (such as reputation, surface behaviors or achievements, and professional activities), the Moon is more concerned with those dimensions of life that are "closer to home"—i.e., more emotional and private, less obvious for the general public to see. In contrast with the Sun, configurations involving the Moon are thus experienced more subjectively, more internally.

Also note how light from the Sun makes any objects or environments appear sharply defined and distinct, whereas the pale light of the Moon makes distinctions seem blurred and colors muted. Symbolically, that hints at how our emotional perception tends to be more integrative and holistic in nature, geared towards relationships and felt connections rather than fine details and rational distinctions.

Then there is the fact of the Moon's changeability over time, as seen in its various phases during the course of a month. At one point one might look up and see a thin sliver hovering above the horizon, whereas two weeks later it will appear as a complete disc radiating in the night. That offers a beautiful symbol for the changeability of our emotional natures, as well as the famed "moodiness" of those born under its influence.

Mercury

The most obvious feature of this body is the fact that it's the closest to the Sun of all the planets, its orbit never carrying it far away from that solar hub. It therefore embodies a faculty of consciousness that operates just outside of spirit—namely, the *mind*. From *The Waking Dream*:

"The planet closest to the Sun, Mercury is symbolic of the mind, which likewise serves as messenger between spirit and soul, consciousness and matter. Through the principle of Mercury (in Greek, Hermes), we understand meaning in all its forms. For this reason, Mercury/Hermes governs all symbolic systems. The word *hermeneutics*, the art of symbolic interpretation, is based on this association. The fastest of the planets, Mercury hints at the speed and changeability of the mind's operations." [2]

For as close as it is to the Sun, it is fundamentally distinct from it, in a way recalling a quote from poet Paul Valery: "At times *I think*, and at times *I am.*" Being separate from that central point of consciousness is what allows the mind to perceive distinctions, to compare and weigh alternatives. As such, Mercury is the source of all the gifts that rationality offers, from philosophy and science to all forms of genius and creativity. But by the same token, that sense of separation from unity is also the source of all our sufferings and sense of alienation from Spirit, even from ourselves. That fateful interval from the Sun to Mercury thus represents the mythic "step out of the Garden" where one now has access not only to the potentials bestowed by the tree of knowledge of Good and Evil, but all of its problems as well.

In yogic terms, that movement relates to the descent of energies from the level of the head down to that of the throat, or the *Vishudhha* chakra—and with that comes what's referred to as *ahamkara*, or "ego-maker": the awareness of one's own sense of separateness and uniqueness. (Notice how we even refer to that lump in the throat as the "Adam's Apple"!) From the standpoint of the

Sun, there is awareness of pure being but not yet of distinctness or separateness; it is only with Mercury that one acquires the gift—and curse—of the comparing mind, and in turn individuated consciousness.

Another telling feature of Mercury involves its closeness to the Sun's intense heat, making it impossible for any moisture or life to exist on its surface. Symbolically, that equates well to how the mind is itself comparatively "dry" in nature, being largely geared towards logic and factual analysis, with little direct grasp of emotions, sentimentality, or empathy. While that can be especially useful in matters of science, business, or the law, it's not quite so helpful when it comes to relationships and matters of the heart!

Venus

It's fitting that one of the most beautiful lights in the night sky should be associated by astrologers with matters of beauty and love. Its brightness in magnitude is second only to that of the Moon, which likely tells us something important about its magnitude as an organ of the human soul as well.

But there is more than meets the eye to this planet, and quite literally so. For starters, it rotates in a reverse direction on its axis from every other planet (excepting Uranus), thus giving rise to the odd fact that its days are longer than its years! This seems to suggest there is something different about this planet, perhaps implying that its romantic or emotional impulses "flow in the opposite direction" of ordinary embodied life.

Even more dramatic is the extraordinary heat which exists at the planet's surface beneath those luminous clouds, which scientists attribute to a runaway greenhouse effect. That gives Venus an average temperature of 864 degrees F—making it even hotter than the surface of Mercury, despite that latter body's closeness to the Sun. What could this mean? From *The Waking Dream:* "...just as the beauty of this planet conceals an inferno of raging heat at its surface, so the hedonistic pleasures of Venus can incinerate the unwary in its fiery crucible—note, for instance, its association with the word *venereal*. Thus this archetype must be approached with greater caution than planets like Mars or Saturn, which exhibit their dangers up front for all to see." Interestingly, in the Vedic cosmologies of India the planet Venus is viewed in a decidedly mixed way, being associated with the figure *Shukra*—guru/teacher to the *Asuras*, the demonic entities locked in eternal battle with the more spiritually-minded *Devas*.

Another interesting feature of Venus is the fact that its orbit traces out a pentagram shape over time. If you were to look down on the Earth from above the plane of the solar system, you would see the Sun appear to go around the Earth, and from that lofty perspective, over the course of eight years you will see Venus go around the Sun thirteen times, and trace out the image of a five-pointed star. In different cultural systems, five-pointed stars have held various meanings. For the ancient Pythagoreans, it was a mystic symbol of perfection; for sacred geometers it is associated with the Golden Section; for some occultists it represents the principle of the *microcosm*, while in a related way some yogic mystics regard it as symbolizing the sacred "doorway" in the heart of the "Third Eye," or Ajna Chakra. In a general way, it all seems to suggest something important about this planet's role as a key toward unlocking our spiritual potentials, while its deceptively hot temperatures may warn us of what can happen when those Venusian energies are unwisely diverted.

Mars

The most obvious feature associated with this planet is, of course, its *redness*, a color often associated with blood, energy, anger, and fire. Scientists inform us that this color is due to the presence of iron oxide, and its resulting rust. Interestingly, in traditional tables of correspondence, iron is the metal most associated with the planet Mars, which was an association made long before scientists knew anything about the chemical composition of the Red Planet.

Aside from its color, astronomers sometimes speak of the surface of Mars as appearing heavily "scarred," due to various geologic and atmospheric factors. Besides an assortment of impact craters, Mars has the largest canyon in our solar system, *Valles Marineris*, as well as the imprints of two massive tsunamis that ravaged its surface at different times in its history. Combined with the fact that Mars also plays host to the largest dust storms of any planet in our solar system, it's natural to wonder if such features don't say something about the turbulent energies and bruises sometimes stirred up by this planet in our horoscope.

Jupiter

At the start of this article we already saw one of the most distinctive facts about Jupiter —namely, how its size establishes the plane of the ecliptic for the entire solar system, and how that correlates well to its role as the symbolic "law-giver" in our own lives.

But more generally, that massive size seems to suggest a quality of expansiveness in whatever areas it touches in the horoscope. Astrologically, Jupiter has long been associated with hope, positivity, and laughter, and wherever it's placed in the horoscope likewise indicates where we, too, have the potential for abundance and "bigger things." But if Jupiter is afflicted, there can be difficulties allowing for that sense of abundance to express itself—or, conversely, where we may be prone to expand *too* much and not exercise judicious restraint.

Saturn

From *The Waking Dream*: "Of all the planets in the solar system, Saturn exhibits the most visible and dramatic ring system. Symbolically understood, that reflects this planet's long-standing association with the archetypal principles of limitation, matter, structure, and time—in all their constructive and destructive aspects. Without its influence, nothing would have structure or shape, all growth would proceed unchecked; yet when overemphasized, structure becomes constriction and confinement, strangling life and preventing development. In our lives, Saturn thus governs all events which provide limits and structures or test us in any way, including governmental figures or law enforcement officials, parents, delays, or constricting conditions of any sort."

Several planets have ring systems, but none so dramatic as those which encircle Saturn. As a symbol of constriction, rings are neither inherently good or bad, but simply a principle that can be experienced in either constructive or destructive ways. We're all familiar with negative instances of constriction, of course—loss, confinement, delays, depression, and so on. But there are many positive expressions, too. Consider how law enforcement keeps us safe and allows us to live every day without fear of danger (or is designed to, anyway). Or consider the fact there would be no beauty in nature, art, or even the human form if there weren't limits, boundaries, distinctions, or shapes of some kind.

Or think of the way we cement our feelings about commitment in relationships by wearing a ring—a constrictive symbol—specifically on the finger associated by occultists with the Sun, the natural ruler of the 5th house of romance, pleasure, and joy. That the ring symbolizes the fact we're now curtailing and channeling our essential life-expression towards a single other, rather than dispersing it in more open-ended, unstructured ways. It's an act of extreme limitation, yes, yet in a way associated with the deepening of love.

Which brings us to a particularly unexpected feature of this ringed planet. Despite its astrological reputation for "heaviness," Saturn has such a low density that it would float if placed in water! Could that be telling us there is something more subtle and "light" to this planet's influence than we've generally realized? Think for example of the happiness that results from having successfully learned the lessons of Saturn, like the aforementioned person who commits to marriage and makes it work; or the yogi who finds liberation as a result of prolonged self-control. When Aristotle said that with discipline comes freedom, he may just as well have been describing a great truth about Saturn. Gustav Holst, composer of the popular orchestral work *The Planets*, said it all a little differently: "Saturn brings not only physical decay, but also a vision of fulfillment."

Uranus

A valuable key to understanding the trans-Saturnian planets lies in the way they circumscribe such broad orbits in space, extending progressively further out from that solar hub. As I mentioned in a previous chapter, this symbolically suggests that they relate to progressively broader and more collective or universal concerns rather than just one's own personal, provincial interests.

As the first of the trans-Saturnians, Uranus therefore takes on special importance as a "threshold" state demarcating the boundary between personal and collective, local and universal. When Uranus is strongly emphasized in a horoscope, the individual straddles the fence between these two domains, and will generally have easier access to the energies of the collective *zeitgeist*. But unlike Neptune and Pluto, this will generally express itself in more *mental* ways, as in the case of an inventor (like Ben Franklin), a scientist (like Albert Einstein), a media pioneer (like Walt Disney), or a political activist (like Karl Marx).

Besides the fact that Uranus rotates on its axis in a clockwise direction, it's also unusual for the fact that its entire axis is tilted sideways, with its north and south poles positioned where other planets have their equators. It's therefore well-suited in symbolism as an eccentric and "revolutionary" influence in our lives, with its location in the horoscope indicating where we will tend to be unconventional, innovative, or possibly even rebellious in our approach to life.

Neptune

Another way to look at the trans-Saturnian planets is not simply in terms of how broad their orbits are, but in terms of their *depth in space*. For observers here on Earth, the fact that they represent progressively distant points in space suggests that they symbolize *progressively deeper levels of the unconscious.*

By comparison, Uranus is—under ideal conditions—partially visible to the naked eye, and therefore represents a kind of threshold state between conscious and unconscious. Note how the glyph for Uranus resembles an antenna, which is a technology designed to pick up electromagnetic waves on the boundary between material and immaterial; while subtle, In other words, those waves are still ultimately physical in nature. That relates well to the borderline symbolism associated with the astrological Uranus, which represents a faculty of consciousness that allows us to pick up subtle wavelengths from the collective mind-field.

But Neptune is the first planet that's *completely invisible* to the naked eye, and therefore represents a true opening to the invisible world beyond surface appearances. For mystics, it's therefore the organ by which spiritual and supernatural realities are perceived and contacted. It's not coincidental that the birth of modern spiritualism, whereby mediums communicate with the spirits of the dead, took place just two years after the discovery of Neptune, when the Fox sisters of upstate New York claimed to have made contact with the spirit world.

In the arts as well, that sense of "lifting the veil on the visible" was paralleled by the important movement known as *symbolism,* exemplified in literature by such figures as Edgar Allen Poe, Herman Melville, and Charles Baudelaire; and in painting with the founding of the Pre-Raphaelites in 1848 and later figures like

Odilon Redon, Gustave Moreau, Jean Delville, and Paul Gauquin. What creative geniuses like these espoused was as an aesthetic of *suggestiveness* that hinted at layers of meaning beyond the obvious, often involving supernatural themes and hidden networks of "correspondence." Though artists and poets had incorporated symbolic ideas and themes in their work before this (William Blake, for example), it was as if the discovery of the first fully invisible planet inaugurated a major new phase of art based wholly on unseen dimensions of meaning.

But precisely because Neptune provides us with a window into the beyond, it can just as easily open us to the darker dimensions of that unseen world, too, and prompt an escape from our existing, more tangible one. I once knew an artist who painted brilliant canvases depicting beautifully imaginative landscapes done in a surrealistic style, and his horoscope displayed several extremely challenging aspects to Neptune. While doing research on an unrelated subject one day, I happened to discover that he shared a birthday with a famed serial killer who used deceit and misdirection to trap victims and fulfill his own dark fantasies (and who eventually died via lethal injection). Though their horoscopes were similar, it underscored for me just how differently two individuals could utilize that channel to the unseen realms represented by Neptune.

Pluto

Whereas Neptune opens the door to the collective unconscious, it's when we get to Pluto that we truly plunge into the watery depths of being. Astronomers have used different methods to convey just how distant this planet is, such as the fact that it takes light traveling 186,000 miles a second a full eight minutes to get from the Sun to the Earth, whereas it takes a full *five hours* for light to reach distant Pluto.

Perched in that far-away point of space, Pluto's mythological reputation as Lord of the Underworld seems fitting. Not surprisingly, the period immediately around its discovery in 1930 was notable for stories involving the *criminal* underworld, centering particularly around Chicago crime boss Al Capone. When strongly emphasized in a chart, it indicates an ability to access the psyche's subterranean realm, with all of the turbulent and dramatic energies contained therein. For psychologists like Sigmund Freud or Carl Jung, it was an invaluable ally in their exploration of the human unconscious, while for singer Mick Jagger it fueled a career based on singing about life's passions, as well as its "darker" impulses—including even a sympathetic anthem for the devil!

Because of the time it takes light to travel, we also know that the further out into space we gaze, the further into *the past* we are seeing. Literally, when we look at Pluto through our telescopes we are seeing how that planet looked several hours earlier. Viewed symbolically, that suggests that Pluto has something important to do with "the past" in our own lives, so that whenever it triggers a point in the horoscope, old issues or memories tend to resurface into present-day consciousness. That's not necessarily an unpleasant thing. When transiting Pluto came along and formed a harmonious aspect to one client's natal Venus, a lover from many years earlier came back into her life and resurrected passions she had nearly forgotten about. I heard no complaints about Pluto that time.

Also, Pluto's orbit is highly unusual in that it's not on the same plane as the other planets, but is inclined at an angle of 17 degrees to that plane, in addition to which its orbit isn't elliptical so much as oval. Combined, these cause it to move far closer to the Sun at times than at others, and even cross over Neptune's orbit on occasion. That seems an appropriate symbol for the extremism often associated with Pluto, which can lead to wide disparities in behavior from light to dark, and from "sacred" to "profane."

And in light of Pluto's association among astrologers with sexuality, snakes, and all things serpentine, it struck me as particularly fitting that when NASA's New Horizons spacecraft took its first close-up photographs of Pluto, its texture was described by astronomers as looking like "snakeskin"!

Bringing it All Back Home

But what about our own home planet, "Mother Earth"? We don't actually use it in horoscopes the same way we do with the other bodies, simply because it's the very basis of the chart and the ground on which we stand. But that doesn't mean it lacks a meaning or significance of its own. Is there anything we can learn about this body from studying its geological or orbital features? I'd suggest a few things.

For starters, the most obvious feature of our planet when viewed from space is the fact that it's largely covered in *water*. Symbolically, that may suggest this is a planet where the lessons being learned are largely *emotional* in nature. While it's possible other planets and celestial bodies have their own range of emotional and experiential states to offer, Earth seems to serve up something unique— namely, embodied life in complex physical forms that consist primarily of water. If there happen to be wayward souls wandering the cosmos looking for a planet where they can engage in the full spectrum of emotional experience in especially vivid ways, ranging from divine compassion to the most intense hatreds and jealousies, this would seem to be the place to be!

Add to that the fact that Earth is perched between Venus and Mars, which suggests that this is a kind of cosmic "way-station" between the energies and lessons of those two bodies. Like children caught up in a cosmic custody battle, humans are torn between the animalistic, warlike impulses of Mars and the comparatively loving urges of Venus, and its challenge seems to be one of striking a balance between these opposing archetypal forces.

But there is another "polarity" involving our planet which may hold another key toward illumining our place on the evolutionary ladder. I'm referring to the fact that our Moon appears to be exactly the same size in the sky as our Sun. In fact, the Moon's diameter is 400 times smaller than the Sun's, but because the Sun is 400 times further away from us, that difference in size balances out perfectly—which makes solar and lunar eclipses possible. While that coincidence is something we take for granted, it's a unique feature in our solar system—nor has it always been the case with our Earth. That's because scientists inform us that the Moon has slowly been moving away from the Earth over millions of years' time, such that it will eventually appear smaller to us than it does now (which of course means it appeared larger to us in the past than it does currently). Perhaps that tells us something important about this stage on the cosmic timeline, in that there exists a certain balance of archetypal masculine and feminine for those of us on Earth now. Could this present epoch in our planet's long history represent a "window" during which its inhabitants can achieve something otherwise hard to attain—namely, the balancing of polarities mystics sometimes refer to as the "marriage of the Sun and Moon"? It would be nice to think so.

CHAPTER 4

DECODING THE MOST ELEVATED
PLANET IN THE HOROSCOPE

Around the time I first became involved with astrology, there was a lively debate amongst some in the astrological community over the horoscope of singer Bob Dylan, who was still riding the wave of popularity that began for him in the 1960s. One well-known astrologer at the time suggested (apparently via rectification) that the singer was born shortly after dawn. This would have placed both his Sun and the majority of his planets in or around the 12th house.

I had a strong hunch that was wrong, though. My own feeling was that Neptune was likely high in the sky when Dylan was born—a difference that would have meant being born sometime in the evening, rather than in the morning. Why did I think that? Simply, because Neptune—the planet of music, inspiration, and spirituality—seemed to be not only a powerful influence in his life and music, but also a particularly *prominent* and *public* one. Throw in the fact that Dylan came to assume a nearly messianic identity for many of his fans, and it all added up in my mind to his having Neptune somewhere near the top of his chart.

Problem was, no one seemed to have access to Dylan's exact birth time. But I was determined to find out whatever I could.

Asking Bob himself was definitely out of the question, so I set out to locate the next best resource: his mom. Surely *she* would know what time of day he was born, or at least have some general idea. After all, she was there when it happened. So, after a couple weeks of phone calls to any and all Zimmermans (Bob's family name) in the Hibbing, Minnesota area, where Bob was born, I finally tracked her down. Following the death of Bob's dad, Abe, it turned out that she had remarried and moved to the Duluth area.

When I rang the number, she picked up the phone herself, and was surprisingly open to talking. When I got around to asking if she remembered what time Bob was born, she paused for a bit, then finally said, "Yes … I think it was sometime in the evening." Years later, when Bob's birth certificate finally surfaced, lo and behold, the time was listed as mid evening—9:05 p.m., to be precise. The conclusion? Neptune was indeed the highest planet in Dylan's chart, positioned in his 9th house.

I bring up this story to introduce an important factor in understanding any chart and, in some cases, possibly the *most* important indicator—namely, the highest (or most elevated) planet in the horoscope. Because of its exalted position, any planetary body located there "lords over" all the other planets in the chart and can exert a powerful influence over someone's entire life. And while that's true, to some extent, of any planet occupying the highest point above the horizon, it becomes even more important if that body is near or conjunct the Midheaven, or MC *(Medium Coeli)*—the zenith point of the horoscope. Any planet aligned with this angle, some believe, is "accidentally dignified" in that its innate qualities are amplified in potentially constructive ways.

Fame vs. "Calling"
Still, there's an important distinction to be made here. On one level, any planet positioned above the horizon in the horoscope represents energies in your life that are more visible to those around you and comparatively more exposed to public view. In

terms of houses, that's something particularly associated with the 10th house, the place traditionally said to govern matters of fame, career, and reputation.

In subtle contrast with the 10th house, however, the MC is more than just a matter of fame or reputation, although it incorporates these things. As the symbolic zenith of the chart, the MC can be considered as also representing the pinnacle of your *life's direction, as something you are aspiring toward.* You might think of it this way: Whereas the 1st house shows who you *are,* in terms of your everyday personality, the MC shows *what you want to be*—i.e., those qualities you feel ambitiously called to realize. If that happens to be Mercury, then communication or mental qualities are what you're striving toward. Or is it Venus? Then your highest aim in life will center in some way around beauty or love. Whatever the planet, though, it's always more than "just another job" you feel inclined to take, or some career you happen to fall into that helps to pay the bills. In short, there's a sense of achievement or sometimes even *destiny* involved with any planet located at this point. [1]

Sometimes this can take very circuitous turns over the course of one's life. Consider my client born with Neptune near the MC, positioned at the focal point of a stressful T-square. As a teenager growing up in a high-crime area, his main goal in life at the time was inspired by a neighborhood drug dealer who wore expensive clothes and drove a flashy car. My client dreamt of someday becoming a big-time dealer like that himself. But as the years unfolded and he matured, he wound up escaping that unhealthy environment, and eventually became a respected addictions counselor who helped hundreds of young men and women grapple with their own drug problems. In retrospect, it's safe to say that, as a young man, he glimpsed something in that drug dealer's life that pointed to his own future destiny and life potential—what psychologist James Hillman might have called his "soul's code"—yet it was still in an unformed and undeveloped state at that point. The influence of Neptune on the MC was always there, but it took time for my client to awaken to its fullest significance.

Public Identity/Everyday Personality

While any energies situated near the top of the horoscope play a role in shaping one's reputation and life direction, these may not always be congruent with who you are on a day-to-day basis, as far as your ordinary personality is concerned.

Take, for example, the highly talented artist I once knew whose chart showed an expansive Jupiter in Leo near the MC. In public, he displayed an almost Dalí-esque personality—flamboyant and dramatic, even brandishing a large upturned mustache similar to that of the Spanish artist. However, that prominent Jupiter in Leo was squared by a far more intense Saturn in Scorpio, down in his 1st house. Hard to imagine a more striking contrast! The general public saw only that sunny public persona, without suspecting that he privately nursed deep emotional wounds from his childhood, which repeatedly surfaced in his adult relationships. Of course, taking a more constructive and holistic approach, one could say his lesson in life was about learning to *reconcile* those contrasting energies, by bringing more Saturn to his Jupiter and more Jupiter to his Saturn; but on an everyday level, it was the *conflict* between those dueling forces that was most apparent to those who knew him well.

This seemingly "split personality" syndrome is especially common in the charts of actors, who are often called upon to play roles very different from their ordinary personalities. A classic example is actress Marilyn Monroe, who had an assertive Venus in Aries near her MC, while harboring a far more vulnerable side in private, as shown by her 1st-house Neptune and a challenging Saturn in Scorpio in the 4th house. She may have convincingly played the "sex kitten" role in films, but her personal life concealed enormous sensitivity and pain stemming from a difficult childhood. [2]

With these basics as our starting point, let's take a look now at the influence of the different bodies in our solar system when positioned near the zenith of the horoscope. Keep in mind that, while we're placing special emphasis on planets that are close to the MC, much of what I'll be describing here applies to *any* planet that's *highest above the horizon,* even if it's farther away from the actual MC. Also, if more than one planet is tightly aligned with that elevated position, then it's important to look to the blended influence of both rather than either body solely by itself. That said, let us begin.

The Sun

When the Sun is positioned near the zenith of the chart, there is a drive to express one's creative essence and core ego values before the world, and to "shine" in a relatively public way. Astronomically speaking, the Sun is of course a star, and metaphorically speaking, you could even say its condition in the horoscope indicates where you are striving to be a "star." Further clues are revealed by what zodiacal sign it's in. Is this Gemini? Then it will likely be intellectual talents, communication skills, or versatility that one aspires to. Taurus? Then it may be a sense of beauty or financial stability. How about Aries? A warrior spirit, competitiveness, and drive—and so on.

The Sun positioned here is one of the primary factors indicating qualities of leadership, fame, or prominence within one's circle of peers, whether that be as head of the local PTA or the leader of an entire country. It's a common placement in the horoscopes of teachers and public speakers as well. But precisely because this part of the chart is such a publicplacement, any mistakes or flaws in one's character will be amplified in more public ways, too. One client of mine with his Sun at the MC trine Pluto became a well-known psychologist, while another client with his Sun *squaring* Pluto gained a reputation in consecutive workplaces for being an efficient manager but overly manipulative and heavy-handed in his dealings with employees.

Again, the zodiacal sign can offer important clues, sometimes in very subtle ways. The Sun in Pisces was the most elevated body in the natal chart of Albert Einstein, and the Theory of Relativity he became famous for represented a more "fluid" conception of reality than what scientists had been subscribing to at the time. In Einstein's view, the boundaries of time and space were seen as relatively elastic compared to Isaac Newton's more rigid and mechanical conception of the cosmos. Likewise, my friend and colleague Richard Tarnas was born with the Sun in Pisces as his chart's highest body, and has gained attention for his work in more theoretical areas like philosophy, psychology, and of course astrology.

Martin Luther King, Jr. had his Sun in Capricorn as the most elevated body in his horoscope, and besides being an important leader in the Civil Rights movement, he wound up becoming heavily identified with a famous speech in which he spoke of getting "to the mountain top"—quite the fitting metaphor for a Capricorn! The 19th-century science fiction writer Jules Verne was born with the Sun and Mercury in Aquarius as the highest planets; he became famous for his futuristic visions of the world, which included imaginative stories of space travel and extraordinary group (Aquarius) adventures. Incidentally, it's worth noting that, since the Sun is never far removed from either Mercury or Venus, it's common to find these bodies closely grouped together, whether near the MC or otherwise.

The Moon
Whereas those born with the Sun highest in the chart may feel an urge toward leadership or expressing their egoic and creative impulses in a public way, those with the Moon highest are more often compelled to project their *personality* or their *emotions* into the spotlight. Singer Joni Mitchell was born with Moon in Pisces

near the MC, and her lyrics are distinctive for exposing her deep-est and most vulnerable emotions to her worldwide audience.

With the Moon in far more assertive Aries close to the MC, painter Salvador Dalí offers a uniquely different case. In some ways, his aggressive personality and distinctive appearance wound up becoming even more well-known to the public than his art. In terms of "lunar" symbolism, it's also interesting that Dalí made his home in Spain a visible part of his career, frequently inviting pho-tographers and filmmakers to showcase its unique features. We see another bit of elevated Moon symbolism in the fact that Dalí prominently featured his wife, Gala, in many of his paintings and drawings, frequently citing her as the source of his inspiration and success. In fact, he was just one of a number of celebrities born with the Moon as their highest body, and whose wives played a prominent role in their careers. Consider the examples of singer/songwriter John Lennon, filmmaker George Lucas, or computer titan Bill Gates.

Lennon's life offers an especially interesting case study of an elevated Moon. Though he became famous as part of an innova-tive collective (Moon in Aquarius), it's obvious that the lunar prin-ciple played an important role throughout his entire life. Having grown up with a largely absent father, he was raised principally by women: his mother Julia (who was struck and killed by a car when he was 17) and his Aunt Mimi. After decades of admittedly misogynistic behavior, he eventually met and married Yoko Ono (an Aquarian), in whom it seemed he'd finally met his feminine ideal, or what Jungians would call his *anima*. Yoko became the cat-alyst that helped him to open up more fully to his feminine side, as he began talking now about the joys of settling down and cooking in the kitchen, and even publicly lying in bed with Yoko for media events (more Moon in Aquarius?). In lyrics like those for the song "Woman," Lennon publicly championed the role and importance of the feminine (and, more controversially, in the song "Woman is the N****r of the World"). Just as we saw with my earlier example of the addictions counselor, it can take a long time to awaken to the potentials of one's highest planet!

Since the Moon also rules "nurturing," the emotions that one chooses to put on display before the public can involve some form of caretaking. Consider the example of my client born with Moon in Cancer conjunct the MC, who gained attention for opening a food pantry for the poor and the homeless; or the chef I worked with who had a similar Moon placement and owned a critically acclaimed restaurant in a major city; or my recent client with the Moon close to her MC who has been a nurse her entire life. In a very different way, those same lunar impulses can steer someone into a life involved with acting or the theater. Actors Robert De Niro, Meryl Streep, Elizabeth Taylor, Jennifer Lawrence, and Peter Sellers were born with the Moon as their most elevated body, befitting lives involved with expressing their emotions and personalities in a public setting.

Mercury

With Mercury highest in the chart, there is an urge to project one's ideas or verbal skills before the world. As such, this is a natural placement for teachers, writers, those in public relations or in any occupation involving communication and mental talents. One finds it in the charts of writers like Henry Miller, Goethe, Balzac, and Renaissance scholar Marsilio Ficino. Writer Sylvia Plath had Mercury in dramatic Scorpio as the highest planet in her chart; her famous book *The Bell Jar* describes a young woman's descent into mental illness.

One aspires toward whatever qualities are symbolized by planets near the zenith, and this provides clues as to the role models or mentors one emulates in life. In the case of Mercury, for instance, those heroes will tend to be more intellectual in nature. One young client of mine, born with Mercury in Aquarius conjunct his

MC, grew up with posters of Carl Sagan and Thomas Edison on his bedroom wall, rather than images of rock stars, sports heroes, or Victoria Secrets' models!

But take note: If this elevated Mercury happens to be in a challenging aspect—especially with Neptune, Mars, Jupiter, or Saturn—one has to be especially careful with any public statements, since these can get one into hot water. I recall a friend with Mercury at the MC squared by Jupiter and Mars. He was a compelling writer and speaker, yet found himself the subject of a libel suit over comments he made in public about a colleague, which cost him dearly in legal fees, not to mention many sleepless nights.

Venus

This placement indicates a desire to project beauty and/or harmony in some way before the public. As noted earlier, Marilyn Monroe was born with Venus as her highest planet, and she became virtually synonymous with mainstream ideals of beauty. Singer and actress Barbara Streisand was born with Venus in Pisces as the highest planet in her horoscope. Naturally, this planetary placement often leads to occupations directly or indirectly involved with fashion and design. Besides being a successful musician and artist, David Bowie, who also had an elevated Venus, became almost as well-known for his sense of style, to the extent of being seen as a fashion trend-setter.

When well-aspected, this placement can confer a certain charm on natives. Actor Tom Hanks is widely regarded as one of Hollywood's genuine "nice guys," and was born with Venus as his highest planet. In some cases, the Venusian energy can take more spiritual forms, with an emphasis on projecting love or kindness to the world. One client of mine with Venus in Pisces conjunct the MC spent years teaching classes and workshops on loving-kindness meditation. I had the pleasure of sitting in on one of her talks one and was struck by her spirit of kindness and her ability to inspire a sense of compassion.

Mars

When Mars is highest in the chart, there is a drive to project energy and strength before the world. Former President Franklin D. Roosevelt was born with Mars close to the MC. He spearheaded America's involvement with World War II, while rallying citizens and soldiers with his call to courage, "The only thing we have to fear is fear itself."

I've seen numerous charts over the years with Mars elevated where individuals were closely associated with sports or martial arts. Muhammed Ali was born with this planet as his highest (with Saturn and Uranus close by), and he famously fought battles both inside and out of the boxing ring, many of which involved his conversion to Islam and a refusal to fight in the Vietnam War. Golfing prodigy Tiger Woods has Mars in Gemini as the highest planet in his horoscope.

Famed tightrope walker Karl Wallenda was born with a T-square to Mars high up in his chart, reflecting a drive to display daring and courage in a very public way. Interestingly, Philippe Petit, the young tightrope walker famed for his walk between the World Trade Center towers in 1974 (chronicled in the brilliant documentary *Man on Wire*) was also born with a T-square to Mars near the MC, but with Uranus aligned there as well. As befits that feisty combination, Petit was not only notable for extraordinary risk-taking but for an almost gangster-like attitude about "breaking the rules," even at the risk of jail time.

The forcefulness of Mars can be channeled in more artistic ways as well, so it's no surprise that Mick Jagger has Mars as the highest planet above the horizon (though just in his 12th house). Singer Iggy Pop, sometimes considered the "Godfather of Punk," is known for his wildly energetic, and sometimes even self-mutilating stage act. He was born with Mars and Mercury in Aries as the highest planets in his horoscope. In a more literary context, Ray Bradbury had Mars as his highest planet and actually became associated with the red planet in his writings (*Martian Chronicles*), while the title of his famed work *Fahrenheit 451* relates to the temperature at which book paper catches fire and burns—fire being another Martian symbol.

Jupiter

With Jupiter highest in the chart, there is often a sense of possibility and confidence about matters of career and in one's dealings with the public. As a result, this is one of the leading horoscopic indicators of popularity and success, as well as general "good luck" when dealing with authorities or those helpful to one's ambitions. Musician Sting has Jupiter as his highest planet.

At its best, this placement can indicate a desire to express a spirit of abundance and positivity into the world, whether through philanthropy, the arts, teaching, or humanitarian projects. The husband of a client of mine was a much-beloved pastor who spearheaded charitable projects over the course of many years; his Jupiter was near the MC. Actress Angelina Jolie was born with Jupiter as her highest planet, and besides her success in the movie industry, she has gained attention for her humanitarian work in Third World countries.

As with both Jolie and Sting, those born with this planet nearest their MC often have lives involving a great deal of travel. Herman Melville's Jupiter was highest in his birth chart, and he became famous for writing books about long journeys to far-off places, most notably *Moby Dick*. David Bowie had both Jupiter and Venus near the MC, and much of his life was spent traveling in connection with his performances.

As always, the zodiacal sign involved is important to consider. For instance, one client of mine, with Jupiter in Aries at the MC, worked as a risk-taking skydiving instructor. But in Libra, that same Jupiterian sense of possibility and abundance can involve matters of law or beauty. The great Renaissance artist Raphael, famous for his idealistic treatment of Biblical themes, was born with Jupiter in Libra in the 10th house. However, we also find this zodiacal placement elevated in the charts of Sophia Loren and Kim Kardashian, both of whom became famous in large part for their attractiveness. My friend and colleague Richard Smoley has Jupiter in Virgo near the top of his chart, and has gained acclaim for his writings on religion, philosophy, and esoteric matters.

And because any planets near the top of the horoscope can reveal the nature and quality of any dealings with those who are above you in rank, Jupiter near the zenith suggests encounters not just with prominent or wealthy individuals, but possibly those involved in religion, spirituality, or philosophy. I once met a man who worked for years with the Pope's office in Rome and had Jupiter exactly conjunct his MC in Pisces. If afflicted, though, Jupiter placed here can show *problems* with such figures, as well as a general tendency toward carelessness and unwise risk-taking.

Basketball legend (and Aquarian) Michael Jordan also was born with Jupiter in Pisces near the MC, where it's manifested quite differently. As many have noted over the years, Jordan didn't simply become successful and popular, he's become an object of nearly religious veneration for many. In one now-famous (or perhaps infamous) exchange with fellow player Reggie Miller, he once referred to himself as "Black Jesus." But he's also become fabulously wealthy through his endorsement of one product in particular: shoes—the feet being ruled by Pisces. (Whereas his peak salary with the Bulls basketball team was 38 million, he's made a billion dollars through shoemaker Nike.) How's that for a well-placed Jupiter in Pisces?

Saturn

Like Jupiter, Saturn near the top of one's chart can show considerable success and prominence in one's life. But *unlike* Jupiter, this usually involves considerably more effort and difficulty along the way. There's often a "late bloomer" quality to the lives of these natives. On the one hand, they generally experience great struggle in building their career and reputation—what one client described to me as feeling like rolling a boulder up a hill only to see it repeatedly roll back down again, Sisyphus-style. Yet these people often live to see great rewards and recognition as a result of all their hard work.

The Spanish artist Picasso was born with Saturn in Taurus as his highest planet, and experienced enormous criticism over his art early on, but eventually found wealth and fame as a result of his considerable discipline and productivity. (It's also worth noting that he's most closely identified with a visual movement known as *cubism*, a style that depicts scenes in a very Saturnine, "blocky" manner.) Jazz musician Louis Armstrong had Saturn as his highest planet, conjunct Jupiter, and he rose from an intensely difficult childhood in New Orleans to become a pioneering artist loved by audiences the world over.

And just as my Sisyphean, boulder-pushing client above pointed out, it's rarely a quick and predictable climb to the top when Saturn is involved. The substantial achievements suggested by Saturn are often coupled with painful reversals or falls from grace—a "three steps forward, one (or possibly two) steps back" scenario. One client of mine, with Saturn conjunct Venus at the top of her chart, became renowned for her artistic talents yet experienced considerable humiliation due to a very public and messy divorce. Singer Johnny Cash was born with Saturn as his highest planet, and besides developing an appropriately Saturnine reputation as the "Man in Black," he endured many ups and downs throughout his career as a result of run-ins with the law and a struggle with drugs.

While Saturn isn't the highest planet in former President Bill Clinton's chart (that would be Uranus), it's next in line in the 10th house, and he, too, experienced prodigious ups and downs in his political life, rising to become the world's most powerful leader but also one of its most humiliated. Saturn high can show deep insecurity over one's reputation, possibly stemming from hardships or criticism during childhood, which can trigger a powerful urge toward achieving status as a way to compensate for those inner self-doubts. But this can have a silver lining, too, since it may serve as the fuel that motivates later achievements and success.

Depending on its zodiacal sign (and planetary aspects), Saturn near the top of the chart can hold clues as to how one may be perceived as an authority. One student of mine, born with Saturn in Cancer conjunct the MC, struggled early on with painful family issues but eventually went on to become a respected authority in the field of family therapy. (Interestingly, actor Leonardo DiCaprio was born with Saturn high in Cancer, and earned his first Academy Award nomination for his role in the film *What's Eating Gilbert Grape*, about a deeply dysfunctional family.)

Someone with Saturn in Taurus as their highest planet might be known more for their expertise in banking, real estate, nature or art, while someone with Saturn elevated in Aries might be respected in sports, martial arts, or military work. One woman I knew well had been a celebrated psychic in her city, and was born with Saturn closely conjunct her Sun in Pisces at the top of the horoscope, while also teaching classes in business skills for fellow psychics. Saturn high in Virgo can be quite difficult early on in life, especially in terms of feeling insecure or criticized, but I've encountered it in the charts quite a few outstanding scholars, writers, and health professionals as well.

Saturn highest in the chart often indicates karmic lessons that natives need to learn around the *use or misuse* of authority and power—whether as wielded by or towards them. For most individuals, this manifests simply through interactions with parents, teachers, bosses, landlords, or the government. But in exceptional cases, this dynamic can play itself out on a much broader stage. Both Adolf Hitler and FBI director Herbert Hoover had Saturn as their highest planet, and not only had problematic dealings with authorities, but became problematic authorities themselves.

Queen Elizabeth II was born with Saturn near the MC. Besides having experienced notable ups and downs throughout her reign (particularly in association with marital scandals involving her children, as well as problems of protocol in the aftermath of Princess Diana's death), she has lived an extraordinarily *structured* life, with virtually every action determined by the formalities of royal tradition.

Uranus

In stark contrast to Saturn, those born with Uranus elevated in the horoscope possess a fiercely independent streak and a desire to pursue uniquely personal or even unconventional life-paths. Needless to say, this can make it difficult for them adjusting to rigid routines or structured environments, and when it comes to career they like to have as long a leash on them as possible. For some years, actor Steve McQueen was the world's highest-paid actor, and was born with Uranus in Aries as his highest planet. He became virtually Hollywood's poster boy for the "rebel" archetype in movies like *The Great Escape* and *Bullitt*; but he was also known for an independent and rebellious attitude in private, too, having spent time in a reform school while a teenager, running afoul of authorities while in the Marines, and battling with movie producers on film sets. [3]

The maverick spirit of innovation signaled by this placement frequently expresses itself in connection with technology or the media. A prime example is Apple computer co-founder Steve Wozniak, born with Uranus as his highest planet, while founding partner Steve Jobs enjoyed a paradigm-busting Uranus–Jupiter conjunction as his highest configuration. Computer pioneer Alan Turing was born with Uranus conjunct the MC, but he experienced the more negative effects of that placement when his (for the time) unorthodox sexuality led to his professional downfall. Astronaut Edgar Mitchell had an elevated Uranus, and besides his own involvement with space travel, he gained attention for promoting research into causes commonly considered "fringe," such as UFOs, ESP, consciousness, and psychic phenomena.

Orson Welles had Uranus conjunct the Moon in Aquarius, near the MC, and became a pioneer in film and radio. Uranus is elevated in the horoscope of director Steven Spielberg, who made a mark as an innovative director and producer of numerous movies and TV shows. Note, too, that one of his most iconic films, *Close Encounters of the Third Kind*, had as its climax the image of alien spaceships appearing out of the sky—a fairly straightforward symbol of Uranus positioned highest above the horizon. With Uranus's connection to the sky and outer space, this planet also features prominently in the charts of many astrologers, such as Rob Hand and Chris Brennan, both born with Uranus as their most elevated planet.

Along similar lines, Uranus generally indicates someone who prefers to "think outside the box," including psychologist James Hillman, who relished playing the gadfly to mainstream psychology with his unorthodox views on therapy and human behavior. Sometimes, this placement propels natives to become involved with social activism and transforming society, fueled by their own "futuristic" sensibility. Karl Marx, author of *Das Kapital* and *The Communist Manifesto,* had this placement, as do philosopher Ken Wilber and motivational speaker Tony Robbins. As mentioned, Orson Welles had both Uranus and the Moon as the highest bodies in his horoscope, and felt drawn from an early age to progressive politics; while still only in his early 20s, he wrote speeches for "New Deal" President Franklin Delano Roosevelt, among others.

But even though Uranus is most often associated with liberal or progressive causes, in some cases it simply indicates a more independent or "lone wolf" streak that can express itself anywhere on the political spectrum. Former U.S. Vice President Dick Cheney was born with Uranus highest in his chart, as were former Secretary of State Henry Kissinger, President Donald Trump, Italian dictator Benito Mussolini, former President George W. Bush, and conservative commentator William F. Buckley. While all of these are generally considered Right-leaning characters, they have all been characterized as very individualistic, choosing to do things their own way, whether others liked it not. The prominent Uranus in their charts also showed itself in all of their heavy involvements with the media.

Alas, Uranus's more rebellious and eccentric tendencies can create problems for natives when their unconventionality flies a bit *too* forcefully in the face of society's norms. Actor Gary Busey found fame early on as an actor but eventually became even more well-known for his erratic and unpredictable personality. A similar situation faced singer and TV show host Tommy Smothers who, along with brother Dick, became a politically controversial voice on TV during the 1960s, but in the following years, his unpredictable behavior on TV talk shows made him a risky bet for booking agents. Orson Welles famously set out to shock the world with his creative projects, such as his 1936 all-black cast of *Macbeth* on Broadway, his *War of the Worlds* radio broadcast in 1938, and of course his thinly veiled send-up of William Randolph Hearst in the great film *Citizen Kane*. Yet that same maverick streak which propelled much of his genius turned out to be the very thing which led to serious problems later in life, when TV and film producers and financiers turned their attention to more predictable figures to shepherd their projects.

Like comedian and actor Jim Carrey, improvisational genius Jonathan Winters was born with Uranus highest above the horizon, and channeled his "weird" impulses in more creative ways through public performances. However, in Winter's case the flip side of that energy was a struggle with mental illness, which he publicly revealed only later in life. Jerry "Nutty Professor" Lewis was born with closely Uranus conjunct the Sun at the MC, and in addition to wildly a successful career in the media (TV, film, and radio), he became known for a comedic style many commentators actually described as "spastic," before it became politically incorrect to do so.

Uranus is the most elevated planet in film director Martin Scorsese's horoscope, and he's clearly earned his place in the cinematic pantheon for his individualistic style. Still, his willingness to push the cinematic envelope ignited major controversy when he chose to depict a very unconventional Jesus in his film *The Last Temptation of Christ*. Actor, comedian, and director Woody Allen has been lauded for his quirky humor and independent spirit in writing and directing films, but the unconventional choices in his personal life led to a severe backlash from audiences when it became known that he married his stepdaughter Soon-Yi.

Neptune

At its best, Neptune highest in the horoscope can indicate a spirit of "reaching for the stars" which sets its sights on lofty goals and inspired dreams of one sort or another. For some, this gives rise to powerful spiritual or creative impulses. Poet Walt Whitman was born with this placement and, as mentioned earlier, so was singer–songwriter Bob Dylan. Neptune is also most elevated in the chart of singer Patti Smith, who gained literary acclaim for her memoir about a relationship with famed photographer Robert Mapplethorpe—photography being another Neptunian symbol. Former President Barack Obama was born with Neptune as his highest planet, and ran his campaign on an idealistic message about the promise of "hope and change"—though it continues being debated how successfully he delivered on that promise.

On a more problematic front, natives with this placement can experience confusion about their career or life's calling, or they might feel compelled to weave an aura of glamour or illusion around their public persona, such as when a performer adopts a pseudonym or "mask" to hide behind. Although raised as a Jewish child in a middle-class Minnesota family, Bob Dylan changed his last name from Zimmerman and crafted a personal history that for years led audiences to believe he'd lived a hard life as a young vagabond riding the rails and traveling with carnivals.

For similar reasons, this placement is another common indicator in the charts of actors, who are ostensibly paid to pretend they're people other than themselves. Neptune is the highest planet in Clint Eastwood's horoscope, as it was for actor and martial arts pioneer Bruce Lee. Interestingly, Lee not only brought martial arts to the attention of millions but also expounded on its spiritual philosophy in writings and interviews. Walt Disney had Neptune as his highest planet, and made a career out of marketing fantasy, usually combined with music, to literally billions of people around the world. A surprising number of my clients over the years born with Neptune high have been beauticians, hair stylists, or make-up artists—presumably reflecting that planet's association with glamour and illusion.

Elvis Presley was born with Neptune as his highest planet. Besides his work in music, he also worked as an actor in many films, struggled with drugs, and privately entertained an interest in mystical and metaphysical writings (including Yogananda's *Autobiography of a Yogi* and H. P. Blavatsky's *The Voice of the Silence*). Comedian, actor, and erstwhile musician John Belushi had Neptune as his highest planet — squaring Jupiter and Venus in his 1st house, no less—and also experienced an extremely public struggle with drugs.

When afflicted, this placement can create problems for one's reputation and a sense of feeling misunderstood. In extreme cases, it can even give rise to a "martyr" complex, where one feels at the mercy of forces beyond one's control. A woman I've known for years was born with a T-square to Neptune at the top of her chart, and I've watched from the sidelines as she's grappled with gossip and misunderstandings from those around her. But those elements of misinterpretation and deception often associated with Neptune can be directed in other ways, too, as it was for talk show host Johnny Carson. His youthful ambition in life was to become a stage magician—a.k.a., the art of deception and misdirection!

I've done charts for quite a few spiritual teachers and yoga instructors over the years, and a considerable number of them were born with Neptune near the top of their horoscopes. But at its most dysfunctional and unbalanced, those same idealistic and inspirational impulses can warp into something far more deceptive, and even dangerous. Even though it wasn't close to his MC, Neptune was the highest planet in the chart of infamous cult leader Jim Jones, who eventually became messianic about his own mission on Earth, leading hundreds of his followers to take their lives alongside him by drinking poisoned "Kool-Aid" —a particularly sobering example of Neptune's delusional and self-destructive side at its worst.

Pluto

Pluto represents an intensely primal energy concerned with matters of life and death, sexuality, power, and transformation. As a result, when perched highest in the horoscope it can indicate that an individual's career or sense of "calling" will be involved with any or all of these areas. On a purely physical level, take a look at the horoscopes of celebrities whose public identities have become closely associated with sexuality, like actress Megan Fox, Ariana Grande, or the late singer Prince. Born with Pluto as his highest planet, Prince was so public about sexuality that he displayed phallic imagery in his 2007 Super Bowl performance, watched by nearly a billion viewers around the planet!

Similarly, Pluto deals with exploring life's "darker" side and with facing aspects of existence less comfortable to those more accustomed to living on the surface of things. We see that probing quality in the work of late singer Leonard Cohen, as well as writer Jack Kerouac, who celebrated the bohemian "underworld" in his classic work *On the Road*. Singer and guitarist Eric Clapton has pursued a lifelong interest in blues, a musical style that explicitly embraces life's suffering and passions. This Plutonian influence is also visible in the personal struggles he endured in his battles with drug addiction and the very public grief he experienced when his young child died after falling from an open window.

Actor Sydney Poitier was born with Pluto close to the MC, and gained attention for his roles in films like *Guess Who's Coming to Dinner* and *In the Heat of the Night*—movies that served to pull back the curtain on America's simmering racism. But Poitier's career was "Plutonian" in another respect: He radically transformed his public persona from that of a poor child with little education, raised in the Bahamas, to that of a sophisticated adult capable of moving among the world's rich and powerful. On the other hand, former President Richard Nixon expressed his elevated Pluto in a very different manner, having become associated with "Machiavellian" power grabs, "dirty tricks," and paranoid snooping on political foes.

Multiple Olympic gold medal–winner Bruce Jenner was born with Pluto as his highest planet (with Mars not far behind), and he gained attention not only for his competitive spirit and success in various sports, but also for a late-in-life gender transition, thereafter being known as Caitlyn Jenner.

Writer Mary Shelley's Pluto was her highest planet, and she gained worldwide fame for her book *Frankenstein,* which ostensibly centered around Plutonian themes of life, death, and resurrection. Actress Ellen Burstyn was also born with an elevated Pluto; she starred in the pioneering 1980 film about near-death experiences aptly titled *Resurrection*, as well as in the blockbuster horror film *The Exorcist.* In a more tragic vein, U.S. astronaut Virgil "Gus" Grissom was born with Pluto highest (squaring his Sun and Mercury), and died in a highly publicized manner when his capsule caught fire on the NASA launchpad in 1967. And though it's just an isolated case, I found it fitting that the one client I've had over the years who managed a funeral home was born with Pluto near the MC!

Final Considerations

A few other points are worth mentioning. First of all, when any planet is close to the top of one's horoscope, the concerns of whatever house that planet *rules* will also tend to come before the public. For example, if someone's Mars is situated near the MC and they have Aries on their 2nd-house cusp, then their assertiveness or conflicts around money will be displayed in a relatively open manner. Or consider the case of someone born with Leo on the 4th-house cusp, with the Sun (its ruler) conjunct the MC. More likely than not, the part of their life they'll become known for will somehow be connected with matters of family, home, or real estate.

But in particular, if the planet near the MC happens to be the ruler of one's Sun sign or Ascendant, then this individual's personal concerns with career or the public will be amplified exponentially. By way of contrast, if a Sun-sign Taurus has Jupiter near the MC, this Jupiter placement may be important, but not nearly as much as it would be if the person were a Sun-sign Sagittarius—the sign ruled by Jupiter. Likewise, someone with Cancer rising who has the Moon near the MC (as we saw in the case of both Joni Mitchell and Salvador Dalí) will tend to project *themselves* before the public more than if another planet were positioned there. Incidentally, considering that the Ascendant rules the head, it's hardly accidental that Dalí's face—specifically his mustache—wound up playing such a crucial role in the public's perception of him.

Finally, whether or not someone has any planets near the top of the chart, the *zodiacal sign* on the zenith needs to be studied closely, since this will also reveal qualities that one is aspiring to express and attain, as well as how the public will see the person. Is the sign Gemini? Then it will involve communication and information. Aquarius? Group or community involvements, the media, or progressive/innovative ideals. Libra? Matters of beauty, the law, or public relations. And so on. In turn, pay close attention to the *ruler* of that sign for further insights into the meaning and direction that the calling will take.

The Midheaven in Different House Systems

Determining what is or isn't the "highest" planet in a chart depends to an extent on the house system one is using. For example, in systems like Placidus, Koch, Campanus, Alcabitius, Porphyry, and Regiomontanus, the MC is identical to the 10th-house cusp; as a result, any planet closest to that angle is automatically the "highest." But in Whole Sign, Morinus, Vedic, or Equal House charts, the MC (or vertical meridian) can be elsewhere—in some cases, a few houses away from the 10th. So, how does one determine what is "highest" in those cases? The simple answer is to focus attention on whatever planet is closest to the *MC point*, and *not* by looking to the "top" of the chart as it visually appears.

As I said, that's the "simple" answer; a more complex response would be to take into account the role of declination, which can alter what is actually "highest" in the sky. As my colleague Jon Parks points out, one can have two planets close to the MC, but the one that's farther from the MC may actually be the "higher" of the two, in terms of having a more northerly declination. For example, 10 South declination is higher than 15 South declination, 15 North is higher than 10 North, and so on. Sound confusing? Well, that's because it is!

This essay first appeared in the February, 2018 issue of The Mountain Astrologer magazine.

CHAPTER 5

THE HOROSCOPE AS A SPECTRUM
OF POSSIBILITIES

Someone sent me an email recently and asked, "If you had to give just one tip for someone just starting up an astrological practice, what would that be?"

Great question, I thought, and a number of possibilities quickly sprang to mind. What I finally decided to tell them was something I'd learned over the decades about how to talk to clients about their horoscopes, which I'd sum up this way:

Nothing in the horoscope is inherently *either "good" or bad." Any given configuration can be expressed on different levels, at varying levels of subtlety. For that reason, the chart doesn't guarantee any single outcome or personality type, but actually represents* a spectrum *of possibilities. There are levels and octaves, in other words, and we need to be careful not to boil down any given aspect or sign placement to a one-dimensional catch phrase, or simple "this-means-that" summary.*

Let me give a real-world example of what I mean. Suppose a client comes into your office who was born with an exact Venus-square-Neptune. (Exact aspects, especially stressful ones, are especially important to note, since they can indicate the part of the chart which sucks all of the proverbial air out of the room, as it were.) There are a wide range of possible expressions for a config-uration like that, so one could discuss some of the possible expres-sions of that energy, preferably starting with the positive. Why? Because people are much more likely to remember the first thing you say about a horoscope or configuration than any subsequent remarks you follow up with.

So what would be some positive expressions of a Venus/ Neptune square? On the one hand, that could show great sensitiv-ity, artistic talent, compassion for the less fortunate, idealism, spiri-tual inclinations, and so on. What about its negative expressions? Well, there can be addictive tendencies with this aspect (whether to drugs, food, pharmaceuticals, or even relationships), illusions in romance, carelessness with money, boundary issues in relation-ships or the urge to "rescue" others (mother, romantic partners, sister, etc.), and so on.

That's a simple example, and it would obviously need to be qual-ified by the rest of the chart. But I've used this general approach with clients for several decades now, and I think there are impor-tant benefits to this type of "spectrum" perspective.

For instance, consider the common tendency to think of hard aspects as "bad" or intrinsically negative. On more than one occa-sion, I've heard someone with an aspect like this one say, in as many words, "Oh, I have a *bad Neptune...*" Not only is that a simplis-tic way of looking at any planetary energy, but it can lead to some-one believing there isn't *any* positive potential to such energies at all. By talking about the positive potentials of an aspect before fully addressing the negative, a client is more likely to approach it with a different mindset concerning its meaning and possibili-ties, and give them a greater range of choices in responding to it. Staying with the Venus/Neptune square for a moment, if a client is simply told that this energy shows addictive tendencies or self-deception in romance, say, they'll likely believe that's *all* it's good for, and consequently feel straightjacketed by those potentials. But if instead they're told that this energy offers a *range* of potentials, some of them quite positive, their sense of possibility about that part of their chart suddenly opens up and expands beyond what it might have been otherwise.

In essence, that's what I told this person who asked me that question. To be sure, this isn't about sugar-coating anything in the horoscope, or glossing over the very real challenges it contains. Rather, I'm simply pointing out the need to strike a balance when discussing astrological patterns, and not overly emphasize *either* positive or negative expressions. To focus solely on one or the other runs the risk of providing a misleading impression of what a person's chart is about, and in turn, their entire life.

In our next chapter we'll explore this perspective further by specifically looking at some constructive possibilities when it's applied to the Moon.

This article first appeared in IAM Infinity Magazine 30, March/April 2020

CHAPTER 6

WHY YOUR "BAD MOON" MAY ACTUALLY BE YOUR BEST FRIEND: TAKING A CLOSER LOOK AT HARD LUNAR ASPECTS

While talking with a young astrologer not long ago, I heard her refer in passing to the "bad Moon" in her chart. When I asked why she called it that, she went on to cite the litany of horrors this celestial body had inflicted on her since childhood.

I suspect the "bad" part of that description stemmed from her exposure to the type of simplistic descriptions found in some older texts, or even in certain quarters of the astrological community today. Whatever the source, I always find it a bit unsettling to hear these sorts of thumbnail descriptions still being bandied about in our discussions of astrology and horoscopes.

There's no denying that emotional problems and frustrations can be part and parcel of this heavenly body's challenges. But as someone who has struggled for the better part of his life with a bad—I mean, *challenged*—Moon (old habits die hard!), I've come to see a different side to those lunar struggles, from watching their effects not only in my own life but the lives of artists, humanitarians, and spiritual teachers who've made their mark on the world, and who, it turned out, also had the dreaded "bad Moon." As for why this might be, I'd suggest a few possibilities.

* It's true that a challenged Moon can often indicate insecurity, hypersensitivity, or emotional dysfunction in someone's life, especially in childhood. But in some cases, that may be precisely what it *takes* to compel someone to jump through all the hoops necessary to become successful, established, creative, or adored and respected by the public. People who are perfectly content in their emotional life will rarely feel driven to exert the energy needed to become successful or even famous. By way of comparison, those with strong Leo energy in their chart or with Venus on their Ascendant may be vain, sure, but unless there are other compelling factors in the horoscope, these individuals are not likely to propel that energy into any high-profile achievements.

* Along a similar line, the sheer backlog of pent-up frustrations and insecurities that accompany a challenged Moon can serve as high-octane "fuel" for one's ambitions later in life. To use an analogy, if you push down hard on a coiled spring, that creates an enormous amount of stored-up energy that, when released, can pack quite a whallop. Likewise, hard aspects to the Moon can have the effect of compressing one's emotions so powerfully that a person will feel compelled to find an outlet for them, either constructively or destructively (perhaps both), when he or she grows older.

True, *any* hard aspect in the horoscope can be a source of emotional frustration, and in turn serve as a stimulus to creative achievement; but there seems to be something particularly important about the role of lunar aspects. Why? Because the Moon symbolizes the emotional core of an entire chart, or what the late astrologer Noel Tyl calls "the reigning need." All planetary energies represent various "needs," of course, but as Tyl noted, the Moon is the *reigning* one. It underlies all the others, similar to the way the headwaters of a major river is the source for all of its tributaries further downstream. As a result, aspects to the Moon drive the personality in fundamental ways that influence all one's other emotional impulses.

* In a very subtle way, the struggle or suffering that arises from a difficult Moon can lead to a development of "soul" which confers an awareness of feelings and emotional depths that might otherwise go unnoticed. For example, if I happen to meet someone who I hear lost a child due to some tragedy, I find myself automatically assuming there's a dimension of depth and sensitivity to them which may well be absent from others who have led comparatively tragedy-free lives. Sure, this individual might have his or her share of character flaws, but shallowness won't likely be one of them. And in the hands of a creative or spiritual temperament, that quality of depth or emotional complexity can become the basis for empathy, creative nuance, or (ideally) wisdom.

Think of how songwriting geniuses Neil Young and Joni Mitchell suffered from polio while young and were confined to their beds for long spans of time during childhood. It's hard to imagine that they would have gone on to compose such musical masterworks as "Heart of Gold" or "Both Sides Now" had they grown up under more carefree circumstances. Similarly, some of the most insightful psychologists and therapists I've known suffered from their own serious challenges early on in life. I strongly suspect that these challenges contributed in important ways to their own later brilliance as therapists, in a way that recalls the "wounded healer" syndrome described in shamanistic studies, where people develop a gift for healing as a result of their own health crises.

To give some idea of how pervasive this pattern can be in horoscopes, I've compiled a list of notable figures born with hard aspects to their Moons, drawing mainly but not exclusively from the creative arts. Easy aspects like the trine or sextile could be included as well, but they tend not to be as common among these notables, likely due to the fact that such aspects generate far less energy. I've allowed for a 10° orb in some cases, although the majority of these examples involve far tighter orbs. I think you'll agree that the list is impressive. I'll start with aspects involving Saturn and, from there, look at other examples involving Pluto and Neptune. As you'll notice, some of these individuals fall into more than one category, simply meaning that they possess more than one of these aspects at the same time in their birth charts.

Moon–Saturn Aspects

Hard contacts between these two bodies often indicates depression, insecurity, or even feelings of inferiority, especially early in life. But aside from motivating a person to compensate for those perceived failings by excelling in some area, Moon–Saturn aspects can also confer an element of depth or gravitas that moves the person's work out of the shallows and into deeper waters. Think about it: Could Bob Dylan have written weighty songs like "Blowing in the Wind" or "Girl from the North Country" at the age of 21 without a tight Moon–Saturn conjunction? Not likely.

But there's another side to Saturn here, and that involves its ability to *crystallize*. Whatever Saturn forms an aspect to in the horoscope indicates something that one is attempting to *structure* or *materialize*. If it happens to be Mercury that Saturn is aspecting, the person will struggle to materialize ideas, whether that take the form of books, blogs, or teachings; if it's Venus, it could be artistic impulses, love, or money one is trying to materialize—and so on. In the case of the Moon, it's *emotions*. So, what better friend to a creative person than having a Saturn–Moon connection, if the aim is to take otherwise invisible emotions and draw them out into structured, tangible reality? Time and again, I find Saturn–Moon connections (or Saturn–Venus and Saturn–Neptune) in the horoscopes of artists, photographers, musicians, dancers, writers, or architects. Here are just a few examples of those with Moon-Saturn aspects:

David Bowie (conjunction)
Bob Dylan (conjunction)
Brian Eno (conjunction)
Ray Davies (conjunction)
Miles Davis (conjunction)
Timothee Chalamet
    (conjunction)
Gustav Holst (conjunction)
Woody Allen (out-of-sign
    conjunction)
Elvis Presley (out-of-sign
    conjunction)
Harper Lee (conjunction)
Joni Mitchell (square)
Steven Spielberg (square)
Louis Armstrong (square)
Judy Garland (square)
Stephen Sondheim (square)
Jane Austen (square)
Leonardo DiCaprio (square)
James Joyce (square)

Ray Bradbury (square)
Martin Luther King, Jr. (square)
Walt Disney (square)
Johnny Cash (square)
Tennessee Williams (square)
Iggy Pop (square)
René Magritte (square)
John Denver (square)
Brian Wilson (square)
Buddy Holly (square)
James Brown (opposition)
Bernardo Bertolucci
    (opposition)
Bruce Lee (opposition)
Jack Nicholson (opposition)
Dalai Lama (opposition)
Napoleon (opposition)
Lorde (opposition)
Randy Newman (opposition)
Judy Collins (opposition)

Moon–Pluto Aspects

These contacts can indicate repressed or turbulent emotions, sometimes resulting from early traumas, sexual conflicts, control issues and manipulation, or even cruelty. Yet, here as well, this linkage connects one with deep emotions or passions that can be redirected and expressed in constructive ways, or lead to powerful psychological or occult insights.

David Bowie (conjunction)
Leonardo DiCaprio
   (conjunction)
Mozart (conjunction)
Barbara Streisand (conjunction)
Brian Eno (conjunction)
Ringo Starr (conjunction)
Groucho Marx (conjunction)
Pierre-Auguste Renoir
   (conjunction)
Amelia Earhart (conjunction)
Fred Astaire (out-of-sign
   conjunction)
Barack Obama (square)
Meryl Streep (square)
Steve Martin (square)

Maya Angelou (square)
Lana Del Rey (square)
Marlon Brando (square)
George Harrison (square)
Jim Morrison (square)
Prince (opposition)
Angelina Jolie (opposition)
George Lucas (opposition)
John Lennon (opposition)
Johnny Carson (opposition)
Isadora Duncan (opposition)
Joyce Carol Oates (opposition)
Stephen Sondheim (opposition)

Moon–Neptune

Though quite different in tone from Plutonian or Saturnian contacts, the Moon–Neptune combination nonetheless poses its own share of challenges, usually due to some blend of hypersensitivity, escapism, emotional confusion, or a general feeling of dissatisfaction and *ennui*—a sense of *"Is that all there is?"* But the flip side here is the enormous capacity for imagination and spiritual sensitivity these aspects can bring as well, and which drive one towards escaping into creativity.

Sting (conjunction)
Dalai Lama (conjunction)
Salvador Dalí (square)
Van Morrison (square)
Jimmy Page (square)
David Byrne (square)
Al Pacino (square)
Sigmund Freud (square)
Tim Burton (square)
Stevie Nicks (square)
David Letterman (square)
George Carlin (square)
Miles Davis (square)
Peter Gabriel (square)
Lord Byron (square)

Harper Lee (square)
Ron Howard (square)
William Faulkner (square)
Peter Sellers (square)
Buddy Holly (square)
Gustav Holst (square)
Ray Davies (square)
Leonard Cohen (opposition)
Robert Downey, Jr. (opposition)
James Taylor (opposition)
Marilyn Monroe (opposition)
Billie Holiday (opposition)
Stevie Wonder (opposition)
Paul Gauguin (opposition)

Final Thoughts

I should add that while I've focused my attention here on Saturn, Pluto, and Neptune, these three planets are by no means the only ones that can take part in this dynamic. For some natives, lunar challenges may result from aspects that involve Mars or Uranus, a Sun-Moon square or opposition, or a conflicted lunar placement in Scorpio, Capricorn, or the 12th house. But there does seem to be something especially pivotal about the influence of those three planets in particular, possibly due to their intrinsically "melancholic" or introspective nature. Needless to say, the best-case scenario for individuals with any of these patterns would be that they resolve whatever dysfunctional issues these energies bring while maintaining whatever positive gifts they hold; but obviously, there's no guarantee of that either way.

Which brings me to a question I've often imagined asking any of the people on this list, be they living or dead, if I had the chance. Simply, imagine you could go back in time and either soften or eliminate those problematic Moon aspects in your chart and, along with them, eliminate whatever difficult emotional challenges they caused—but in doing so, you'd also eliminate whatever *gifts* those aspects brought, creatively, psychologically, or spiritually. Would you still do it? Or would you choose to *keep* that problematic Moon—warts and all?

I still haven't decided what *my* answer to that would be.

This essay first appeared in the October, 2016 issue of The Mountain Astrologer magazine.

CHAPTER 7

DEGREES AS YEARS: A SURPRISINGLY SIMPLE "TIME LORD" TECHNIQUE

S imply put, the horoscope could be described as a symbolic blueprint encoding the diverse potentials of someone's life. But not all of the potentials indicated in the chart activate at the same time during that person's life. So what determines when those different planetary energies "come alive"?

In the minds of most Western astrologers these days, the primary triggering mechanisms used for that purpose have generally been transits or progressions. For example, when Jupiter comes along and crosses over your Venus, your romantic or aesthetic urges will tend to be amplified. Or when Saturn first comes back around to where it was when you were born, during your late 20s, the potentials in that part of your horoscope will be activated in a significant way.

In ancient times, however, one of the most common triggering mechanisms was something known as the "time lord" technique, or what in the Vedic astrological tradition (both ancient and current) has been known as the *dasha* system. Whereas conventional transits are based more solidly on actual astronomical phenomena, time lord techniques tend to be more symbolic in nature.

For instance, a person's life may be divided into "chapters" based on certain assigned periods of time associated with different planets or houses. Consequently, in the Hellenistic system of "profections," every one of the twelve houses of the horoscope can be seen as relating to a successive year of one's life, such that the 1st house reveals clues about a person's first year, the 2nd house about their second year, and so on, all the way around the twelve houses (with the system repeating itself after age twelve, so that the 1st house then relates to age 13, the 2nd house to age 14, etc.).

One common time lord–type technique found in the Western tradition involves something referred to as the "planetary ages." The 20th-century mystic and philosopher, Rudolf Steiner, had his own version of this technique and viewed human development in terms of seven-year cycles, each one associated with the classical planets. According to that system, the first seven years of life are governed by the Moon; the second seven years (7–14) are governed by Mercury; the third seven years (14–21) by Venus; the *next three seven-year segments* (21–42) are governed by the Sun; the next seven-years (42–49) are governed by Mars; the next seven-years (49–56) are governed by Jupiter; and the "final" seven-year period (56–63) is governed by Saturn. Steiner himself didn't suggest any planetary rulerships for the years past 63, but other writers have suggested various possibilities, such as assigning Uranus to the years 63 to 70, Neptune to the years 70 to 77, and Pluto to the years 77 to 84.

In this article, I'd like to look briefly at one technique that has received relatively little attention but which I've found to be surprisingly accurate and astonishingly simple. It was related to me by my first astrology teacher, Maureen Cleary, who summed it up this way: *"Look to the zodiacal degree a planet in your horoscope occupies, and that will tell you what year of your life that planet's energy will manifest in an especially important way for you."*

Is your Venus located in 25°33" Aries? Then look to the period around your 26th year for something important to unfold relating to your Venus. (Remember, when a planet has actually entered the 25th degree, that means it's now into your 26th year. Is your Saturn several minutes into the 17th degree of its sign? Then it's likely that sometime during your 18th year, you had an important development pertaining to Saturnian lessons or challenges. Is Jupiter located somewhere in your 21st degree? Then look to what happened in your 22nd *year*—and so on.)

I've generally found that we can extend the orb of this influence a degree or so on either side, in terms of when that planet will reveal its influence. For example, if someone's Saturn is positioned within the 21st degree of a sign, one might see Saturnian influences strongly manifesting anytime between ages 20 and 22. However, in some cases I've been astonished to find that by looking even to the *actual minutes of arc*, one sometimes sees that influence climaxing during a *specific month or even week*. Say that your Jupiter is at 21°30" Scorpio. Jupiter may "activate" exactly six months into your 22nd year (since 30 minutes of arc represents one-half of a degree, and thus one-half of a year).

As for how this technique works *beyond* the age of 30, that's simple enough. As with Hellenistic profections, simply repeat the numbering sequence once you've reached the end of that cycle. For instance, suppose a person has their Sun at exactly 5°00" Cancer. That degree would activate not only near the 5th birthday, but again around the 35th birthday, the 65th birthday, and the 95th birthday.

I distinctly remember that when I first heard of this technique, I was frankly skeptical since it seemed almost *too* simple. Yet the more I worked with it over time, the more surprised I was by its efficacy. (Several years after learning the technique from Maureen, I asked another astrology teacher of mine, Goswami Kriyananda of Chicago, whether he had ever heard of the technique. Indeed, he had—and he added, seemingly almost as perplexed by its simplicity and power as I had been: "I find it *frighteningly* accurate.")

What I'd like to do here is present a handful of examples to illustrate this technique in action, and I'll begin with my own horoscope.

First, let's take the placement of my Sun, which was at 13° Gemini when I was born. The period around (and following) my 13th birthday was perhaps the most significant turning point of my young life, one I often look back on as my key "creative awakening." Besides discovering books about spirituality and "alternative" topics, this was a time when my mind was opening to a host of new subjects, ranging from lost civilizations and paranormal phenomena to musical influences like Bob Dylan and Claude Debussy. That was the year I started painting in oils (which led to my attending art college several years later). It's also when I met a famous movie actor (and solar figure), Vincent Price—which, for a childhood movie fan like myself, was somewhat akin to meeting Jesus Christ himself.

Now, add 30 years to *that* in order to find the next activation of my Sun degree, and you arrive at my 43rd year of life. What happened between my 43rd and 44th birthdays? This was when my first book, *The Waking Dream*, was published—a truly Geminian manifestation.

My Venus is at 7° Gemini, and while I have no memory of what happened during my seventh year (other than some dabbling in watercolors), when I add 30 years to that date, I come up with age 37, which is the year I got married.

My natal Neptune is positioned in the 19th degree of Libra, and the period between my 19th and 20th birthdays was another pivotal time of my life. Among other things, this was not only a key period for me in my experiments with hallucinogens, but it was also when I started studying mysticism more intensively and began attending classes with yogi/mystic Goswami Kriyananda. I was a sophomore in art college at the time and was heavily involved in filmmaking, which led to an eventful trip to California with two fellow students and one of our film instructors that year. The trip was ostensibly for the purpose of shooting footage by the ocean, but it also proved to yield two life-changing LSD trips in the Big Sur region—all obvious Neptunian symbols. On the more negative side, unfortunately, it was a romantically disillusioning year for me as well—a pattern that repeated 30 years later at age 49 when, as a then-divorced bachelor, I discovered that a powerful new love interest went up in smoke.

Let's look now to a couple of famous examples. John Lennon was born with his Uranus at 25° Taurus. Since he was born on October 9, 1940, this means that 25 years after his birth, we would need to focus on the twelve-month period between October 9, 1965 and 1966. Did anything innovative, radical, media-related, or even disruptive occur for him during that period? Aside from the brilliantly innovative musical work he was doing with the Beatles at that point (both the *Rubber Soul* and *Revolver* albums came out during that period), this turned out to be one of the most disruptive times of his life. In the course of an interview during the spring of 1966, Lennon infamously remarked, "Christianity will go. It will vanish and shrink ... We're [the Beatles] more popular than Jesus now ..." In the ensuing months, that single remark circulated through the media and ignited a firestorm of controversy around the world, leading to the burning of Beatles' records by religious fundamentalists and even threats against Lennon's life.

Or let's take one of Lennon's early idols, Elvis Presley. Born on January 8, 1935, Elvis had his Jupiter at 18° Scorpio. His 18th year was in 1953. Did anything important or "expansive" happen for him that year? As it turned out, in August 1953 Elvis walked into the offices of Sun Records and made his first-ever record, a two-sided disc with "My Happiness" on the one side and "That's When Your Heartaches Begin" on the other. Though he wasn't formally signed to a record contract until a short while later, that first acetate signaled the beginning of his recording career and brought him to the attention of producer Sam Phillips.

Finally, let's consider the case of singer Bob Dylan, who was born on May 25, 1941. As I wrote about in chapter four ("Decoding the Most Elevated Planet in the Horoscope"), Dylan's Neptune is a particularly prominent feature of his chart, since it's the most elevated planet. It's positioned at 24°56" Virgo—which would place the Neptunian period in question somewhere between 1965 and 1966. So, what happened then? In the minds of many, it led to the most brilliant songwriting efforts of his career, with the extraordinary release of his albums *Bringing It All Back Home, Highway 61,* and *Blonde on Blonde,* all within a relatively short time.

Dylan's Sun is at 3°33" Gemini, and while we don't know what happened for him at age 3, if we simply add 30 degrees to that, it brings us up to a point midway through his 34th year—which would have been the 1974–75 period. What happened then? After being famously reclusive for a number years following his fabled motorcycle accident, he suddenly exploded back onto the music scene with a much-heralded world tour, backed up by The Band, while also recording his masterpiece album *Blood on the Tracks,* released in early 1975 and widely considered his finest work since the mid-1960s. (*Rolling Stone* magazine ranks it #16 on its list of the 100 Greatest Albums.) Dylan also wrote and recorded his celebrated song "Hurricane" during that period (mid-1975), and last but not least, he initiated his extraordinary touring ensemble, the "Rolling Thunder Revue," which hit the road from late 1975 into 1976.

Let's fast-forward to the next major activation of Dylan's Sun in Gemini. If we add another 30 years to his 3° Gemini Sun, this brings us to his 63rd year, which would have been between 2004 and 2005. Did anything of consequence happen for him during that period? Indeed—that's when he published his much-awaited autobiography, *Chronicles: Volume One.*

Dylan's chart points up an interesting aspect of this technique, namely, that when you find two or more planets occupying the same (or similar) degrees, even if in different signs, it seems to amplify the importance of those corresponding years even more dramatically. For example, Dylan's Mercury is at 23° while his Neptune is at 24°; those two years of his life were an exceptionally creative time for him (but also a problematic one, in terms of stress and substance abuse).

An even more dramatic example of this principle is that of my client whose chart showed an exact square between Saturn and Venus at 17° of their respective signs, with Pluto also being positioned at 17° of another sign. Three planets in the exact same degree, in other words. Did anything significant happen for her romantically around age 17, I asked? When she heard that question, her eyes widened considerably, as she solemnly went on to tell me about a sexual assault she experienced at 17, which left her traumatized for years. On the other hand, I have another client who was born with a near-exact conjunction between Jupiter, Venus, and the Moon in the 22nd degree of Scorpio (in the 5th house of pleasure, no less), who told me that in her 22nd year she experienced the most profound sexual awakening of her life.

These are just a few examples that illustrate this technique at work. But I strongly encourage readers to put it to the test with their own charts, as well as their clients' charts, and see for themselves what it has to offer.

This essay first appeared in the October/November issue 2018 of The Mountain Astrologer magazine.

CHAPTER 8

DOES ASTROLOGY DENY FREE WILL?

One of the criticisms commonly leveled against astrology concerns the thorny question of free will. If our lives are somehow influenced or even predetermined by the stars, the argument goes, does that mean we have no real choice, and that we're little more than puppets manipulated by some overarching cosmic fate?

The simple answer to that is, no—not exactly, anyway. A helpful analogy to explain this point is a simple weather forecast. When the weatherperson on TV announces there will be rain during the coming weekend, you have a wide range of options in how to react to that news. You can choose to stay in and watch TV, sit and meditate, play with your dog, or even go out and enjoy a walk in the rain. An astrological prediction is a bit like that, in that you may not have total control over the planetary "weather patterns" affecting your life, but you have considerable free will in how you *respond* to them.

For me, an even better analogy may be the one I used near the start of this book—that of sheet music. Give a musical score to two different musicians, one of a jazz artist and the other a classically-trained pianist, and the odds are they'll play it very differently, even though they're looking at the same notes. Indeed, the jazz musician might improvise wildly around those basic notes on that sheet music, in the process transforming that work into something nearly unrecognizable at times. Just as with that piece of sheet music, you can "play the notes" of your horoscope in a variety of different ways—or even improvise around its themes and create something wildly different from what appears on paper. That's why two different individuals born at the same time in the same city can wind up leading surprisingly different lives, although there will be certain structural commonalities between them.

Another key to understanding this point is the fact that astrology speaks in a language of *symbols,* and for that reason there are "octaves of meaning" involved. For example, a Mars-Mercury square in the chart of a five-year-old will not manifest the same as it will for that person when they're 70 years old. They'll experience that basic energy but at different levels of expression, some considerably more constructive than others. It would be ludicrous to propose a singular, fixed prediction for how a pattern like that would manifest for someone without knowing the level of maturity or experience they'll bring to it. Symbols are multi-leveled, and we experience and express them in widely different ways, sometimes within the same lifetime.

That goes for transits and progressions, too. If that same five-year old were to have transiting Jupiter come along and conjunct his or her natal Venus, he/she might fall in love with the new puppy that mom and dad brought home; or perhaps feel delighted at the new toy received as a special gift. But at the age of 45, transiting Jupiter on that same natal Venus might manifest as getting married, going on a trip to Paris, or even making a killing at the roulette tables! It's the same archetypal symbolism, but at different levels and forms of expression.

Here is an experience from my own practice which hit that point home for me in a particularly fascinating way, while underscoring the role that choice plays in how we relate to our horoscopes. I had two clients come to me separately who were born within days of one another, who had extremely similar charts. As it so happened, they both experienced the effects of transiting Saturn over their natal Neptunes around the same time, just one week apart, before meeting me.

I asked each of them what happened that previous week to find out how that Saturn transit had manifested for them. The first one sheepishly admitted he was arrested for drunk driving, while the second one said that he joined Alcoholics Anonymous in order to quit drinking!

Think about that for a second.

Very similar planetary symbolism was at work in both cases, but in the one case the client chose to manifest that energy *from the inside out,* as it were, by using his Saturnian discipline to take control of his Neptunian escapism, while the other client wound up letting that symbolism manifest from the *outside in,* by not using discipline and letting the outside world manifest it *for* him. It reminds me of the old line by Carl Jung: "When an inner situation is not made conscious it appears outwardly as fate." So despite the similarities in their charts and transits, they chose to manifest those patterns in dramatically different ways, one more constructively, the other more destructively.

So when it comes to astrology and free will, it's all a matter of balance. One way or another, the energies of our horoscopes will manifest, but there is an element of choice in how we respond to those energies, and what forms they'll take. Or as Richard Tarnas once put it, "Astrology is not concretely predictive, but archetypally predictive."

CHAPTER 9

SATURN AS THE KEY "KARMIC" CHALLENGE OF THE HOROSCOPE

More years ago than I care to remember, I heard a visiting astrologer make the offhand comment that Saturn's placement in the horoscope indicates where one's "key karmic challenge in this lifetime is."

If indeed reincarnation is real, as I personally believe it to be, I think it's probable there are various factors in the horoscope that relate to "karma," rather than just one—Pluto, the 12th house, the Nodes, one's closest hard aspect, and still others. For that matter, the *entire horoscope* is likely "karmic," insofar as it all results to one extent or another from momentums set into motion over many lives.

But having thought about that astrologer's comment quite a bit since first hearing it, I've come to believe there is indeed something unique about Saturn as representing *an especially focused symbol* of one's current life-challenges. Saturn is commonly referred to by astrologers as the planetary "taskmaster" of the horoscope, and that's not a bad way to put it. Without question, wherever Saturn is in the chart is where fate doesn't let you get away with your mistakes very easily!

But I'd like to add a further layer of meaning beyond what that astrologer's comment initially suggested to me, which is this: beyond simply indicating a particularly focused point of difficulty or frustration, the placement of Saturn also signals where we can potentially achieve *our greatest success and achievement in life, too.* There are a couple of possible reasons for that.

One is those is that, from a reincarnational standpoint, it's possible that Saturn shows where we have the greatest reservoir of past-life experience stored up from previous lifetimes, and with that naturally comes a considerable backlog of learned skills, too— however slow those might seem in unfolding this time around. By analogy, think of how much longer a 100-car freight train takes to pick up speed than one with only five or ten cars attached.

But another reason for the enormous potential contained within Saturn centers around that very element of difficulty and struggle it faces us with. In other words, precisely because of the enormous effort Saturn requires to deal with its problems, the end result can be a considerable level of mastery, too—what I've often referred to as the "late bloomer" side of Saturn. [1] As the old saying goes, the "squeaky wheel gets the grease," and Saturn might well be thought of as the squeaky wheel of the horoscope. But all of that heightened attention brings a heightened degree of learning and expertise as well. As the key taskmaster of the horoscope, Saturn keeps pounding away at us until we finally get things right!

Whatever your preferred explanation, I'd like to take you on a quick tour through the zodiac to see how this dual effect of Saturn can manifest in each of the signs, with a "karmic" look at both the negative and positive sides of this planet in our lives.

SATURN IN ARIES:
Negative: At its most difficult, the hard lessons of Saturn here tend to revolve around matters of assertiveness, anger, or self-centeredness. One is likely to find that fate has a way of exacting an especially

heavy toll for missteps involving impulsiveness or impatience in life. There can also be deep-seated issues around self-confidence early on, involving one's core sense of "*Me!*," as well as major challenges with overcoming fears. Overly competitive impulses can lead to painful consequences in the lives of these natives.

Positive: In its more evolved form, Saturn in Aries can bring a serious degree of mastery when it comes to expressing qualities of courage, and accessing one's "inner warrior." Those early struggles with fear or confidence can eventually transform into a capacity for leadership and considerable fearlessness when venturing onto life's battlefields. In both positive and negative ways, this sign placement is similar in influence to that of a Saturn/Mars aspect in the horoscope.

Notable figures with this placement: As with virtually all the examples of Saturn through the various signs, the lives of famous notables often display both the positive and negative sides of its influence, frequently at different stages of their lives. A classic example is George Washington, who experienced an especially steep learning curve with regard to Saturn in Aries. While most famous for his extraordinary prestige and glory in the Revolutionary War, his younger impulsiveness led to horrific mistakes on the battlefield early on, such as the skirmishes culminating in the battle of Fort Necessity—blunders which led to the Seven Years War between England and France, called by one historian "the first truly global conflict in human history"[2]—not to mention his early defeats in the Revolutionary War. But he learned from those mistakes and went on to claim victory for the American forces. A darker exemplar of Saturn's influence in Aries was that of Iraqi leader Saddam Hussein, whose iron fist brought him great wealth and power but ultimately rebounded in the form of crippling defeats and a humiliating demise.

The discipline that Saturn potentially brings to one's "war-rior" nature is especially obvious in the case of martial artists like Chuck Norris and Jason Stratham, as well as actress Lucy Lawless, who played the fictional warrior princess, Xena, on TV. Similar to Scorpio, Aries is associated with sexuality and desire, so Saturn's placement here sometimes gives rise to natives known for their attractiveness and sex appeal, like Tina Turner, Pamela Anderson, Julia Roberts, Christy Turlington, Jennifer Aniston and Natalie Wood. When that sexual energy goes off the rails, though, Saturn can bring down the hammer especially hard on its natives—as it did for disgraced comedian Bill Cosby, rapper Bobby Brown, and even actor Dustin Hoffman, whose later career was marred by accounts of early indiscretions.

SATURN IN TAURUS
Negative: The most challenging lessons for these natives tend to involve matters of materialism, security, practicality, and of course money. Insecurities over feeling unloved cause these natives to compensate via material acquisition or worldly achievements.

Positive: At its best, Saturn in Taurus instills a profound sensitivity to (and awareness of) nature, wealth, and materiality generally. When well-aspected, individuals with this placement have an instinctive understanding of how to survive in the real world. It can also indi-cate someone who is a great builder, whether that be of physical structures, institutions, or works of art. They often have a keen sense of legacy, and of the mark they want to leave on the world.

Notable figures with this placement: The Greek military figure Alexander the Great was born with Saturn in Taurus, and besides being an impressive builder (e.g. the city of Alexandria), he was famously driven to acquire ever-greater tracts of real estate during his brief life. On a fictional front, Orson Welles' film *Citizen Kane* premiered during a major stellium in Taurus, including Saturn, and it fittingly portrayed a man whose need for love drove him to amass ever more worldly possessions to fill that emotional need.

Artistically, figures like Vincent van Gogh and Picasso showed genius in their approach towards the natural world and its forms. But whereas it gave Picasso a businessman's savvy in acquiring wealth, van Gogh experienced the Saturnine influence in terms of an ongoing struggle with scarcity and poverty. American founding father Benjamin Franklin expressed this planetary placement through his ability to innovate and invent in practical ways, while it gave scientist Stephen Hawking extraordinary insights into the natural world—in particular, gravity (a Saturnian force). Franklin Delano Roosevelt also had this placement, and was faced throughout his presidential term with issues of physical hardship, and became intensely involved with economic and banking reforms and working to lift the United States out of depression. American Senator Bernie Sanders was also born with this placement, and likewise focused enormous attention on economic reforms and battling big banks. In a quite different fashion, Mother Theresa expressed the more austere aspect of this zodiacal placement with her vows of poverty and a focus on the world's poor.

SATURN IN GEMINI

Negative: The most difficult lessons here tend to revolve around issues of communication and thinking patterns. With Saturn in Gemini the individual can not only experience a struggle with expressing and articulating ideas and feelings, but they have to be especially careful with their choice of words, since misstatements or verbal gaffes can lead to problems. Negative thought patterns can also lead to depression and cynicism, with a "glass is half-empty" attitude towards life.

Positive: On the other hand, Saturn here can bestow a genuine talent for structuring and expressing one's thoughts into words, whether through writing, teaching, or simply ordinary conversations. It can give rise to a deep and thoughtful mind, with an ability to put profound ideas into relatively simple terms. This placement gives a sense of discipline and an ability to focus deeply on intellectual and creative work.

Notable figures with this placement: Among the great communicators sometimes found with this placement is philosopher Alan Watts, who had an extraordinary gift for expressing profound spiritual and philosophical concepts in easy-to-understand terms, while singers Paul McCartney, Joni Mitchell and Mick Jagger penned songs and lyrics which spoke to audiences the world over. Writer Franz Kafka used the "dark" side of Saturn in Gemini to write imaginatively about issues of confinement, control, and anxiety.

Film director Orson Welles justly received attention not only for his brilliant cinematic works but his distinctive, deep-throated voice, displayed not just in films or theaters but countless TV and radio commercials. On the other hand, important works like *Citizen Kane* or his infamous "War of the Worlds" broadcast of 1938 caused him major problems—the former because of its thinly veiled critique of media mogul William Randolph Hearst, the latter due to the controversy caused by the Halloween night broadcast. Similarly, Wikileaks co-founder Julian Assange first gained worldwide fame for his role in unleashing confidential government information onto the worldwide web, but later suffered considerable repercussions (and confinements) due to the many high-leveled feathers he ruffled along the way.

Inventor and entrepreneur Elon Musk is another Saturn in Gemini native who has learned hard lessons about carefully choosing his words, such as when critical comments he made about a celebrated Filipino figure (a man who rescued young children from a cave) resulted in a high-profile lawsuit. Bobby Fischer became world-famous for his brilliance as a chess player but found himself heavily ostracized for anti-Semitic remarks he made. Critic and writer Roger Ebert became celebrated for his elegant and simple-to-understand prose (being the only film critic ever to win a Pulitzer Prize), but experienced the more challenging side of Saturn in Gemini when mouth cancer prevented him from communicating in ordinary verbal ways towards the end of his life.

SATURN IN CANCER

Negative: The most painful lessons associated with this placement tend to center around matters of the family or home, as well as the emotional capacity to give or receive nurturing. This may include issues of loss in the family, contending with the weight of family legacy, or feelings of being unloved or uncared for. These individuals must guard against becoming consumed by worry and fear.

Positive: Domestic matters can become deeply meaningful areas of experience, while ancestral legacies and family tradition can hold deep riches and rewards. Even though there may still be frustrations involving issues of nurturing or parenting, this placement can also drive one to excel in those very areas, through cultivating a deep caring for others.

Notable figures with this placement: The life of actress Angelina Jolie offers an example of both the positive and negative aspects of this energy. In a positive vein, there is her humanitarian work in Third World countries, as well as her role as doting mother to a seemingly endless caravan of children; while on the other hand there is her famously turbulent relationship with actor-father, Jon Voight, and her even more famously turbulent marriage to (and divorce from) actor Brad Pitt. In an earlier chapter I mentioned one client of mine born with Saturn in Cancer who was raised in difficult family conditions but eventually developed a successful family therapy practice. In a more artistic vein, Renaissance genius Michelangelo had this placement as well, and there's something fitting about the fact he was drawn to put into solid form one of history's most famous expressions of maternal love and sorrow—the famed Pieta, a marble statue depicting the Virgin Mary lamenting her dead son, Jesus.

It's fascinating how many well-known natives with this placement come from families which are themselves distinctive or famous in some way, or that suffered from emotional troubles. Besides Angelina Jolie, there is Liza Minelli (whose mother was Judy Garland), Donald Trump (whose wives and children became celebrities in their own right, and whose father was also a notorious New York real estate mogul); president George W. Bush (the son of a president); both Kirk Douglas and son Michael Douglas were born with Saturn in Cancer and both were famous and powerful in their own spheres; while John F. Kennedy of course came from one of America's most prominent families.

At its most painful, though, this placement sometimes brings greater-than-average hardships or losses beyond any garden-variety divorces or infidelities. Guitarist Eric Clapton tragically lost his infant son when the child fell out of a high-rise window; singer Neil Young was faced with the daunting responsibilities of raising a special needs child; singer Dean Martin was traumatized by the early death of son Dino in an aviation accident; Liza Minelli suffered with her mother's turbulent life while growing up; and John F. Kennedy experienced a wide range of family tragedies, including the death of brother Joseph during WWII, sister Rosemary undergoing a prefrontal lobotomy at age 23, sister Kathleen Agnes dying in a plane crash in 1948, and most famously, wife Jacqueline suffering a miscarriage, a stillbirth, and their son Patrick dying two days after being born.

SATURN IN LEO

Negative: The hard lessons for these natives can center around matters of ego, the misuse of power, or even an unbridled quest for pleasure. At its worst, it inclines towards dictatorial tendencies, and the possibility of humiliating falls from grace involving very public blows to one's ego.

Positive: At best, the discipline and laser-like focus brought by Saturn can bring extraordinary success through the sheer application of will, and the ability to crystalize creative impulses in superior ways. As with Saturn in Aries or Capricorn, this placement can also indicate leadership potentials.

Notable figures with this placement: The enormous creative potentials of this placement can be seen in such diverse figures as Beethoven, David Bowie, Steven Spielberg, Charlie Chaplin, and Elton John. The quality of raw willpower it can confer is especially obvious in the life of Arnold Schwarzenegger who, despite a series of daunting obstacles—an unpronounceable name, unconventional looks, and a thick accent—still managed to become successful in several different fields, including real estate, bodybuilding, acting, and politics. Likewise, Ludwig von Beethoven achieved his creative artistic success in the face of continued romantic frustrations and a growing profound deafness. Charlie Chaplin made his cinematic efforts seem almost effortless, yet as a mountain of uncovered film outtakes have since revealed, his creativity was a constant struggle, and he labored to get individual scenes "right" even to the extent of reshooting them repeatedly over weeks of time.

Leo is the archetypal sign of kingship/queenship, so Saturn placed here can indicate a tremendous rise to prominence but also great falls from power and respectability. Besides his creative work, Chaplin experienced scandals and criticism not only over his romantic involvements with younger women but his political views. President Bill Clinton became a powerful figure on the world stage but also found himself at the center of a major scandal over his romantic missteps. Arnold Schwarzenegger may have been successful in various professional fields but he, too, was scandalized when an affair with his child's nanny led to a very public divorce from wife Maria Schriver.

Wife of Henry VIII Anne Boleyn came close to kingly power, but literally lost her head in the process. Adolph Hitler achieved astonishing influence on the world stage but his hubris ultimately led to a truly Wagnerian downfall. Singer, rapper, and music producer Kanye West became a distinctive talent in the entertainment world, but has also fielded enormous criticism over the years because of his inflated ego.

SATURN IN VIRGO

Negative: Virgo represents the critical and analytical faculties of the soul, so natives with Saturn here must be careful not to become overly focused on negativity or imperfections, whether in themselves or the world around them. If not unchecked, this can cause one to become paralyzed with worry and negativity, or simply become overwhelmed by details. On a bodily level, that analytical capacity for "breaking things down" can sometimes manifest in terms of problems with digestion, the intestines, and assimilating nutrients.

Positive: At its best, this placement can confer deep insights and a profound commitment to learning and knowledge. These natives can concentrate well, and have an ability to grasp the deeper meanings of books, philosophies, or life in general—"digesting life experience," as it were. These are not shallow thinkers! While this placement can go overboard with self-criticality (or criticism of others), at best it can confer modesty and humility, and an impulse to be of service to one's community and the world-at-large. While this placement can, when afflicted, lead to health concerns, it can also give rise to considerable expertise or authority in health-related matters.

Notable figures with this placement: Johann Sebastian Bach was born this placement, and we see its influence not only in his breathtaking productivity and work ethic but also for the intricacy of his musical compositions. The analytical side of this placement can be seen in philosophical figures like Madame Blavatsky, Rudolph

Steiner, and Ken Wilber, but we also see its influence in the penchant of these writers to accrue mountains of details, not to mention their occasionally hypercritical style. Actress Meryl Streep displays the extraordinary sense of precision and eye for detail in her crafting of characters for the big screen, while TV "pop psychologist" Dr. Phil expressed its influence through his incisive approach towards guests and their problems, as well as his general focus on health, both psychological and physical.

SATURN IN LIBRA

Negative: In this sign, the hard karmic lessons center around relationships and social interactions generally. There can be limiting experiences in marriage or romance, but this may also involve struggles with feeling appreciated or loved by the public-at-large. When unbalanced, it can lead to a painful sense of social rejection or simple awkwardness in interactions. One's perception of one's own "popularity" can be a major concern. Through trial-and-error over years or decades, one is forced to learn hard lessons about the art of compromise and social interaction.

Positive: Saturn is exalted in Libra, so the very struggles that arise with this placement can eventually lead to considerable mastery when it comes to socializing and diplomacy. Since Venus is the planet associated with Libra, this can also give rise to formidable achievements in the arts or performing, with a keen sense of structure in creative works.

Notable figures with this placement: Singer/songwriter Sting has a Sun-Saturn conjunction in Libra, and besides being a successful performer and songwriter he's experienced both the ups and downs of relationships. In interviews he's remarked that he considers the collapse of his first marriage to be the one area where he's "failed" in life, while his second marriage has seemingly been a happy and successful one. Disgraced movie producer Harvey Weinstein was born with Saturn in

Libra, and we see both its positive and negative sides in his extraordinary success with the arts but also through serious crimes and misdemeanors in relationships, affairs, and several failed marriages.

Donald Trump's first wife Ivana also experienced the positive and negative sides of this placement, having attained extraordinary popularity and wealth as a result of her marriage but also heartache, humiliation and rejection. The famed yogi Paramahansa Yogananda had this placement, but apparently manifested his Saturn through prolonged austerity in relationships and a lifelong vow of celibacy. But it was also apparent in the painful legal problems he experienced with his long-time friend Dhirananda, as well as the oft-negative (and frequently racist) attention he received in American newspapers, coupled with the social rejection he sometimes experienced because of his dark skin.

Novelist Jane Austen was born with Saturn in Libra, and her plots often involved matters of social commentary exploring women's dependency on marriage in the pursuit of social standing and security. Interestingly, the United States was "born" with Saturn in Libra, on July 4, 1776, but here that influence seems to have manifested through this nation's reputation as a "nation of laws" (and of lawyers).

SATURN IN SCORPIO

Negative: The hard lessons for these individuals tend to center around issues of anger, manipulation, and power. Mistakes or missteps in these areas are amplified exponentially and can lead to severe recriminations or regrets. Sexuality in general is an area of major learning for these natives. There can be festering resentments over early emotional wounds, along with tightly-held secrets around lingering hurts. At its very worst, it can lead to vindictiveness or even cruelty, whether expressed or received.

Positive: When the intense energy of this placement is successfully harnessed, it produces an extraordinary sense of power and determination, and a true mastery of the "warrior" spirit. When balanced and cultivated, it can also confer deep insights into the workings of sexuality, magic, and the occult.

Notable figures with this placement: In the movies, we see the warrior side of this placement in such figures as *Wonder Woman* actress Gal Gadot, or martial arts megastar Jackie Chan. In a more real-world context, that warrior energy surfaced in the life of revolutionary figures like Fidel Castro and civil rights leader Malcolm X. Tech giants Bill Gates and Mark Zuckerberg became notorious early in their careers for a "take no prisoners" attitude towards competitors, although that seems to have softened greatly during their later lives (some say because of the tempering influence of their wives).

As with Saturn in Aries, it's fascinating how many celebrities with this zodiacal placement are associated in the culture with sexual charisma—Marilyn Monroe, Scarlett Johanssen, Marlon Brando, Katy Perry, Richard Burton, Olivia Wilde, and Nicki Minaj, among others. But we also see some of the problems around sexuality in some celebrity's lives, such as Marilyn Monroe's early abuse, Brando's famous sexual addiction, and Oprah Winfrey's early experience with rape. Architect Frank Lloyd Wright experienced the dark side of this placement not only through an early scandalous affair with a colleague's wife but the horrific murder that took place on the grounds of his Wisconsin home, Talesien. Hugh Hefner, founder of the hugely influential Playboy empire, experienced both sides of Saturn in Scorpio, having enjoyed countless sexual escapades and great wealth as a result of a business based on sex, but also contending with numerous scandals and controversies over rape accusations, obscenity charges, and unflattering tell-all books by former lovers.

Actor Mel Gibson was born with Saturn in Scorpio, and became associated with films of considerable depth and dramatic power but also startling violence bordering on sadomasochism, torture and cruelty. He also experienced enormous blowback in his personal life over comments uttered in moments of drunken rage, when years of repressed emotion erupted to the surface in the form of anti-Semitic comments.

SATURN IN SAGITTARIUS

Negative: The hard challenges facing these natives often center on matters of freedom and their adventurous desire to expand horizons. The deep-seated urge to "run wild" may be constrained by practical limitations, be those social, bodily, or legal in nature; while in some cases there can be frustrations dealing with rigidly conservative religious or political figures in their lives. For some, this placement manifests as a deep fear of taking chances—sometimes with good reason, since miscalculations over knowing their true limits can result in serious problems. There can be a powerful, and sometimes painful, struggle in the search for meaning. Dogmatism and a deep-seated need to be "right" can become lead to serious problems. These individuals may even find themselves wrestling with their belief (or lack of) in the existence of God.

Positive: At best, this placement can bring genuine wisdom or insight in philosophical or political matters. The very struggle with philosophical or religious ideals can even lead to these figures becoming respected authorities in these areas. Their concern with morality and matters of principle can lead them to crusade for justice and become agents of change in the world.

Notable figures with this placement: It's fascinating how many famous figures born with this placement led lives closely involved with ideology, religion or philosophical matters. Consider the list: Mahatma Gandhi, Martin Luther King, Abraham Lincoln, Vladimir Lenin, Charles Darwin, Osama bin Laden, Che Guevera, Rasputin, and Iranian politician Mahmoud Ahmadinnejad. Osama bin Laden expressed the ultra-conservative religious side of this placement as a crusader for ultra-conservative Islam, whereas Charles Darwin found himself on the receiving end of criticism from conservative religious figures over his theories of evolution (and internally, he struggled with his own religious principles). Comedian and TV personality Bill Maher has expressed the more atheistic impulses of this placement with his openly contemptuous views on religion and "God." My friend Richard Smoley was born with Saturn in Sagittarius, and is a respected authority in the field of philosophy and religion, and even wrote an entire book on the subject of God, titled *How God Became God.*

Novelist and journalist Earnest Hemingway was born with Saturn in Sagittarius and encountered blowback from conservative authorities for his "scandalous" stories, but also experienced frustrations trying to balance the limitations and responsibilities of marriage with his deep-seated need for freedom. He traveled widely throughout his life, and experienced both praise and criticism for his many stories set in distant locales. But he also encountered major problems on many of those journeys, from losing manuscripts while traveling to serious injuries on the battlefield, and several near-fatal plane crashes. And while his stories superficially seemed to be more existentialist or even cynical in tone, there was frequently a deeper philosophical or mythic undercurrent to many of them.

SATURN IN CAPRICORN

Negative: The painful lessons of these natives often involve the misuse of authority, the downside of raw ambition, and the negative effects of status and fame. When afflicted, there can be painful falls from grace and a tarnished reputation.

Positive: This placement can also confer an intuitive understanding of power dynamics in the real world, along with an innate talent for navigating the echelons of power. Ambition can result in enormous productivity and achievement in the world, and lead to considerable respect in one's community.

Notable individuals with this placement: Clint Eastwood was born with Saturn in Capricorn, and parlayed its energies into successful careers not only in acting but business and politics. For billionaire Warren Buffett, Saturn in Capricorn gave rise to extraordinary instincts in the business world. That intuitive grasp of how to ascend the worldly ladder is also apparent in the lives of figures like Barack Obama, Walt Disney, Tony Robbins, Simon Cowell, and Rupert Murdoch.

Princess Di was born with Saturn in Capricorn, and experienced both the positive and negative aspects of this placement, ascending to extraordinary fame but equally extraordinary disgrace, both of those as a result of her marriage to Prince Charles. That extreme positive/negative polarity is visible in the lives of many other natives born with this placement, including Marie Antoinette, Louis the XVI, Julius Caesar, cult leader Jim Jones, and actor Kevin Spacey.

SATURN IN AQUARIUS

Negative: Those born with Saturn in this sign encounter some of their most difficult lessons in connection with groups or one's community, and with learning how to integrate with society at large. At worst, there can be feelings of alienation or social rejection, and frustrations over issues of hierarchy amongst colleagues or even friends. There can also be major challenges in learning how to reconcile one's conservative and progressive tendencies.

Positive: While there can be difficulties and frustrations in connection with social interactions generally, these individuals sometimes find themselves ascending to positions of great respect or authority in groups. They are often drawn to organize or manage collective enterprises, whether that be in business, political activism, or simply garden-variety social gatherings and parties.

Notable individuals with this placement: Jeff Bezos was born with Saturn in Aquarius and serves as the leader and CEO of a global network connecting millions of people via internet technology, while also spearheading a futuristic effort to develop his own space travel company. Winston Churchill expressed both the positive and negative of this placement by becoming the respected leader of his nation, but also a much-criticized figure by political opponents.

Yoko Ono achieved lasting fame through her association with the world's most famous musical group, the Beatles, but also became widely viewed as being instrumental in their break-up. Carl Jung and Aleister Crowley were both born in 1875 with this placement, and both became influential leaders of groups while also experiencing considerable problems with associates. Painter Salvador Dali was born during Saturn's next sojourn through this sign in 1904, and not only experienced his own share of ups and downs with groups—in particular, the Surrealists—but expressed the more scientific side of this placement in his growing fascination with quantum physics.

Elvis Presley was most well-known a solo performer, yet was inextricably tied to groups throughout his life, both constructively and destructively. Besides his back-up musicians and numerous fans, he was also surrounded throughout his career with an assortment of undesirables and hangers-on, who contributed substantially to his unhealthy (and ultimately fatal) lifestyle. Actress Shirley MacLaine was famously associated with the "Rat Pack," but experienced the downside of Saturn in Aquarius through the enormous criticism she received for her progressive, "New Age" beliefs. Astronomer Carl Sagan expressed both the progressive and conservative sides of this placement—on the one hand, promoting various futuristic and progressive scientific or political ideas, while on the other hand evangelizing against "New Age" beliefs in books like *Demon-Haunted World*. Howard Hughes was a larger-than-life visionary in both the film and aviation industries, but also became increasingly reclusive and agoraphobic in his later years, virtually cutting off all social ties with longstanding friends and associates.

SATURN IN PISCES

Negative: There can be hard lessons for these natives around learning the proper balance between selfishness and unselfishness. The impulse to "escape" or avoid responsibilities can result in painful repercussions. Failure to set proper boundaries or keep one's gullibility in check can also lead to disastrous results. There can be disillusionment in those areas of the chart where a Piscean Saturn is placed, frequently resulting from unrealistic expectations. There may also be a feeling of "bearing life's heavy burden" with these individuals, as though they've been constrained by fate or obliged to pay off some heavy debt from past lives somehow. As with Saturn in Sagittarius, there can be struggles with religion or religious figures with this placement.

Positive: The disciplining force of Saturn can help to structure the spiritual and imaginative impulses inherent in Pisces. Though there may be struggles with religious ideals and situations in life, these can lead to spiritual depth and profound insight—sometimes even enlightenment. And while this placement can sometimes indicate considerable suffering or a heavy sense of obligation, it can also give rise to deep compassion and an acute sensitivity towards the suffering of others and the needs of the less fortunate. In both positive and negative ways, this sign placement is very similar to the effects of a Saturn/Neptune aspect.

Notable individuals with this placement: While the more spiritual potentials of this placement is evident in figures like the Dalai Lama or the "sleeping prophet" Edgar Cayce, we also see the "heavier" side of this energy in the sense of heavy obligation and suffering they both experienced at times in their lives. Early on, writer J.K. Rowling experienced her share of struggles as a poor single mother, but also expressed the more creative side of Saturn in Pisces through her ability to crystallize an entire fantasy world into books and cinema, while also becoming known for her compassion as a humanitarian and philanthropist.

Among movie actors, Keanu Reeves was born with Saturn in Pisces and has become almost as well-known for his melancholic demeanor ("sad Keanu") as for his movie roles. Actors Anthony Hopkins and Robert Downey Jr. utilized the energy of Saturn in Pisces to craft scores of extraordinary performances on film, but both experienced the negative side of this planetary influence through their early (and fortunately, successful) struggles with alcoholism, too. Singer Sinead O'Connor expressed a very different side of this energy when she stirred up worldwide controversy with a very public crusade against the Catholic church (ruled by Pisces). She also struggled openly with emotional problems for much of her life, including contemplating suicide at times.

Final Note
On an even simpler level, one can look to the placement of Saturn in the different *elements* for important insights into this planet's workings in charts. When positioned in the Water signs (Cancer, Scorpio, and Pisces), the potential challenges and achievements brought about by Saturn tend to be more emotional in nature; in the Earth signs (Taurus, Virgo, Capricorn), they largely center around practical or worldly concerns; in the Air signs (Gemini, Libra, Aquarius), they're more social and intellectual in nature; while in the Fire signs (Aries, Leo, Sagittarius) the challenges tend to involve matters of assertiveness, courage, or ego.

This essay first appeared in the June/July 2019 issue of Mountain Astrologer magazine.

CHAPTER 10

THE LIMITS OF ASTROLOGY: OR, DOES THE HOROSCOPE REALLY SHOW *EVERYTHING?*

Not long ago a first-time client asked me, somewhat haltingly, "Does the horoscope really tell you *everything* about some-one?" I'm not sure if that look of concern on her face was because she feared that her deepest, darkest secrets might somehow be revealed by the glaring X-Ray vision of astrology, or she was worried she might be told when she might die—or something else entirely. Whatever the reason, I responded by telling her, no, there are plenty of things the horoscope can't reveal. And that's actually a good news/bad news situation, as I hope to make clear here.

At any rate, it was shortly after that exchange with my client that I started thinking about some of those things the horoscope doesn't show, and I compiled a short list of them. They include such things as these:

* *Your gender.* (The horoscope can't tell whether you're a man or a woman.)

* *What race or ethnicity you are.* (A horoscope won't tell you whether its owner is black, white, yellow, polka-dot, or for that matter Japanese, American, or Italian.)

* *What religion you are.* (It's true, a chart can indicate important things about your religious attitudes, such as whether you are more conventional or unconventional in your beliefs, more devotional or analytical, and so on, but it can't actually reveal whether you are Christian, Muslim, Buddhist, Jain, or some other faith.)

* *Whether you're gay, straight or bisexual.* (Here, too, the chart can give certain general clues about sexual attitudes, such as whether you're more uptight or uninhibited, conventional or unconventional, and so on, but any of those qualities could exist within *any* sexual lifestyle.)

* *Whether you are a human, an animal, or for that matter a building, idea, event, or even a question.* (If someone hands you a horoscope without any information about what it was cast for, you'll have no way of knowing whether it's for any of these things.)

* *When you're going to die.* (This one's a biggie. Yes, the horoscope can pinpoint critical times in a person's life, but not their date or time of death, at least not with any certainty. True, there are systems and techniques which *claim* to target the date or time of death, but there are obvious limits to that approach. For instance, a given horoscope could just as easily be for a pet hamster as for a person, each of which has a radically different average lifespan. So how could the horoscope by itself reveal a definitive date or time of death, without taking into account the baseline longevity of who or what it's cast for?)

* *What someone's exact level of genius is.* (While the horoscope can show certain genius-like tendencies, it won't reveal whether those potentials will actually *rise to the level* of genius. If it could, then we would expect someone born around the same time and location as Einstein, Isaac Newton, or James Joyce to rise to the same level of achievements as they did, when that's clearly not the case.)

* *What group karma you may be bound up with.* (Imagine an asteroid coming down and wiping out all life on the North American continent. Would that show up in the chart of every single inhabitant of North America? Of course not. That's because our own horoscope is embedded within larger blocs of group karma that extend beyond ourselves. If you're meant to be obliterated in an asteroid strike that will wipe out millions, it's unlikely that will be shown in the chart of every one of those victims!)

* *What specific form the various triumphs or tragedies of your life may take.* (A seriously afflicted Mars in someone's natal 4th house could manifest in many different ways during a person's life, such as through sexual issues, domestic conflicts, a home fire, and so on. But we can't be 100% certain of the specifics involved, as far as which way it will go for any single individual.)

* *What a person's true level of spiritual growth or maturity is.* (The horoscope shows the general nature of the challenges and potentials you'll encounter in this life, but not *your response to them.* A common example of that would be the lives of twins. Two individuals can be born only a few minutes apart with nearly identical horoscopes, with afflicted Neptunes in the 12th house, say; yet one of them might become an alcoholic while the other one becomes a monk. There is an element both of uncertainty and free will in our response to the chart. For much the same reason, the chart can't really show a person's level of *spirituality* with certainty, since that involves a function of self-control and inner balance in responding to the challenges of life.)

* *Your future.* (Well, not in detail anyway. The horoscope can describe the general trends that are coming up in your life, such when you might experience good luck with someone living far away; but it won't tell you that on May 21st of 2023 you will meet a person named Domingo from Spain who will hand you a check for $945!)

* *Lastly, and perhaps most subtly, the chart doesn't tell you what a person* should do *in confronting their major life decisions.* That is, while the chart provides useful information as to how things might turn out, that's quite different from saying what someone *should do,* in terms of what the wisest choice of action for them will be, since that's a highly personal matter depending on various factors unique to them. Here's an example. Several decades ago, I was invited to the wedding of a friend, and couldn't help but notice he planned the ceremony to take place on the exact day Saturn was set to square Venus. It took all my willpower to keep from warning him away from that date, since this was hardly an auspicious aspect for a blissfully happy romantic undertaking. But I felt that saying something unsolicited would be unethical, since he hadn't actually asked me for my opinion. So I kept quiet—which turned out to be a good thing. That's because even though the marriage ran into problems, predictably, it wound up serving as a valuable lesson for my friend, who was a double-Aries born with a natal Saturn/Venus square himself. The ensuing marital disaster faced him like nothing else could with his own self-centeredness and narcissism; consequently, as painful as the entire episode was for him, he learned something important from it and made changes for the better. In short, the fact that the planets were difficult at the time didn't necessarily mean he *shouldn't* get married, simply that it would be difficult—which is an altogether different thing. Lots of useful or important life experiences are difficult, but that doesn't mean one shouldn't experience them!

These, then, are a few of the things I believe the horoscope can't reveal. But why is it important to even know understand what these limitations are? I feel there are several reasons.

The first of those simply has to do with *context.* The horoscope delineates the broad contours of a person's life, but those contours are heavily modified by the specific life-context for that person. For example, reading the chart for a child will be different from reading for them when they're 70. While the planetary patterns may be the same, the outer circumstances and internal psychology they bring to bear on those patterns will be radically different. By the same token, reading a chart for someone from Japan will be different than reading for someone from Italy—just as reading for someone living in the Amazon jungle will be different than reading for a Wall Street broker in Manhattan. (You wouldn't tell the Amazonian tribesman that the upcoming Uranus trines to their midheaven might manifest as great new opportunities in the futures markets!) Context is nearly everything, and having a better understanding of it can only benefit our readings.

For example, when doing predictive-based readings for clients, I often find it helpful to begin by asking a few questions about what's been happening in their lives recently. True, a big part of the reason they've come to me in the first place is to find out *from me* what's going on for them. But learning a little bit about them at the start of our discussion actually allows me to be more precise in looking ahead for them. Suppose transiting Uranus is about to conjunct someone's Venus, and they tell me they've been married for ten years. That Uranus aspect will manifest very differently than if they'd told me they've been single for the last ten years! In the first case, it's likely their marital commitment will be seriously put to the test, while in the latter case they could find themselves facing new romantic opportunities. Obtaining a certain amount of information about them up front gives me a useful springboard for understanding what may lie just ahead for them.

But an even more serious value to understanding astrology's limitations has to do with the perspective—and safety—of the client. As I touched on in opening this piece, I occasionally encounter the misconception (especially among first-time clients) that the horoscope shows *everything*, and that the astrologer is some sort of omniscient, all-knowing oracle. That can set the client up for false hopes, or even false fears. Suppose the astrologer tells someone they're going to become rich, or famous, or that they will get happily married. If those things *don't* come to pass, that person will likely be very disappointed—especially if they believe that the astrologer is an all-knowing, omniscient oracle. Conversely, if the astrologer tells them they will be unlucky in love, or that they'll die at a certain time, that will obviously impact the client's well-being in other ways.

But there's also this to consider. That perceived aura of oracle-like authority projected onto the astrologer can make vulnerable clients open to potential abuse, if they happen to be working with a predatory astrologer prone to seducing clients with comments like, "I can tell from our charts that you and I were meant to be together in this life," or "There's great sexual chemistry between our horoscopes!" For that reason, I think it may be healthy for some clients—especially those completely new to the discipline—to be aware of astrology's limitations, and the fact that astrologers *aren't* omniscient or infallible. Needless to say, problems like this aren't exclusive to the astrological community, since they can happen in virtually any helping profession, but it would be naive to pretend they never happen in our field at all.

In the end, I'd add that the assorted limitations we're discussing here actually speak to something quite positive about astrology—namely, that the horoscope *is not* in fact the whole picture. To my mind, that means that we enjoy a certain degree of freedom in our lives, that there is actually some "wiggle room" in our response to our charts. An analogy I used earlier in this book is how the chart is like a piece of sheet music, in that it can be played many different ways and in many different styles—jazz, rock, ballad, classical, etc. Even if we can't easily change the notes, we can certainly influence the *style*. The same goes for horoscopes, which can be played in different "styles."

So coming back to that question originally asked by my client when I started this article, "Does the horoscope really tell you *every-thing* about someone?" No, it doesn't—and that's something we should probably be grateful for.

This essay first appeared in the October/November 2019 issue of The Mountain Astrologer magazine.

CHAPTER 11

ON THE ROLE OF INTUITION
IN CHART INTERPRETATION

O ver the years I've increasingly found it helpful paying attention to intuitive impressions that crop up while talking to
clients, however odd or off-the-wall those impressions might seem
at first.

As an example, I had a female client come to me who was born
with Mars in Pisces near her Midheaven. While preparing that
reading and contemplating that chart pattern, the image of the
Joan of Arc flashed quickly through my mind. Reflecting on that
for just a second, that actually made a certain sense, considering
that Joan was a religious warrior-figure, which could fit quite well
with Mars in Pisces.

So I cautiously decided to ask the client if this held any particular meaning for her. She was surprised, and told me she owned a
small statue of Joan of Arc, and it was the only heirloom handed
down to her after her parents had passed away. This exchange
then became a useful point of departure for me in discussing not
only her family legacy but her own very assertive idealism on various fronts, from animal rights activism to promoting the arts, and
so on. My intuition had proved useful in that case.

Here's another example. I was talking over the phone with a client living in the American Southwest about an upcoming transit of Neptune in Pisces crossing over the top of her horoscope, when an image of people on a beach surfing suddenly appeared in my mind. That seemed bit odd, not only because she lived in a land-locked area but because I'd never had an image like that come up for me during a reading. It turned out that the upcoming time frame I was describing for her was the period she was planning to travel to San Diego to learn surfing! Here as well, the Neptunian symbolism of the situation provided me with a jumping-off point for discussing other developments in her life currently taking place, of which surfing was just a symbol.

Another instance was my client who had spent his life as a psy-chotherapist, and who was simply curious what I saw in his chart. I spoke at length about the various patterns which stood out for me, but towards the end of our discussion something drew my atten-tion back to the Pluto/Moon conjunction up in his 9th house. Out of the blue, an image formed in my mind of a young man standing in a cave in or around Greece, conducting some type of ritual or invocation likely connected to the Eleusinian myster-ies and the cult of Persephone and Demeter. This was so striking that I decided to tell him about it and ask if it meant anything to him. He was surprised upon hearing this, because as a young man in his early 20s he actually traveled to both Greece and Crete, and at one point spent time exploring a cave in that area while doing research into the Eleusinian mysteries! Here as well, that exchange became a starting point for a more in-depth discussion of his Moon/Pluto conjunction, and how it tied into his involve-ment with psychology and studies into the ancient mystery cults (and caves!).

Here's one last example, this one having more to do with the art of synthesis in interpretation. I was having a particularly hard time with a horoscope I was scheduled to do, since it displayed so many oppositions and squares, indicating various contradictory tendencies—outgoing and introverted, selfish and unselfish, rebellious and conformist—that I wasn't sure how to tie it all together without seeming like I was just throwing a lot of spaghetti against the wall in hope something might stick. I stopped for a few moments, closed my eyes, and just waited to see what impressions arose. What appeared in my mind was a medieval engraving I'd seen weeks before of a person being drawn and quartered—i.e., someone literally being torn limb from limb. While I certainly didn't want to mention that gruesome image to her, I did mention the possibility she could feel sometimes as though she was being "torn in several directions" with her varied responsibilities. On hearing that, *she* actually brought up the historical image of someone being "drawn and quartered"! To my surprise, it turned out she had a degree in medieval history (something I didn't know), and explained how that form of punishment often haunted her because of the way it seemed to symbolize the way she felt on so many occasions in her life.

For me, experiences like these raise a number of questions, one of which is whether a computerized chart reading—however sophisticated—could truly ever replace that intuitive element which almost all seasoned astrologers experience from time to time. Whether you ascribe that intuitive faculty to something metaphysical or simply to some higher form of logic doesn't really matter; either way, it's real, it's effective, and over time seems to play an ever-greater role in whatever divinatory system one is practicing.

But it also reminded me of something a colleague online remarked not long ago when he asserted that astrology would ideally be broken down into a series of precise formulas, and that if one really truly understood those formulas it would take the "guesswork" out of readings. To him, it was all really just a matter of "quantifiable principles," and he predicted we'd ultimately find a way to bring these all together in order to provide highly accurate horoscope readings, even in computerized form.

But can any number of formulas, however intricate and precise, ever really replace that intuitive, synthesizing component? I wouldn't say "never," but let's just say my intuition tells me not to hold my breath.

CHAPTER 12

RELATIONSHIPS AND THE SEVENTH HOUSE

S ome of the most common queries astrologers find themselves grappling with involve matters of romance and partnerships. "How will I fare in love?" "Will I get married?" "What kind of partner will I become involved with?"

Needless to say, these are complex questions, since "romance" can mean different things to different people, and various astrological factors can factor into their outcomes. For instance, someone's sexual drives or satisfaction can be indicated by the condition of their Mars and Venus, as well as their 5th house. The luminaries (Sun and Moon) are also important to consider, since they embody the fundamental masculine and feminine principles in someone's life, which is true whether one is straight and gay.

But the 7th house tends to show one's fortunes in terms of actual *partnerships,* and by that I mean romantic relationships that are more formal or long-lasting in nature. As a result, someone's chart may have a Jupiter/Mars conjunction in their 5th house, which tends to show a relatively lively sexual life, while also having a conflicted Saturn in the 7th house, which points to more frustrating challenges in areas of marriage or partnerships. (The converse is true as well, of course: someone may have Jupiter/Venus in the 7th house but a stressed-out Saturn in the 5th, which points to more stable partnerships but not necessarily the happiest time in the bedroom.)

In the broadest sense, the zodiacal sign on the 7th house can be extremely revealing as to the types of partners one will become involved with, as well as one's attitudes towards partnerships generally. What follows are some brief synopses I've put together for each of the twelve signs on the 7th house, and what general tendencies these signify. For a more refined analysis, one should also carefully examine the condition of the planetary ruler for that sign and house, which will reveal further clues into how and where that energy will express itself.

ARIES ON THE 7TH HOUSE

With Aries on your Seventh House, you may find yourself attracted to highly energetic, motivated types, with a possible interest in (or involvement with) sports, business, or other high-octane activities. Their self-confidence or forcefulness serves to complement your own tendency to deliberate in situations, and can help to light a fire beneath you. You prefer someone with whom you can engage in energetic activities with, such as sports, hiking, or (of course) sex. Couch-potatoes? Extreme introverts? They're not for you. At a deeper level, all this is because you are attracted to the "fire" in their personalities, which can ignite your own potentials in various ways. In turn, your sense of harmony and fair play can serve to counterbalance *their* tendency towards impulsiveness or impatience at times. But you need to be cautious that the very thing which attracted you to them in the first place—their energetic, forceful nature—doesn't also become a source of conflict and argumentation between you. They can be fighters, in both the best and worst ways. But remember: it takes two to tango, so make sure you're not contributing to that dysfunctional dance without realizing it. The essential key is this: always look before you leap, and never rush headlong into any relationship without first carefully examining your prospective partner's personality, as well as the dynamics between you. Take it one step at a time at first, and see where it goes. After all, what's the hurry?

TAURUS ON THE 7TH HOUSE

With Taurus on your 7th house, you are drawn towards practical and financially stable types who provide an element of material security to your life. Simply put, they *ground* you. They don't necessarily need to be wealthy, but it's certainly preferable if they are self-sufficient and balanced in worldly matters. It's even possible you could find yourself involved in financial or business dealings with them. Despite that, you'll want to be cautious of individuals who exhibit signs of extravagance, indulgence, or materialistic traits. Venus rules this sign, so those with this house placement are frequently drawn toward artistic types—painters, sculptors, designers of one sort or another. They may also have a connection to nature somehow, and this can be an area where the two of you share quality time together, whether through enjoying the outdoors, gardening, or traveling to beautiful places. Cooking can be a point of connection between you as well. Since Venus rules this sign, you definitely prefer your partners to be physically beautiful or sensual, though be wary of basing long-term relationships solely on sexual gratification! They're probably more conservative than you in important ways. You also need to be careful that the very thing which drew you to them in the first place—their practicality and ability to ground you—doesn't conceal a hidden stubbornness, or that their relatively conservative tendencies don't wind up boring you.

GEMINI ON THE 7TH HOUSE

Gemini on the Seventh House indicates you place a premium on partners who are intelligent or with whom you can communicate. There certainly needs to be a strong mental rapport. They may themselves may be involved in a profession where communication is vital, like writing, media, sales, or teaching. They can be versatile, the proverbial "jack of all trades," and you definitely prefer them to be flexible and ready for any change of plans. More than the average person, you like to have fun with your partner, and enjoy stimulating activities together. They may be younger than you, but watch for immaturity or irresponsibility. They can be involved with travel, which may even be a point of connection between you. Like you, your partners also values freedom and independence, which can make the dance of commitment a lively one over the course of your entire life, where you are the one wanting commitment in one relationship, only to be the person wanting freedom in the next! Gemini harbors a certain mischievous or even deceptive streak at times, so be on your guard for duplicity or infidelity on their part, though you may yourself be tempted to engage in more than one partnership at the same time. That comes with its own share of risks, needless to say.

CANCER ON THE 7TH HOUSE

With the sign Cancer on your Seventh House, emotional security is the dominant priority of your partnerships. You are drawn to highly sensitive, even intuitive types. Because Cancer governs the home and domestic matters, the role of family is a central one in your relationship, not only in terms of creating and managing your own but negotiating the sometimes perilous straights of your extended families, with both in-laws and "out-laws"! This emphasis on family can cut both ways, being potentially a source of extraordinary emotional richness as well as soul-wrenching dramas. This zodiacal sign relates to the maternal principle generally, so your partner may be called on to nurture or mother you—or, conversely, you may find yourself playing the nurturer and mother to them. It is especially important to strike a mature balance in that way, both emotionally and financially, so that it never veers towards an unhealthy extreme where one partner is more like the dependent child and the other the responsible parent. Watch early on for signs of possible problems in this area, should they reveal indications of neediness or dependency. Above all, seek out a partner who simply accepts you, with whom you can be emotionally vulnerable and set aside the stiff formality of your Capricorn Ascendant so that you can just be yourself.

LEO ON THE 7ᵀᴴ HOUSE

With Leo on your Seventh House, you are attracted to strong personalities who have a certain flair or sense of style about them. They may be involved with performing or coming before the public in some way. It's definitely a plus if they have a creative streak, whether that be in the music, acting, or the entertainment field. Their inspired playfulness and ability to engage fully in life serves to counterbalance your own tendency towards detachment or mental observation. On a deeper level, you're drawn to their confidence and self-esteem because it embodies qualities you strive to awaken in yourself. Be on your guard, though; this placement can indicate being drawn towards powerful personalities, so be careful that you don't simply "give away your power" to them in ways that blind you to your own potentials or degree of control in situations. It's good to remember that the health of your partnerships will always mirror the strength or weakness or your own ego, so if your own self-esteem is lacking, you'll probably attract partners who either reflect that lack, or else compensate for it through domineering behavior. In those cases, power struggles between the two of you can ensue, with your partner's strong personality causing you to feel overshadowed or even bulldozed at times. It's especially gratifying when you find someone who can engage in creative activities with you, and who is supportive of your own goals.

VIRGO ON THE 7ᵀᴴ HOUSE

With Virgo on the Seventh House you prefer partners who are intelligent and analytical while being responsible and practical at the same time. It helps if they are well-educated, and you prefer them to be conscientious and good-workers. They can be concerned about health or involved with the healing professions in some way. They may be more conservative than you, which can actually be a good thing in helping to ground you and compensate for your own idealism or even casualness about ordinary matters. Whereas you can be nonchalant or even dreamy about life at times, your partner will be the one who dots the "i's" and crosses the "t's." That may involve areas of hygiene, too. But watch that their conservative tendencies don't conceal an overly prim and proper sensibility that ultimately frustrates you—or, on the other hand, that your own "casual" style doesn't wind up driving them crazy, too. Be especially careful of those who seem critical towards you, or who you in turn wind up criticizing. Together, you complement each other well, but guard against a general atmosphere of negativity or mutual fault-finding. It's ideal if you can find a cause that the both of you fully support and share energies with.

LIBRA ON THE 7TH HOUSE

With Libra on your Seventh House, you are drawn towards someone who is refined, graceful, or even beautiful. They are likely to be involved with the public in some capacity, either as a performer, artist, teacher, or perhaps even lawyer. They are good communicators, and can be skilled diplomats. Though they can be quite attractive, guard against those who show signs of vanity or self-centeredness, or even superficiality. They have a soothing effect on you, and serve to counterbalance your own tendency to be impulsive or react to situations emotionally. It's especially important that you go that extra mile to see each other's viewpoint on matters, since you may have dramatically different opinions about situations and approaches to problems. Also, make sure your naturally competitive nature doesn't get in the way! Your partner represents a side of you that you'd like to develop more of in yourself—namely, a refined and more emotionally balanced nature.

SCORPIO ON THE 7TH HOUSE

With Scorpio on the Seventh House, sex appeal in a partner is especially important to you. Though surface beauty may be a part of that, it's really their deeper sense of passion and charisma that draws you in. You prefer there to be an air of mystery about them, and the old saying 'still waters run deep' could well describe your choices in partnerships. They may even exude a sense of hidden strength. But watch for signs that this doesn't lead to power struggles or possessiveness. It's important that neither of you bury your emotions too deep or conceal important secrets or resentments, so try to get issues out in the open in a healthy way, even if that means seeking the help of a third party or therapist. Otherwise, you may be surprised by unexpected eruptions that transform the relationship in serious ways. In marriage, be especially cautious when dealing with the temptations of extra-marital dalliances. And while sex appeal is important, it's important not to base long-term relationships solely on sexual chemistry. Especially watch that you're not attracted to "bad boy" or "bad girl" types simply because you find that undercurrent of danger strangely alluring. Shared finances are very possible with this placement, but they need to be watched carefully lest you find yourself squabbling over money or harboring resentments over possessions.

SAGITTARIUS ON THE 7TH HOUSE

With Sagittarius on your Seventh House, personal freedom is of enormous importance in partnerships, and you may attract a partner who feels that same need for freedom as well. In any event, don't be surprised if your relationship starts feeling a bit claustrophobic. To help avoid that problem, it's important that you establish ground rules for maintaining personal space, so that you and your partner can enjoy sufficient breathing room to keep the partnership from suffocating either of you. At their best, partnerships have an expansive quality for you, and can expand your horizons.

You'll likely enjoy traveling with your partner, and they may even hail from a far-off location. It's ideal if they have a great sense of humor. There is a considerable amount of good luck with this placement, and that enables you to draw in partnerships more easily than most. Be careful not to treat them too lightly, though, lest the individuals you leave behind wind up nursing their broken hearts as you ride off into the sunset! Religion or philosophy can play a key role in your relationships, and can enrich your connection, whether that be through a shared religious faith, spiritual practice, or ideological viewpoint. But be on your toes for signs of extreme opinions or dogmatism on their part, so that personal philosophies don't wind up driving the two of you apart.

CAPRICORN ON THE 7TH HOUSE

With Capricorn on your Seventh House, you can find yourself drawn to individuals who are professional, ambitious, or have achieved a fair amount of status and position in life. Slackers need not apply! There can be a significant age difference with this placement, too. Many of those with Capricorn on the Seventh can find that establishing a serious relationship occurs later in life than most, or certainly later you'd they'd prefer. This can be due to a certain cautiousness or shyness on your part, or to more external factors—but remember that delay doesn't necessarily mean denial! Guard against an attitude of negativity regarding relationships and marriage, and work to keep a positive and constructive attitude towards this area of your life. Being in partnership can seem challenging in many ways, and may feel like you're required to take on heavier responsibilities than you originally expected. Since Cancer is on your first house, this combination usually shows that one partner is more focused on caretaking the home and family, while the other is out in the world playing the more professional role. If so, it's important that you strike a healthy balance in that regard, so that it doesn't cause conflict or resentments. If your prospective partner is indeed older or enjoys an elevated status, that can be very beneficial but you should watch for early warning signs of coldness or excessive detachment on their part.

AQUARIUS ON THE 7TH HOUSE

With Aquarius on the Seventh House, you're likely drawn to a partner who is unconventional, or at the least quite different from you. They will be unique in certain respects, and stimulate your own personality and imagination more than you might first realize. They're "ahead of the curve" in their own way, and may be an innovator in their respective profession or hobby. In extreme cases, they might seem like a bit of an oddball by society's standards—such as an astrologer, scientist, inventor, or social activist. But that difference is part of what attracts you, since it mirrors qualities in yourself you hope to draw out more. You definitely require freedom in relationships, and may well enjoy an unconventional arrangement with your partner. It's extremely important that you respect each other's independence and create a good deal of time and space to be on your own. Because Aquarius relates to groups, your partner can be involved with organizations or community projects of some sort, and may also be heavily involved with technology and media. But watch for signs early on that they're not too detached or mentally removed from their emotions, or that they don't appreciate your more fun-loving, spontaneous nature. On the other hand, be careful that your own need for attention or desire for control doesn't get out of hand! The two of you balance each other very well, and shared creativity is especially recommended; but extreme tendencies on either side can become a major stumbling block if not addressed early on.

PISCES ON THE 7TH HOUSE

With Pisces on the Seventh House, you prefer partners who are sensitive, spiritually-inclined, or artistic. They can balance out your more analytical, logical qualities in good ways. But your ideal-ism about relationships may not always mesh with cold reality. If not tempered by common sense, that can lead to problems when you discover that those traits you originally found so appealing in them turn out to have other kinds of baggage attached. You are capable of giving wholeheartedly in partnerships, but there are times when that can feel like a heavy sacrifice or obligation. Especially be on guard early on that your partner doesn't harbor secret dependencies or addictions, or health issues that grow more serious over time if unattended. In such cases, that could lead to some emotionally draining caretaking on your part later on. And while your partners may be good souls at heart, realize that if they can't pay their bills, those responsibilities may well shift over to you. But it's also possible that, deep down, caretaking is something you actually feel comfortable with, since a part of you may be drawn to helping partners in extreme ways. One way or another, there is always something karmic about your significant relationships, a feeling that, one way or another, you've been drawn together by fate.

CHAPTER 13

ASTROLOGY'S HARD LESSON

Astrology has many insights to offer, but one of the most profound happens to be one that many people have the hardest time accepting. It goes something like this:

Suppose a person grows up in a painful or even traumatic family environment, and winds up developing considerable anger as an adult over that early upbringing, perhaps even believing those early family members were responsible for his or her later dysfunctions, relationship issues, general failures, and so on.

Needless to say, those early life-challenges will surely be indicated in some way within that person's horoscope, whether it be through hard aspects to the Sun or Moon, the placement of Saturn or Mars in the 10th or 4th house, or some other configuration—there are many ways this type of situation can be indicated.

But here is the bitter pill that some find hard to swallow. Those horoscopic patterns, whatever they may be, *were present in that person's horoscope from the moment they were born.* Why is that important? Because it suggests that before any family member had a chance to do anything at all to them, or facilitate any of the problems they've held grudges about since childhood, the celestial patterns indicating those things were *already present in their life from the very start.*

So what should we make of this? It almost seems as though those family members were simply the conduits or triggers for those problems encoded within the birth chart, rather than their Sole cause.[1] That isn't to absolve those family members for whatever abuses or negligent acts they may have committed, of course, but it does suggest that those early life-dramas were intimately connected to something in that individual's life-destiny from a very early point.

Like I said, it's one of the more difficult lessons astrology has to offer, and actually applies not just to early family traumas but to *any and all* painful situations we experience in life with their reflection in the horoscope. Understandably, this idea triggers defensive reactions for some, probably because it can easily be interpreted as "blaming the victim," or suggesting that life-problems may be payback for past "bad karma." But there are actually a few different ways of looking at this.

For example, yes, it's possible some of the troubling things we encounter in life are "karmic," and that we're reaping what we've sowed in one past life or another, perhaps even stemming from many lifetimes ago.

But it's also possible, as some mystics have suggested, that a person can take on difficult situations in life specifically to learn something new, or to elicit potentials that can only be cultivated as a result of challenging situations. In these cases, it has far less to do with "bad karma" than with one's spiritual evolution, or what some might call *dharma*. As Goswami Kriyananda remarked, "… one of the mistakes that many modern western astrologers make is they believe that squares or oppositions are due to 'bad karma.' And they're not. *Many times we induce difficult squares into a chart when we're born in order to accomplish something.*" (Emphasis mine) [2]

In fact, rather than see this as somehow blaming victims for their misfortunes, I'd suggest a different reframe—namely, that it's actually a way of taking responsibility for our lives and refusing to see our various triumphs and tragedies as the random workings of a meaningless universe. Are we simply victims of a cosmic crapshoot, unwitting recipients of the "slings and arrows of outrageous fortune"? Or is there some meaning and purpose to the challenges we experience?

The German philosopher Schopenhauer framed the question this way: "Is a complete misadjustment possible between the character and the fate of an individual? Or is every destiny on the whole appropriate to the character that bears it?" [3]

Looked at deeply enough, astrology seems to have its own answer for that.

CHAPTER 14

FUTURE SHOCK: CONTEMPLATING URANUS'S NEXT RETURN TO ITS DISCOVERY DEGREE

W e all know about the doctrine of "planetary returns," and how a celestial body circles back around to where it stood at the time of one's birth. At such times, that body's meaning is reconceptualized, reformulated, and can even reach a new plateau of expression. Whether they realize it or not, even non-astrologers know about this principle, more or less. I say that because it lies at the root of one of the most common rituals we humans partake in: the birthday celebration, when the Sun makes a full revolution around the zodiac 360 degrees from where it was at the time of one's birth.

Yet returns don't simply affect individuals but entire nations, possibly even the entire Earth. I'm not simply referring to national horoscopes and how planets return to their natal positions in those charts, although that's true, too. I'm talking about the fact that the three outer planets of our solar system—Uranus, Neptune, and Pluto—were discovered on specific dates in recent history, which allows us to construct charts for their positions and then determine when they will return to the zodiacal degree they occupied when they were discovered. Such times could well be thought of as planetary returns not just for specific individuals or even nations, but *for everyone, everywhere—indeed, For the entire Earth*

For example, Pluto was discovered in 1930, but its orbit around the zodiac is so lengthy (roughly 250 years) that it won't return to its discovery degree in Cancer during the lifetime of anyone now reading this. Neptune doesn't take quite as long to make that complete circuit (roughly 164 years), and it finally experienced its first full return somewhere between 2009 and 2010. (There is disagreement about the exact timing, due to the role that precession plays in these calculations, but that's a relative quibble when talking about a planetary cycle lasting over a hundred years.)

Uranus was discovered by William Herschel in 1781, and is slated to return to its discovery degree at 24° Gemini in 2031, with an orb of several years on either side. So it's natural to ask: What will this bring for humanity?

Fortunately, since Uranus's orbit around the zodiac takes only 84 years, we already have two Uranus returns under our belt to look to for clues as to what might be expected this next time around. Let's take a quick look at some of the events surrounding those previous returns, along with symbols around the original discovery of Uranus, to help us make some educated guesses about this impending one.

Looking Back: The Discovery of Uranus

As I explored in my book *Signs of the Times* (Hampton Roads, 2002), the entire period around the discovery of Uranus in 1781 saw a number of dramatic trends taking shape throughout our world, of which three are especially noteworthy for our purposes. The first of those is political in nature. The period of the late 1700s has often been called the "era of revolution," since popular uprisings upended governments in America and France, and spurred unrest in other parts of the globe. With the emergence of modern democracy, this was a time when "people power" was emerging as a force for change, and along with it a newfound sense that ordinary citizens could seize the reins of power and control their own destinies. It was a transformation of popular consciousness, and the seeds planted during this period would have lasting effects for centuries to come.

Another dominant trend of the era was technological, as reflected in the rise of the Industrial Revolution. This was a period of extraordinary innovation, with such diverse developments as the modern steam engine, the cotton gin, and myriad early investigations into electricity. [1]

However, in some ways, the most iconic technological development of the period was the advent of aviation. In 1783, just two years after the discovery of Uranus, the Montgolfier brothers staged a public demonstration of the first hot-air balloon capable of carrying passengers. It was, in a very real sense, the birth of modern aviation, since it signaled the start of humanity gaining mastery over gravity, and it eventually led to the emergence of such technologies as airplanes, jets, rockets, and even spacecraft. Modest as it was, that single balloon lifting skyward was a profound sign of the times, not just technologically but also in terms of humanity's breaking free from the Saturnian limitations of the past in other ways—religiously, politically, economically, and creatively.

Planet Earth's First Uranus Return: 1863
Uranus made its first full revolution to its discovery point in 1863, although its influence extended at least ten years on either side. Throughout the mid-1800s, the concern for personal freedom and civil rights grew exponentially, as reflected in the abolition of slavery in countries around the world and the growing sympathy for the rights of the poor and disenfranchised. Lincoln's Emancipation Proclamation was signed during the peak of that return in 1863. Although the American Civil War was the most conspicuous manifestation of this social ferment in the United

States, similar developments were occurring elsewhere, too—for example, Russia's abolishing of serfdom in 1861.

Technologically, this was a time when mechanical innovation was transforming our world in dramatic ways, too. The mid-to-late 19th century saw the emergence of such innovations as the telegraph, electric lights, the transatlantic cable, photography, the steamship, and ever-expanding railway systems. In science, Charles Darwin ignited an intellectual revolution with the publication of *The Origin of Species* in 1859, a book that forever altered the way humans viewed both the world and themselves.

But significantly, this was also a time when lighter-than-air travel was gaining momentum as an idea in popular culture. Jules Verne's *Five Weeks in a Balloon* was published in 1863, while his book *From the Earth to the Moon*, published in 1865, introduced readers to the possibility of journeys beyond the Earth, and even fantasized about humanity's interaction with alien beings. In fact, the term "aviation" itself was coined in 1863 by French pioneer Guillaume Joseph Gabriel de La Landelle.

The Second Uranus Return: 1947

The 1940s marked yet another period of extraordinary social ferment around the world. In addition to the profound impact of World War II, this decade also became a major turning point in the emergence of individual rights, not simply with the wartime overthrow of fascism but with the establishment of key democratic governments around the globe—the most dramatic example being India, which in 1947 became the largest democracy in the world (and remains so to this day).

The flip side of Uranian "people power" was the overthrow of China's established government by revolutionaries spearheaded by Mao Zedong, giving birth to the People's Republic of China. Though reformist in several positive respects (e.g., the virtual elimination of prostitution and China's drug problems), this created another form of tyranny with its own problems and social issues. And in the U.S., the Central Intelligence Agency was formally established in September 1947, bequeathing its own decidedly mixed legacy to the world.

Technologically, the late 1940s ushered in a period of unprecedented innovation and mechanization. As writer and blogger Christopher Loring Knowles expressed, "In historical terms, this is as if your three-year-old were in nursery school one day and then graduated from Harvard at the top of her class as soon as she turned four. There's simply no precedent for the high-tech explosion that began in the late 1940s." [2]

Scientists had unlocked the powers of the atom, and in 1945 unleashed them to devastating effect in Hiroshima and Nagasaki. The transistor was developed in 1947, and went on to become the most popular electronic communications device in history. Computer technology was developing at a rapid pace, with the first stored-program computer (nicknamed *Baby*) running its first program in 1948 at the University of Manchester. The 1940s were also an historic time for developments in aviation, with the development of rocketry and sophisticated new aircraft, as well as the establishment of the U.S. Air Force in the summer of 1947.

But a far more unusual "aviation"-related development also took place during this period—namely, the so-called Roswell incident, in which two or more alien spacecraft purportedly crashed in the New Mexico desert. A source of heated controversy ever since, the event itself occurred in early July 1947, literally within days of Uranus's return to its discovery degree at 24° Gemini. Whether this was in reality an encounter with alien races or something far more prosaic, the omenological symbolism of this story is worth pondering, as we're about to see.

The Third Uranus Return: 2031

The next return of Uranus to its discovery degree is set to occur in 2031, though its presence will naturally be felt for years on either side. [3] (That breadth of influence is amplified by the fact that the United States' third Uranus return will be occurring shortly beforehand, around 2027, suggesting there could well be considerable overlap or intersection between these two, symbolically.)

So what will this bring? To a large extent, it will undoubtedly usher in a culmination of those trends which began around 1781, and that were reinforced during that planet's subsequent returns—that's the approach I'll be taking here.

In our previous encounters with Uranus, there were seismic changes in the world's political order, so it's safe to say this return could bring a good deal of that, too. Does this portend the advent of major wars or revolutions, like those which occurred during the late 1700s, the mid-1800s, and the 1940s? That's a possibility. Also, considering the roles that China, India, and Israel played during the last return period in the late 1940s, it's conceivable these three nations could become especially important players in the coming global changes within this coming period.

Technologically, the late 2020s and early 2030s will likely usher in startling new inventions and scientific breakthroughs in areas like computerization, atomic research, astronomy, as well as media and telecommunications technologies. But there could well be a dark side to all this, too, such as nuclear accidents *à la* Fukushima, and perhaps even continuing repercussions from Fukushima itself. There could be accelerating environmental collapse, as well as the ever-mounting problems posed by our surveillance technologies.

Here's another possibility. The period around the discovery of Uranus during the late 1700s saw the growing popularity of "automatons"—complex mechanical contraptions designed to mimic human or animal behaviors. I find it curious that, as Uranus swings back around again, society seems to be careening toward the wholesale robotization and automation of society, to the extent that some analysts are predicting humans could be eliminated from the workforce almost entirely. Perhaps the next Uranus return could be a time when that trend reaches critical mass, culminating in what some imaginatively call *the rise of the machines.*

An even stranger possibility for our next Uranus return might be inferred from the Roswell incident of 1947. Viewed as an omen, what could that portend for this coming period? My own suspicion is that this could be a time when humans could finally establish open contact with nonhuman intelligences—and if the events of 1947 are any indication, this might even take place in the days or weeks immediately around the first exact return during the first half of July, 2031. Whatever form this takes, it would obviously represent a profound turning point in human history, with untold consequences for our religious, scientific, and social institutions.

Coda

One last thought. Because of the symbolic connection that many modern astrologers perceive between Uranus and the sign Aquarius, it's possible that these occasions of Uranus returns provide us with "sneak previews" of the next Great Age. What will the Aquarian era bring, in terms of cultural, technological, and political changes? It's possible that the period around 2031—like those of our two previous Uranus returns—will offer us more than a few important clues. Stay tuned!

This article first appeared in the August/September, 2017 digital edition of the Mountain Astrologer magazine.

CHAPTER 15

THE SEVEN TRADITIONAL PLANETS: DO THEY CORRESPOND TO MATHEMATICAL PRINCIPLES?

If the planets are truly "archetypes," or universal principles, it's natural to wonder whether they might relate to fundamental principles found in other symbolic systems. For example, I've wondered over the years whether the seven traditional planets could be equated with certain basic mathematical functions. Take a moment to consider the essential meanings associated with the planets alongside these following principles of math and see if you don't find the correspondences intriguing:

Venus = *addition*
Jupiter = *multiplication*
Mars = *division*
Saturn = *subtraction*
Sun = *power*
Moon = *square root*

What about Mercury? One possibility is that it doesn't relate so much to any specific function as to the *essence of mathematics itself,* which—like thinking—is founded on the principle of relationship, or the "ratio" between two or more quantities. (Note, too, how the word "ratio" lies at the root of *rationality*.)

Let's take a closer look at these correspondences for what they might suggest.

Recall how in traditional astrology Venus is referred to as the "Lesser Benefic," whereas Jupiter is considered to be the "Greater Benefic." This presents an interesting analog to the mathematical functions of addition and multiplication in the way each of these "expand" on something.

For instance, if you *add* the numbers 3 and 7, you simply get 10. But if you *multiply* those two, you get 21—a considerably greater amount. As such, multiplication represents a "greater" form of expansion, whereas addition represents a "lesser" form of expansion. (Notice, too, how Venus is associated with love, which is generally thought of as the *adding* of two beings together; whereas Jupiter could be equated with the expansion of that pairing via procreation into other living beings, as in "go forth and *multiply…*").

Likewise, one of the astrological qualities commonly associated with Mars is *divisiveness*, and the tendency to "cut into." That's a feature that equates well with the mathematical principle of division, whereby one quantity "cuts into" another, as if with a knife, thus splitting that original quantity into two or more quantities beyond the initial one.

But whereas Mars represents the ability to "cut into," Saturn is more often known as the ability to *cut out,* or *cut away.* Fittingly, a common association of Saturn is that of "loss" (sometimes symbolized as the Grim Reaper bearing his scythe), which obviously implies something being *subtracted* from one's life.

But what about the Sun and the mathematical function of "power" (an association I first heard from Shelly Trimmer)? Unlike multiplication, which involves one quantity amplifying another, the mathematical principle of power relates to the *amplifying of any quantity by itself*—such as 4 squared, 10 to the 20th power, or 45 to the 3rd power. In a very similar way, the Sun symbolizes the principle of self-awareness, the Leonine egoic ability to *expand upon and amplify one's own being*. (Also, note how astronomers explain the way suns are born out of gaseous intergalactic clouds that have become so compressed back on themselves that the energy stored within them breaks loose and sets off a chain reaction—with light exploding outward as a result.)

In contrast, the Moon represents more of an internal awareness or emotional reflectivity, and is sometimes even described, symbolically, in terms of "roots." So its association with the function of the "square root" is clear, since that, too, deals with the core root-essence of any quantity.

The Outer Planets

Where do the outer three planets Uranus, Neptune, and Pluto fit into this scheme, if at all? Interestingly, they correspond surprisingly well with the mathematical associations we saw with Saturn, Jupiter, and Mars.

Consider the relation of Mars to the principle of division and that of "cutting into." In the case of a planetary aspect like a Mercury-Mars square, for instance, we often see a propensity for "cutting" or "divisive" speech. But much the same thing occurs with Mercury-Pluto squares, albeit in more covert or subtle ways, as with sarcasm or passive/aggressive criticism.

And Neptune is expansive in a way similar to Jupiter, but with a subtle difference. For example, someone born during a Sun-Jupiter square may exhibit an exaggerated or expansive sense of identity or goal-setting; by contrast, someone born with the Sun-Neptune square will also exhibit an expansive sense of identity and goals, but in a way that might be considered more diffused or perhaps even "spacey."

And while Uranus might seem to be very different from Saturn, it is actually very similar in certain respects. For example, whereas someone born with a Sun-Neptune square will tend to have a comparatively expansive or diffuse sense of self, perhaps to the point of lacking clear boundaries, someone born with a Sun-Uranus square will instead be *extremely* individualistic, with *strongly* defined boundaries. That Uranian concern with differentiating oneself from the crowd is a far more eliminative, comparatively Saturnine process of "subtracting" one's identity from those of others, quite unlike the blurring of boundaries seen with either Neptune or Jupiter. [1]

Final Thoughts

As far as what usefulness we might draw from this cross-pollination of systems, here are a few points to consider. For one, it could serve as a teaching tool for helping to convey the essential meanings of the planets to novice astrologers. (After all, who isn't familiar with the basic principles of math?) On a more philosophical level, this correspondence between systems suggests that archetypal principles—wherever we find them—are, at root, simply *qualities of relationship.* In a sense, neither the archetypes nor the planets are so much "things" as *patterns of behavior,* or *ways of becoming.*

Then there's this. As I believe we've demonstrated here, there's a striking correspondence between the meanings of the planets and certain mathematical principles; but what about other solar systems, with their own sets of planets and moons? Would we discover that those systems have their own versions of "Jupiter," "Saturn," "Venus," and so on, and that there are certain archetypal commonalities among all solar systems (based, perhaps, on harmonic principles similar to what was originally associated with "Bode's Law")? Or would we learn that our solar system is completely unique in the way it embodies these fundamental principles?

Definitely food for Pythagorean thought!

This article first appeared in the February, 2017 issue of Dell Horoscope magazine.

CHAPTER 16

"IT'S NOTHING PERSONAL!" ON THE FINE ART OF RELAYING HARD NEWS TO BELEAGUERED CLIENTS

A woman came to me several years ago with some of the most difficult planetary aspects I'd seen in years. Saturn, Mars, Neptune, and Pluto were all hitting her chart in challenging ways, by *both* transit and progression. This had all been unfolding for a year by the time of our meeting, and it looked to me like this planetary onslaught might continue for at least another six months.

I could tell just from the weary look on her face that she'd definitely been feeling the burn of those horoscopic heavy-hitters, and from the start of our talk seemed to be holding back tears. So over the next few minutes, I did my best to explain the impact of these energies in a way that gave her a sense of their magnitude but also provided some insight into their constructive possibilities, too.

I also felt it important to give her some sense of the time frame involved with all of this, to help her realize that the problems she was enduring weren't going to last forever. That seemed especially reassuring for her—as it does for many clients I've met who are experiencing challenging aspects. Clients not well-versed in astrology often fear that the difficult circumstances they're experiencing in the moment will remain that way for the rest of their lives!

Then, off the top of my head, I said something I hadn't really articulated to a client before, but which seemed appropriate at the time. That was this: "Probably the most important thing for you to realize about these energies right now is *not to take it too personally.*"

I went on to explain how for many clients during difficult times, it's tempting to believe that they're somehow to blame for what's gone wrong—and as a result can feel like they're a failure, a "loser." I know from first-hand experience that it's important to keep a sense of perspective on such situations, lest one fall prey to guilt or shame over what is happening. That's because what's happening is often simply the result of the astrological "weather"—the natural ebb and flow of impersonal forces which you can only do so much to change. To use an analogy, imagine you're living in a house in the country, when one day a huge storm blows up and a tornado damages your home. Do you think to yourself, "Somehow this must be my fault! This all happened because I f&$% up..."? Or do you chalk it up to simply being a case of difficujlt timing, an unfortunate shift in the weather?

In much the same way, the astrological energies sometimes converge in such a way as to disrupt our lives—marriage, job, health, and so on—and it's not necessarily anyone's "fault." Sure, karma may be involved, but that's just one piece of the puzzle. Watch any nature documentary from Africa where an animal on the savannah dies horribly at the hands of an attacking predator, and ask yourself: Was it that animal's "karma" which caused that fate? Or was it just the natural vicissitudes of life? As humans, we also have to contend with the extreme ups and downs of mortal existence—and when life's roller coaster careens down to its lowest point, sometimes all you can really do is simply hang on for dear life, knowing it will be over soon. Do the best you can, yes, but don't become too invested in the outcome.

To my surprise, my simple statement seemed to make a big difference for her. She breathed a sigh of relief, as though a weight had been lifted off her shoulders. Because, on top of all the problems she'd been facing, she had been beating herself up for everything that had gone wrong in her life, including even things completely beyond her control—like her husband leaving her for a younger woman after she was diagnosed with cancer.

Since that time, I've made a point of telling other clients who were going through especially hard times much the same thing, that it's helpful to not take those circumstances too personally, as if it's all their fault. Sometimes, it's just a matter of difficult timing, the result of a confluence of converging planetary cycles happening all at once—what I'll refer to in a later chapter as a "perfect storm" of astrological forces. An especially brutal winter comes and it turns frigidly cold outside, and it's not anyone's "fault," and certainly not punishment for someone's bad behavior.

So, if you're a working astrologer and this feels right to you, try it with your own clients who may be going through difficult times, using whatever words feel right to you, and see whether it makes a difference. If so, it may be just the thing that transforms an otherwise unbearable situation into something considerably more manageable.

CHAPTER 17

SEARCHING FOR PLANET X: HOW WILL ASTROLOGERS UNLOCK THE MEANING OF A NEW PLANET?

O f all the discoveries made by astronomers during the last few centuries, few if any have held as much excitement for astrologers as the possibility of new planets being discovered in our solar system.

And it just so happens that we've been hearing lately about mounting evidence for a new, previously unknown body at the fringes of our solar system—possibly the size of Neptune and orbiting the Sun once every 10,000 to 20,000 years. For some astronomers, faithfully abiding by Pluto's official demotion from its former status as a "planet," this new body is sometimes referred to by the unofficial title "Planet Nine"—though I'd personally prefer the alternative moniker suggested by others, *Planet X*.

If confirmed, this would of course be a special cause for celebration amongst astrologers, but also a certain amount of hand-wringing. Why either?

I say "celebration" because, for astrologers, a new planet represents a novel state of consciousness in the collective psyche, and with it a new set of symbolic possibilities. Think of it as similar to a painter acquiring a new color to add to his or her palette. (Of course, "new" is a relative term here, since any newfound planet would have existed for eons of time, just hidden from sight, with its discovery symbolizing those energies emerging more prominently *into consciousness.*)

On the other hand, a discovery would inaugurate a certain amount of "hand-wringing" since it would begin the thorny process of determining just what that new body *means*—something that could take years or even decades for astrologers to determine or agree upon.

While it's obviously too early to say anything concrete about Planet X, there are some general guidelines we could draw up as to what we might look for once an announcement has been made. We have some experience in these matters, actually, in light of humanity's encounter with the previous three trans-Saturnians: Uranus in 1781, Neptune in 1846, and Pluto in 1930. By looking to what occurred in the years surrounding those three discoveries (as I did with Uranus in chapter 14), we'll find some useful pointers as to how we could approach any newly discovered bodies. What follows are a few simple examples of what I mean.

The Revolutionary Impact of New Planets

Perhaps the most obvious point to make about the earlier bodies is that the discovery of each coincided with the rumblings of social revolution. That makes a certain archetypal sense when you consider how each new planet represents a disruption in the established order, with literally a new world of knowledge opening up for humanity.

Will that happen with the discovery of the next new planet as well? Almost certainly—and to my mind, that possibility is underscored by the body's likely orbit. Whereas Pluto extended the boundaries of our solar system far beyond their previous limits, the new planet has been theorized to be roughly *10 times farther out from our Sun than Pluto.* If nothing else, that suggests the state of consciousness it represents could be *very* out of the ordinary! But let's see if we can narrow this down a bit more, by speculating on a few specific areas.

Politics

As we also saw earlier, during the era of Uranus's discovery in the late 1700s our world was in the throes of a monumental shift due to the rise of modern democracy, exemplified by the American and French Revolutions. The period around the discovery of Neptune also represented a period of upheaval, as reflected not only in the European riots of the late 1840s but in the growing concern over the rights of the downtrodden and the enslaved. The years on either side of Pluto's discovery were turbulent as well, coming in the immediate wake of the so-called "Roaring 20s" and then a worldwide depression. There was growing anger amongst ordinary citizens across the world over our broken political and economic systems, which led to reforms in America by "New Deal" president Franklin Roosevelt and, in Germany and Italy, to the rise of fascist dictators who channeled that populist rage very differently.

Note how the social shifts during all three of these periods represented a rising up of oppressed and ordinary peoples in response to growing injustices and inequalities. Does that give us some clues as to what might happen with the new planet? If so, it could well explain some of the unrest we already see simmering in countries around the world.

Technological Changes and New Energy Sources

Each of these previous three discoveries has also been accompanied by stunning developments in science and technology, and in our ability to access and exploit Nature's resources. The highly Uranian 1700s saw the rise of mechanization and the Industrial Revolution, including assembly-line mass production, steam power, and early investigations into electricity. During Neptune's century, humanity awoke to the potentials of another major fuel source—oil. (The same year Neptune was discovered, businessman Samuel M. Kier from Pittsburgh found oil seeping into his salt well, which he then bottled and sold as medicine, and in 1859 the world's first oil well was drilled.) And the years around the discovery of Pluto witnessed the unlocking of the atom, and with that came the daunting specter of atomic energy.

What might a new planet signal, in terms of energy sources? It's notable that we're already seeing a growing number of stories in the media about alternative energy sources, including renewables and clean energy, along with a renewed interest in cold fusion. Or will it turn out to be something entirely different from anything previously known? Or perhaps all of the above?

Aviation

As we also saw earlier, the discovery of Uranus coincided with the birth of modern aviation, with the launch of the first hot-air balloon in 1783 by the Montgolfier brothers in France. In the years around Neptune's discovery, George Cayley built the first manned gilder, and Henri Gilfard built the first airship powered by an aircraft engine (unsuccessfully). And the 1900s saw the rapid rise not only of conventional aviation but the first liquid-fueled rockets in 1926, culminating eventually in space travel.

It's tempting to speculate about another quantum leap in aviation or space exploration. Perhaps that will involve the much-discussed "EmDrive" technology, designed in 2001 by aerospace engineer Roger Shawyer and theorized by some as revolutionizing space travel. Or could it be the development of anti-gravitational technology, so often discussed in UFO-related circles?

Archaeology and History

To my mind, one of the more intriguing aspects of all the trans-Saturnian discoveries has been how each one coincided with a shift in our understanding of *history*. To understand this, we need to look at something I touched on in chapter 3. Because of the time it takes for light to travel, this means that the further out into space we look, the further into the *past* we are seeing. When we look at Pluto through a telescope, for example, we're actually seeing how it appeared five hours earlier. As a result, the uncovering of these previously invisible bodies in our solar system can be viewed, synchronistically and symbolically, as mirroring a corresponding opening up of previously hidden knowledge about our deep past.

The same decade as Uranus's discovery, for example, geologist James Hutton presented a paper to the Royal Society of Edinburg arguing that the Earth was far older than generally believed—and ever since then our understanding of the past has continued to exponentially push beyond previous boundaries, from the once-thought 6000 years suggested by the Bible to the 13 billion years theorized by modern cosmologists.

Nor is it just our *planet's* age that has undergone a major overhaul. As a result of Darwin's theory of evolution, we've revised the antiquity of the human species itself, as new discoveries in archeology have also continued to alter the way we date civilization's origins, too. Archaeological discoveries at sites like Gobekli Tepe in Turkey and Gunung Padang in Indonesia have forced us to rethink the true birth of human culture by thousands of years. It's interesting to contemplate how our grasp of history could change with the discovery of a planet many times farther out than Pluto!

Economics

Interestingly enough, there have even been shifts in our economic philosophies with each new planetary discovery. The birth of modern capitalism is often associated with the publication of Adam Smith's *An Inquiry into the Nature and Causes of the Wealth of Nations* in 1776, simultaneous with the birth of the U.S. and just five years before the discovery of Uranus. The birth of modern socialism is associated with the publication of Karl Marx's *Communist Manifesto* in 1848—coinciding closely with the discovery of Neptune in 1846. Besides witnessing the rise of the modern "Plutocrat," the years around Pluto's discovery saw the rise of "Keynesian economics," with the publication of *The General Theory of Employment, Interest and Money* by John Maynard Keynes in 1936. In addition to ushering in the concept of *macroeconomics*, Keynes work has been called "revolutionary" because of his views about the role of government in regulating free markets. It's not far-fetched to imagine that a new planet could signal a new phase in our global economic system, and how we view money—especially considering the already-revolutionary impact the internet is having on business and such developments as Bitcoin, not to mention controversial proposals about a cashless society.

Some Technical Considerations

There are a few other points that could be useful when approaching a new planet and gauging its importance in our own lives.

* One of the classic methods used by astrologers for understanding a new body is by studying the mythological name assigned to it by astronomers, the underlying belief here being that a certain synchronicity exists between that naming and the planet's inherent nature. Despite some disagreement among astrologers over the usefulness of this method, my own feeling is that, despite its limitations, it remains a useful tool for unlocking a planet's symbolism and meaning. [1]

* Some further clues may also lie in studying the Sabian Symbol of the zodiacal degree occupied by the planet when it's found. For example, Uranus was at 24° Gemini 27" when it was discovered, thereby placing it fully in the 25th degree of that sign. The Sabian symbol for that degree? *A GARDERNER TRIMMING LARGE PALM TREES.* Considering the legacy Uranus has bequeathed to us in terms of modern technologies, there's something fitting about

the fact that its discovery is associated with an image of humans manipulating and reshaping nature. In much the same way, it's possible that the Sabian Symbol for a new planet could shed light on its meaning and subsequent role in humanity's future.

* There have already been some discussions as to what zodiacal sign Planet X could possibly rule. Presuming that Venus now rules Libra and that Mercury rules Gemini (though some dispute even those associations), then the new planet could conceivably rule either Virgo or Taurus. It's also possible this new planet could fall outside the conventional rulership scheme altogether. Or, might it enjoy another "co-rulership" status similar to the way Uranus, Neptune, and Pluto are viewed by many as sharing rulerships with Aquarius, Pisces, and Scorpio? (See chapter 27) One approach that might help settle the matter would be to closely study current events around the time of the planet's discovery, to see if they resonate to one sign more than another.

* Yet another way to gather insights into a planet's symbolism is to track the ephemeris and watch what happens each time another planet comes along and conjuncts, squares, or opposes it. By way of illustration, a search of major transits to Uranus over the years, coupled with a scan of news or historical accounts, clearly suggests it has something to do with technology and social change (among other things). Similarly, what would we learn from studying what happens whenever Jupiter, Saturn, or Uranus align with the new planet? This could also be done retroactively, by looking back over recent decades and centuries to see if any common threads emerge from its encounter with other planetary bodies, especially during conjunctions.

* Last but not least, once an ephemeris for the new planet has been established you could look at your own date of birth to see where the body fell in *your* horoscope, to understand what significance

it might hold in your life. Because of its great remoteness, Planet X's orbit would necessarily be so slow that it could remain in the same zodiacal region for long periods. As a result, it's important to see if the planet specifically lands on an angle in your horoscope, such as the Ascendant or Midheaven, or if it's conjunct a personal planet like the Sun or Moon. Contacts like these would suggest a far more intimate significance for you than for the average person. Here as well, carefully watching transits or progressions to that planet in your horoscope over time could reveal important clues as to is meaning and influence.

These are just a few ideas to keep in mind should an announcement about the new planet be forthcoming anytime soon. I'll be watching to see what the astronomers find!

This essay first appeared in the August, 2017 issue of The Mountain Astrologer magazine.

CHAPTER 18

ASTROLOGY OF THE WEIRD: STRANGE
LIGHTS OVER PHOENIX

On the night of July 22, 2015, Julia Graham and her husband were driving near historic Rosehill Cemetery in Chicago when they caught sight of a figure in a clown outfit standing near the cemetery entrance. On being illuminated by the car's headlights, the figure slowly waved, then turned and ran toward the cemetery entrance, proceeding to scale the 7-foot-tall main gate— not an easy feat, especially for someone dressed in a clown outfit. Without saying a word, the unusual figure disappeared into the darkness of the cemetery. After being reported by a local TV station, the story quickly became viral on the Internet, yet the person in the clown costume was never identified and investigators never found any clues as to a possible motive.

I've always been fascinated by odd stories in the news like this, by unusual or even anomalous events that hover at the fringes of what's considered normal or even believable. The early 20th-century writer Charles Fort was one of the first to collect and study such accounts, compiling them into books like *Lo!* and *Book of the Damned.* It's in homage to Fort's single-minded research that contemporary researchers even refer to freakish events by his name now: *fortean!*

For me, though, my own interest in these happenings lies in a more astrological direction, for what they might tell us about the prevailing zeitgeist. As ancient cultures like the Babylonians and the Romans believed, the more unusual an event is, the more importance it assumes as a potential "sign of the times," as a barometer of broader changes taking place in society. As astrologers, we have the added advantage of being able to unlock the deeper significance of such anomalies using our knowledge of the heavens.

Take the story of the gate-crashing cemetery clown. When I first read about it in the news, I wondered: What astrological signature could possibly account for something like that? I knew that clowns were commonly associated with Jupiter (humor), while gates or fences are associated with Saturn (boundaries, limitations), and as for cemeteries, well, that could be Saturn or possibly Scorpio or Pluto. So, what was the dominant planetary aspect in effect at the time of this event? Lo and behold, it turned out that Jupiter in Leo was forming a tight square to Saturn in Scorpio! The odd encounter with the clown gave expression to the astrological energies at the time in a way that might have seemed cryptic but was hardly meaningless, at least when viewed through the eye of symbolism.

In that spirit, I've long turned my attention to select events of "high strangeness" with an eye to some of their astrological meanings. The times they occur are hardly random, they coincide with the shifting heavens in fascinating ways. Along with the astrology, I've also found that these events are embedded in larger networks of synchronicities related to their historical periods and other developments at the time. As a good example of that, let's take a look at one spectacular event that startled residents of the American Southwest late during the late 1990s.

The Phoenix Lights

There have been countless reports of unidentified flying objects around the world over the years, but one of the most dramatic of these took place on March 13, 1997, when thousands of Arizona residents looked up to see an extraordinary display of anomalous lights moving through the sky. In fact, there were two separate incidents that night, the most dramatic of which involved an enormous V-shaped craft seen gliding slowly over Phoenix and its neighboring regions, completely silent. The Arizona governor at the time, Fife Symington—an Air Force veteran—witnessed the incident himself and stated in no uncertain terms afterwards that this was no conventional aircraft. But to avoid alarming the citizens, he initially made light of the event in media appearances and only later admitted to having witnessed the craft himself.

So, what might account for this event, astrologically? As I've made clear in various writings over the years, I'm not especially fond of the conventional "snapshot" approach to historic events, where one focuses *solely* on horoscopes drawn up for the exact moment they occur. That's because a microscopic approach like that runs the risk of missing the proverbial forest for the trees, by overlooking the broader, longer-term patterns at work over time. As a result, I'll focus primarily on the longer-term transits in effect throughout the early months of 1997, rather than just those which occurred on March 13th.

And by using that approach, what we find is that the configurations in play were unique and significant. Among other things, there was a conjunction of Jupiter and Uranus in effect throughout that period—an alignment often associated with important breakthroughs or cultural advances, whether that be the first Moon landing in July 1969, the premiere of *Citizen Kane* in May 1941, or Charles Lindbergh's famous transatlantic flight in May 1927. Adding to the power of that Jupiter–Uranus alignment in 1997 is the fact it also served as a late-term trigger for the once-every-170-years conjunction of Uranus and *Neptune*, which was exact in 1993 but whose influence clearly extended throughout that entire decade and was punctuated by Jupiter's late entry into the picture.

But that's not all. Pull back just a tiny bit further, and we see that the March 13th sighting took place in the immediate wake of a powerful convergence of planets, or stellium, in the tropical sign of Aquarius several weeks earlier. The Sun, Mercury, Venus, Jupiter, and Uranus were all in Aquarius, with that stellium argu-ably reaching its climax during the exact Jupiter–Uranus conjunc-tion that occurred on February 15.

As I've argued elsewhere, lineups like this are hugely important engines of change in society and exert their influence for months or even years beyond their completion. By analogy, think of how a gong will continue reverberating long after it's been struck, not just at the exact moment of the strike. All major astrological pat-terns are like that, actually, but that seems to be especially true of stelliums.

The fact that this particular stellium not only included Uranus but took place in a sign co-ruled by Uranus suggests that its influ-ence would be heavily concerned with Aquarian-style changes in the world—revolutionary technological and scientific advances, along with a possible surge in alternative or "fringe" interests. And as it turns out, that's precisely what took place throughout 1997.

The Cloning Revolution

Among the more historic media stories of 1997 was the announce-ment on February 22, almost exactly on the Uranus-Jupiter con-junction and just a few weeks prior to the Phoenix event, that Scottish scientists had successfully cloned a sheep they named "Dolly." Aside from its technological implications, this became an explosive story because of all the hot-button moral concerns it trig-gered for people, including the sobering specter of assembly-line humans, eugenics and population control, the usurping of God's creative powers, and even the danger of mutant experiments gone wrong, *à la* H. G. Wells' tale *The Island of Dr. Moreau.* The controversy came to a more explosive head later that same year when an eccentric doctor (and my former next-door neighbor), Richard Seed, publicly proclaimed that he would become the first person to ever clone a human being. ("God made man in his own image," he told National Public Radio correspondent Joe Palca on December 5, 1997. "God intended for man to become one with God. Cloning is the first serious step in becoming one with God.") Though Seed never succeeded in his quest, it was directly as a result of his comments that 19 European nations and 18 American states rushed through legislation permanently banning the cloning of humans. For some, the cloning breakthrough was as "Promethean" a development as any the world had seen in decades, on a par with the harnessing of atomic energies in 1945.

One Step Beyond?
There were other highly "Aquarian" developments during that period as well, some of them with explicitly extraterrestrial or Space Age overtones. For instance, the month of March 1997 saw an unusual number of prime-time TV shows about aliens, including a nightly series about UFOs on the Learning Channel. In a more strictly scientific vein, NASA released a set of spectacular new photos that month of outer space taken by the Hubble telescope. It's also worth noting that February and March saw the re-release of all three original *Star Wars* films, in advance of the much-anticipated "prequels" to George Lucas's sci-fi movie franchise.

The heavens were on our minds in other ways as well. The March 24 issue of *Time* magazine had as its cover story "Our Changing Perceptions of Heaven," while the March 31 issue of *Newsweek* featured a cover story on "The Mystery of Prayer"—both of these articles underscoring the public's growing interest in the popular network TV show *Touched by an Angel.* One way or another, it seemed that the public's eyes were turning toward the skies, both literally and metaphorically, as if expressing a heightened fascination with the "beyond."

The Heaven's Gate Cult

But that fascination had its more sinister side, too, which became clear with the tragedy of the "Heaven's Gate" incident that unfolded roughly one week after the Phoenix lights sightings. Cult leader Marshall Applewhite and his partner Bonnie Nettles, along with 37 of their followers, committed suicide at their compound in San Diego, California, ostensibly to reach what they believed was an alien spacecraft hiding behind the Hale-Bopp Comet. Applewhite and Nettles (a.k.a. "Bo" and "Peep") convinced their followers that the UFO would transport their souls to "another level of existence above the human," which Applewhite described as being both physical and spiritual in nature. [1]

Needless to say, their cult reflected Aquarian/Uranian ideals in a number of ways. Besides its obsession with UFOs, space travel, and even the TV series *Star Trek,* the group's urge to transcend the mundane concerns of earthly life was distinctly Aquarian in tone. By contrast, Pisces can also be concerned with escapism and transcendence but in a way that tends to be more ethereal and *truly* otherworldly, as exemplified by Christianity's and Islam's emphasis on a *heavenly* paradise. Filtered through an Aquarian prism, however, the urge to "transcend" took on a more secular and *this*-worldly guise for the Heaven's Gate cult, with its hoped-for "promised land" that resided in the *starry* heavens, to be attained via high-tech spaceships!

In a further intriguing touch, it's worth mentioning that some male members of the Heaven's Gate cult voluntarily chose to be castrated, in an extreme effort to help maintain their ascetic lifestyle. Why is that worth mentioning? Note that, in Greek mythology, the tyrannical sky-god Ouranos—our eccentric planet's namesake—inflicted pain on Gaia, the feminine deity associated with the Earth, by persecuting her children, but as a result was himself castrated by one of them. Viewed symbolically, that can be taken to read what happens when that uniquely Aquarian form of detached rationality goes to extremes and loses touch with the more emotional and visceral aspects of ordinary, embodied life. In much the same way, the Heaven's Gate cult lost touch with earthly values and practicalities, and as a result sought its salvation in the distant stars.

Conclusion

So, what are we to make of all this?

For one, the events of early 1997 reflected an emergence of Aquarian impulses in the collective psyche in ways that proved both constructive and destructive. The Phoenix lights—along with developments like the cloning breakthrough, media stories about outer space and UFOs, and the re-release of *Star Wars*—signaled an opening of the group mind to progressive ideals and technological innovations, signaling a time when humans were thinking "outside the box" in new ways. It's even possible to see some of that same influence in the children born during that remarkable year, including Malala Yousafzai, the young Pakistani activist and youngest-ever Nobel Prize laureate (born July 12, 1997), or Jack Andraka, the award-winning American inventor and cancer researcher (born January 8, 1997).

On the other hand, the Heaven's Gate tragedy shows us what can happen when those same energies are perverted in more dysfunctional ways. The cult's top-heavy fixation on fringe ideals and outer space mirrors the Aquarian imagination when it has become overly detached from reality and—analogous to a futuristic spaceship floating above the Arizona desert—operates fully untethered from ordinary emotions and realities.

In fact, this also has something important to tell us about the effects of *any* major astrological configuration that unfolds on the global stage. When a powerful archetypal force emerges into consciousness, as signaled by significant planetary transits, the energy itself is ultimately neutral but people can choose to respond to it either constructively or destructively. Consider how the Uranus–Pluto square of the 2011-to-2016 period gave rise to horrific acts of terrorism—but also a renewed spirit of activism and humanitarianism. It was the same essential energy in both instances, but responded to in very different ways. With any astrological pattern, the outcome isn't predetermined or one-sided, since we have a say in how it will manifest. The events of early 1997 made that clear in fascinating and unusual ways.

This essay first appeared in the April, 2016 issue of The Mountain Astrologer magazine.

CHAPTER 19

LOOKING BEYOND THE HOROSCOPE: INCORPORATING SYNCHRONICITY INTO OUR INTERPRETATIONS

Though I first became curious about astrology during my mid-teens, it was only in my early 20s that I began to seriously explore the deeper workings and applications of this art. As it so happened, that also happened to be the same time I first became aware of Carl Jung's theory of *synchronicity*—the concept of "meaningful coincidence," which explores how disparate events come together in ways that seem to seem to defy the normal workings of chance.

In contrast with ordinary cause-and-effect relationship like we see with billiard balls interacting on a pool table, synchronicities seemed to involve "acausal" connections, where there was no direct, obvious relationship between things, other than one of *meaning*. For example, you're looking through some old photographs in a family album and come across a picture of a friend you hadn't seen in 20 years, when suddenly the phone rings and it's that very friend calling up to say hi. That sort of thing.

But the more I delved into both these subjects, the more I began realizing just how much they had in common, not just in their theoretical foundations but their practical applications.

For example, I saw that astrology could be viewed as a beautiful example of synchronicity *writ large*, in that the patterns of our horoscope illustrate how "meaningful coincidence" permeates every aspect of our lives. Every facet of our daily experience, from the trivial to the profound, is embedded in a network of acausal connections and correspondences that symbolically relate back to the planets, aspects, and houses of the horoscope. In a way, then, *one's entire life is* "synchronistic" in the sense that *everything co-incides*.

But on a more practical level, I also saw how specific instances of "meaningful coincidence" could actually enhance our understanding of individual horoscopes. Consider the case of my friend who said she'd just met a man she was attracted to while working at the local health food store she managed. But an odd thing happened during that first encounter, she explained. Literally during that first conversation while waiting on him at the store's front counter, a car parked outside the front door suddenly burst into flames, prompting the fire department to show up and douse the flaming vehicle with water. Not exactly the best possible omen for a new relationship, I thought to myself. As it turned out, she became romantically involved with the man but, not too surprisingly, the relationship also "went up in flames," causing her enormous heartache and anger in the process.

Naturally, I was intrigued by this turn of events, and set about erecting a horoscope for the exact time of that first meeting, which she remembered by heart. Would that disastrous outcome be shown in the planetary configurations of that day? Lo and behold, it did portend big problems for the star-crossed lovers: in addition to a nearly exact square between Mars and Venus, Pluto and Saturn were conjunct right on the cusp of the 7th house, the segment of the horoscope related to partnerships. The chart revealed a considerable potential for passion in the relationship, but also great potential for conflict and struggle as well.

But anyone with a bit of symbolic discernment could have learned much the same thing just by looking at those omens during that first encounter. In that same way, the more I paid attention to such events over time with friends and clients, not to mention my own life, the more apparent it became that while horoscopes were incredibly useful tools, there are actually *many* ways of "reading" what is happening in the world besides what's offered solely by horoscopes; there are *many* sources of symbolic information in the environment besides what can be found simply in the patterns of the stars and planets.

Here's another example. A client showed up for a consultation, and during the course of our talk asked my thoughts about the outcome of a legal battle she was engaged in. At the exact moment she posed that question to me, I heard the sound of loud cheering from a soccer competition being held in a nearby sports field. I noticed in her horoscope that Jupiter would be trining her Sun around the time of the trial, but there were other, more challenging energies at work, too. So which way would it go for her? The indicators in the horoscope were decidedly mixed, but that background cheering from the sports field at the moment she asked her question gave me some confidence things would turn out well for her in the end. As it happened, the court case was eventually settled in her favor—an outcome revealed as much (if not more) by the omens in my environment during our reading as by the positions of the stars.

An Ancient Way of Seeing

The notion of looking to sources other than the stars for insight is hardly a novel idea, It's been a staple of traditional cultures since time immemorial, for whom "signs" and "symbols" have always played a role. When a child is born, contemporary astrologers generally assume the primary way to decode the life of that child is by erecting a chart for the moment of its birth; but for many traditional societies, it was the custom for the parents to look at what was happening in the immediate environment for a "sign" related to that child's life. For instance, in many Native American tribes if a deer happened to be running by at the moment a child was born, the child might have been named "running deer," in the belief that the deer somehow represented a living cipher into that child's character and destiny.

We know that the classical world has its own share of such stories. The ancient Greek scholar Plutarch tells the story of how Alexander the Great's father knew of his son's extraordinary destiny from the various omens that attended Alexander's birth—and there are similar stories surrounding the births of other great figures from ancient times, both East and West. In much the same vein, I've often asked clients whether anything unusual or noteworthy of any sort happened around their births, as told to them by their parents, and the stories I've heard invariably reflect their horoscopic patterns in intriguing, sometimes even comical ways.

Of course, there are those astrological purists who might argue such events won't really tell you anything you can't learn simply by examining the horoscope for that same moment in time. But I'd argue that within those environmental images—like the deer running by at the birth of the child—we find uniquely *concise* symbols for potentialities only revealed by the horoscope in *comparatively abstract* form.

Yes, the horoscope effectively reveals the deeper archetypal dynamics of a situation, but when you consider how those archetypal dynamics can unfold in so many different ways, and on so many different levels of symbolism and subtlety, it becomes clear that the very *specificity* of that manifest event reveals a great deal about how those archetypes *are actually unfolding.* Consider the example of pioneering scientist and inventor Nikola Tesla, who was born in the midst of an electrical storm. That fact alone foreshadowed his lifelong involvement with electricity as well as—if not even better—than anything shown in his horoscope.

As mentioned, I'll sometimes ask a client or student if they know what happened around the time of their birth. One student of mine, born with Neptune on her ascendant, asked her mother if she remembered anything about the period around her birth; she was told that their neighborhood flooded the same week she was born, causing damage to their home. Similarly, I'll occasionally look up what major world events happened on the day someone was born, to see if any striking synchronicity presents itself. A good example of that was famed actor-filmmaker Orson Welles, who was born on May 6, 1915. Looking through the historical records, I was intrigued to learn that was the same day baseball icon Babe Ruth hit his first career home run—and the very next day the Titanic's main rival, British ocean liner RMS Lusitania, sank. As anyone familiar with Orson's career arc knows, that two-fold progression is a pretty good metaphor for how things unfolded for him later in life.

A Synchronistic Approach to Mundane Astrology
Much the same approach can be applied to studying developments on a global scale, customarily the province of *mundane* astrology, also described as "the astrology of world affairs." For the majority of mundane astrologers, the primary method for understanding a historic event is to simply draw up a horoscope for the moment it occurred, or to correlate cultural trends with planetary cycles, especially those involving the slower-moving planets. But here as well, we often find important symbols or synchronicities constellated around these events which shed important light on their significance. Let's look at a few examples.

It was very early in 1979 that social unrest in Iran caused then-reigning Shah Mohammed Reza Pahlavi to fly out of that country to avoid being violently deposed by an increasingly angry populace. That departure proved to be a pivotal event which led not only to the infamous Iranian hostage crisis but the ultra-conservative Islamic segment of that population taking control of that nation's politics and cultural values for decades to come. What's interesting to note is that within just 60 seconds of the Shah's plane leaving the runway, a major earthquake shook the nation—a coincidental intersection of events that told symbolists like myself that Iran was in for an extremely "shaky" time ahead. Which is of course exactly what happened. Iran found itself in a state of enormous upheaval for years. Astrologically, one could have drawn up a horoscope for the moment that plane departed, it's true, but I doubt it would have conveyed that sense of impending instability quite as concisely as that earthquake did.

It was several months later, in the Spring of 1979, that media-watchers were treated to an unusual news story involving then-U.S. President Jimmy Carter. While sitting in a small boat on a lake in Georgia, the President suddenly found himself attacked by a wild rabbit swimming in a seemingly threatening way towards his boat, which he then batted away with one of the boat's oars. The event became a source of humor and even ridicule in the media for weeks afterwards. But one person I knew saw it as holding symbolic importance. Precisely *because* it was so unusual, and happened to none other than the President of the United States, my early teacher, Shelly Trimmer, predicted in writing that the U.S. could soon find itself "under attack" by a smaller but disproportionately bothersome nation. It was shortly afterwards that we found ourselves embroiled in the Iranian hostage crisis. Here as well, it's conceivable the hostage crisis could have been foreseen using conventional astrological methods (though I'm unaware of any such predictions). But the fact that it was indeed foreseen solely through omenological symbolism speaks to the value of non-astrological sources like this in helping us understand and sometimes even predict historical developments.

Humanity's exploration of outer space has yielded numerous examples of dramatic synchronicities. When Americans first landed on the Moon in 1969, astrologers promptly drew up horoscopes for the key moments involved—the initial launch, first touchdown on the lunar surface, Neil Armstrong's first steps on the lunar surface, and so on. But as I mentioned in *The Waking Dream*, it's worth considering what further insights might be had by learning that the moment we were setting foot on the Moon's surface, archaeologist Iris Love was uncovering the most important of Aphrodite's ancient temples in present-day Turkey. (Note, too, that for the ancient Greeks, the worship of Aphrodite was always associated with the Moon). Or consider the fact that same weekend also witnessed Ted Kennedy's tragic incident at Chappaquiddick—an event replete with "lunar" symbols all its own, from water and drinks to women. Approached symbolically, if we see the Moon mission as reflecting a collective opening to the archetypal feminine, we could read such synchronicities as illuminating various *aspects* of our collective relationship to the feminine—with Kennedy's scandal revealing the more dysfunctional side of that national connection.

In my book *Signs of the Times*, I devoted a chapter to the extraordinary set of omens and synchronicities that attended the explosion of the space shuttle Challenger in January of 1986, all completely separate from any conventional horoscopes or classic delineations. [1] But there were significant omens and synchronicities surrounding the mid-air destruction of the space shuttle Columbia in 2003 as well.

Upon its return into the Earth's atmosphere in early February of that year, the Columbia lost pressure and disintegrated over Texas, causing the deaths of all its crew members. Significantly, this happened at a time when President Bush and his advisors were drawing up plans for an invasion of Iraq, which would get underway several weeks later and lead ultimately to the deaths of many American soldiers and Iraqi citizens. We were assured up front that the entire undertaking would be "swift," and likely lead to few American casualties. But the fact that the shuttle disaster took place precisely during the build-up to the war—not to mention the fact that it occurred over that part of the country where President Bush's personal home was—signaled that the Iraqi incursion could be considerably less "swift" and more costly than anyone imagined. Here as well, astrology might have provided some insight into the war's outcome, but that singular tragic image spoke volumes of its own.

Another example of the synchronistic approach to cultural developments can be found in the field of UFO studies. As I mentioned in earlier chapters, one way that astrologers have approached this subject in the past has been to erect horoscopes for key events or encounters described by witnesses over the years. But just as we also explored in previous chapters, an alternate approach would be to examine the various events or synchronicities *constellated around* those events, or even explore the striking number of anomalous phenomena associated throughout history with those particular dates.

As one example, take the singular event commonly cited as the key turning point in popular consciousness regarding the UFO phenomenon: Kenneth Arnold's sighting of June 24, 1947, when he observed a series of unusual objects while flying his private plane through the skies of Washington state. Not only did the famous "Roswell incident" take place shortly after this sighting, and the Maury Island incident several days before, but June 24th is historically the date of St. John's Day and Midsummer Night's Eve—a time of the year commonly associated with strange apparitions and the proverbial "thinning of the veil" (recall Shakespeare's tale about midsummer happenings). That date was also associated in Elizabethan England with fairies and the appearance of little people generally, and further associated with the legend of the Pied Piper. Historical connections like these not only provide historical context, but can help illumine some of the more out-of-the-box theories associated with UFO studies like those pioneered by Jacques Vallee, for whom the answer to this mystery resides less in nuts-and-bolts explanations involving metallic spaceships and "little green men from outer space" than in humanity's timeless encounter with the mythic and archetypal dimensions of reality.

As those familiar with my other writings know, I've long viewed movies as a rich source of symbols and synchronicities that could be mined in understanding historical patterns. That's particularly apparent when we see several films on the same general theme premiering around the same time, as if synchronistically under-scoring a given idea or archetypal theme in the zeitgeist. In late summer of 2006, for example, the high-profile films *The Illusionist* and *The Prestige* were released close to one another, with strikingly similar stories about the interplay between reality and illusion, truth versus falsehood.

In fact, that dynamic beautifully illustrated not only the key planetary pattern in effect at the time, Saturn oppose Neptune (hard reality versus illusion), but what was happening throughout the culture. That's because those same themes were percolating through the media in a number of ways, including public debates involving prominent atheists like Sam Harris about the existence (or non-existence?) of God; or discussions in the media about the balance between skepticism and gullibility; or in more political circles, the problem of lies told by our elected leaders and the chal-lenge of distinguishing truth from fiction in political discourse. Of course, configurations involving Saturn and Neptune can man-ifest in many different ways and on many different levels, but the stories shared by those two films provided us with a fairly concise window into the level at which those energies were manifesting for many of us at that time.

Let's look at one final example. One of the most significant developments in the annals of modern science was the discovery of the sub-atomic realm in 1897, by Nobel Laureate in physics J.J. Thompson. More than any other development, Thompson's discovery of the electron led the way to opening up the previously hidden subterranean world of the atom—and in turn the subsequent zoo of sub-atomic particles we've come to recognize like the proton, neutron, lepton, and quark, among others. It was an epochal turning point, hinting at the discovery of a vast new world at our fingertips much larger than the obvious, tangible one we're normally familiar with. [2]

But how could we possibly go approaching its broader significance as a historic development? One approach would be to take the "field thinking" approach and carefully scour other historic events or synchronicities from that period to see if those might offer some further clues as well. And to my mind, the most dramatic of those was the fact that during that same period researchers in a seemingly unrelated field were announcing the discovery of another "vast new realm of reality," largely unknown until then, and likewise lying just beneath the surface of everyday life. I'm talking here about the discovery of the *unconscious mind.*

Just two short years later, in 1899, Sigmund Freud published a work that would be forever associated with the discovery of the unconscious, *The Interpretation of Dreams.* More than any other, this was the book that suggested our conscious experience was just the tip of a far larger iceberg of experience largely hidden from view, but which influenced our surface motivations and behaviors in myriad profound ways.

The fact that these two developments—the discovery of the sub-atomic realm and the unconscious—occurred so close to one another struck me as a potentially important synchronicity. Viewed symbolically, it strongly suggested that some new dimension of consciousness was opening up for humanity, and with that an unveiling of previously hidden potentials.

As it so happened, this all coincided with a major astrological configuration taking place during that decade: the once-every-five-hundred-year alignment of Pluto and Neptune. Consider that fact that Neptune and Pluto are completely invisible to the naked eye, signifying that they symbolize forces rooted deep within the human psyche. Their coming together in a conjunction thus pointed to profoundly deep stirrings taking place in the collective unconscious, and along with that a host of new possibilities. Among other things, that period saw the birth of cinema, an extraordinary flowering of symbolist art and "Impressionistic" music, the emergence of global culture, and an awakening of mystical sensibilities (exemplified by movements like The Theosophical Society and The Golden Dawn), among other developments.

So as useful as knowing the nuts-and-bolts astrology of that time may be, those twin developments heralded by Freud and J.J. Thompson provided us with an especially graphic image of what was taking place at the time, in a way that enhanced our astrological understanding of the period, in terms of humanity's opening up to previously hidden potentials of consciousness.

Appreciating the Symbolic Imagery of Events
This all brings me to an important point—namely, that while horoscopes can convey important clues into the meaning of both personal and historical events, we shouldn't overlook the tremendous amount of symbolic information contained within *the imagery and actual forms of the events themselves*. I can explain this with a simple analogy.

Imagine if someone asked you to interpret a dream they had the night before. Would you set about trying to do that by drawing up an astrological chart for the moment they had the dream? Or, would you simply spend time reflecting on the actual imagery and events in that dream? While the horoscope would indeed hold some useful clues, I think it's obvious that enormous insight could also be had simply by examining the symbolism of the dream itself, without necessarily resorting to anything *outside* the dream.

In a not-dissimilar way, horoscopes can indeed reveal much about the inner dynamics of personal or historical events; but when you consider how these same archetypal dynamics can unfold in so many different ways, then the *specificity* of those manifest events can prove enormously insightful as to how those archetypes are *actually unfolding.*

For instance, consider the blockbuster movie *The Joker,* which came out at the exact peak of a Pluto station in early October of 2019, when that planet's influence was especially strong. The film's story exemplifies Plutonian themes to a remarkable degree, with its tale of buried secrets and old wounds coming to light. Now, there are many ways Pluto energies can manifest—an archaeological discovery, a volcanic eruption, a hazardous toxic spill, political power struggles, acts of mob violence, and so on. But that film gave expression the one manifestation which seemed particularly active at the time—and which I saw unfolding in the lives of friends and clients at the time, in terms of buried issues and old wounds coming to light for them, too.

As I said at the outset, within the manifest event for a given horoscopic moment we find a uniquely concise symbol for potentialities only *abstractly* suggested by the chart. As a result, *instead of using the chart to explain the event, it can be useful sometimes to work "backward" from the event to better understand the chart.*

Conclusion

It's tempting to believe that astrology is somehow sufficient unto itself, requiring no other methods or systems to enhance its efficacy. I'm reminded of the astrologer I knew who, when asked whether she thought studying subjects like psychology, I Ching, palmistry, or the Tarot might help her own astrological practice, replied, "There's no need, really. Astrology covers all the bases." Well, not really. In this essay I've tried to demonstrate how knowing different symbolic systems can provide us with different perspectives onto a given situation that aren't available through any one system. Understanding the language of synchronicity and "meaningful coincidences" offers us one such avenue, and should rightly be part of any truly holistic approach to astrology, whether we're focused more on personal interpretations or on world events unfolding across the global stage.

This article first appeared in the August/September 2020 issues of the Mountain Astrologer

CHAPTER 20

THE CLUSTER EFFECT: WHEN PLANETARY TRIGGERS CONVERGE

In October of 1991 there occurred a confluence of three weather systems off the coast of Nova Scotia so violent it produced waves over a hundred feet high and resulted in the deaths of over a dozen people. It was such a rare convergence of forces that meteorologists came to calling it "the perfect storm," with the event eventually becoming immortalized in Sebastian Junger's 1991 book of the same name and later, a 2000 film starring George Clooney and Mark Walberg.

As astrologers, we carefully chart the celestial "weather" at any given time, and it goes without saying some periods are more highly charged, active, or turbulent than others—astrological "perfect storms," you might say. One of several possible reasons for that is how multiple planetary or zodiacal triggers will sometimes converge and pool their energies around the same time, leading to what I've sometimes called a "cluster effect."

Over the years I've found such clusters can be hugely significant factors in our lives, for better or worse. A simple example would be my client whose chart showed a Mars Return firing on the exact same day as transiting Uranus squaring his Sun, with both of those happening near a full Moon. Since this took place shortly before he came to me, I naturally asked if anything significant happened around that time. He said he had a huge blow-up with his boss at that point, which in turn led to him getting fired—hence his reason for looking for an astrologer to get some explanation as to what happened. It was a "perfect storm" of stressful planetary triggers, that was obvious, and I'd like to believe that knowing about it in advance might have helped him cope with those turbulent energies better than he actually did.

Another example of clustering involved a female client of mine whose horoscope showed transiting Saturn coming up to conjunct her natal Moon within just two days of her progressed Moon squaring her natal Saturn. There was no way to know for sure what that would bring, but I could at least let her know this could be an emotionally challenging time, and would most likely involve her home or family somehow. It turned out that her mother fell gravely ill that week and had to be rushed to the hospital, where she passed away several days later. While knowing those astrological triggers ahead of time certainly didn't erase the pain of losing her mother, it at least helped her emotionally brace for what was coming, rather than simply feeling sucker-punched by fate.

To be sure, the cluster effect isn't always a negative thing, a proverbial clusterf*%k, as some call it. Take the case of my friend who experienced Jupiter trining his natal Venus just as a progressed Venus trined his natal Jupiter. What happened? That was exactly when he was in Las Vegas making a killing at the gambling tables! It was a "perfect storm," all right, but one involving quite pleasant forces coming together.

Another example of "positive" clustering was my client who had Uranus trining his 10th house Sun precisely as Jupiter was crossing over his Midheaven. It was then that he landed a plum job as a news anchor for a local news station. Clusters like these can be approached as windows of opportunity we can take advantage of, and maximize to their fullest potentials, if we put our mind to it.

Clusters We All Share in Common

The point here is that in all these cases it wasn't just a single celestial trigger involved but multiple factors occurring around the same time, which combined to trigger significant life changes. In a more general way, it's much the same principle during those times in all our lives when similar transits converge at similar ages.

One of the most notable of these occurs between the ages of 20 and 22 when we all experience a combination of Uranus squaring its natal position and Saturn squaring *its* natal position, too. This famously causes considerable tension for many, it being a time when we're trying to reconcile the urge to break free and "find ourselves" while struggling with the heavy weight of parental conditioning and youthful insecurities.

Another well-known cluster occurs between the ages of 27 and 30 when all of us experience the combined effects of our first progressed lunar return and our second nodal reverse, followed shortly after by our first Saturn return, our second transiting Uranus trining its natal position, and Neptune sextiling its natal position. This is generally a time of intense personal reflection and re-evaluation, and often involves a struggle between contrasting feelings of aspiration and disillusion. As one friend of mine put it, "This was when I had to grow up, and realized I had to start acting like an adult." Although some use the energies of this time to their professional or creative advantage, others find it a bit more than they can really handle—something sadly illustrated by the early deaths of so many rock and pop stars around this age, such as Jimi Hendrix, Jim Morrison, Amy Winehouse, Janis Joplin, Tim Buckley, Brian Jones, and Kurt Cobain, among others. It's a formative time for many, but not always a very comfortable one.

Another such clustering takes place during our early 40s, when the average man or woman experiences a major convergence of slow-moving transits which include Uranus opposing natal Uranus, Saturn opposing natal Saturn, and Neptune squaring natal Neptune. As with our previous clusters, the cumulative power of this one makes the early 40s a particularly vulnerable time for some, one often associated with the dreaded "mid-life crisis" when we become more aware of fading youth alongside the looming specter of old(er) age. Similar to those earlier transition points, one may feel torn between the growing urge to "find oneself" and the obligation to deal with responsibilities and existing routines. In my own case, this was a time of extraordinarily mixed emotions, since I was struggling with the need to break free of problematic situations in my professional and personal life exactly as I was experiencing some important creative breakthroughs as well (among other things, this was when my first book was published).

Especially notable are those times when such "universal" clusterings coincide with other major transits or progressions in one's chart, as if to suggest particularly significant transition points in life. Just a week before starting this article, for instance, I had a young woman in her early 40s come to me who was undergoing the abovementioned cluster of Uranian, Neptunian, and Saturnian energies, on top of which she was *also* contending with such heavy-hitter transits as the recent Pluto/Saturn conjunction sitting exactly on her Midheaven, which was in turn closely squaring her Sun—in addition to which transiting Uranus was conjuncting her Taurus Ascendant. Now, *that's* a full plate!

What happened? She had been a psychologist teaching at a university who became so frustrated by the politics and bureaucratic machinations of her department that she finally resigned, which sent her into an occupational free-fall that had her wondering what her next step would be. Fortunately, her natal chart showed some harmonious and constructive aspects between some of those same planets (in particular, she had a tight natal trine between Saturn and the Sun), so I suggested this period was really about a radical reconstruction of her life, a professional "course correction" she could use to regroup and reconnect with the core dreams and creative aspirations that motivated her earlier in life. In addition to having dreamt of being a writer when she was young, she had recently begun thinking of starting up her own business. Her new occupational status was giving her an opportunity to seriously consider both those options.

The Cluster Effect in Mundane Affairs

It's also worth recalling the way this clustering phenomenon manifests on the collective level, too, where we find it at work behind some important historic developments. A dramatic example of that took place during the first week of February, 1962, when a rare stellium of seven celestial bodies in the (tropical) Aquarius coincided precisely with a total solar eclipse in that sign. As I mentioned earlier in this book, and elsewhere, the full significance of stelliums is rarely felt at the exact time of their occurrence and can they exert powerful ripple effects for weeks, months, sometimes even decades afterwards. While there were some important political developments during that period—most notably a particularly tense stand-off between the U.S. and Russia later that year with the "Cuban Missile Crisis"—it inaugurated a particularly fertile time in the arts. Not only did Bob Dylan release his first album just a few weeks later, but the next few months saw the Rolling Stones play their first live show, the Beatles record their first record ("Love Me Do"), and the Beach boys signing their hugely successful contract with Capitol Records.

Another extraordinary confluence of energies which I mentioned previously occurred in 1941, during the last few days of April and the first few days of May. Not only did Uranus exactly conjunct Jupiter then (a combination frequently associated with cultural breakthroughs), but both of those bodies exactly trined

Neptune at the time, and all of this happened in connection with a powerhouse stellium in Taurus involving the Sun, Mercury, Venus, Saturn, Jupiter and Uranus. Now, *that's* a cluster! As it so happened, May 1st saw the world premiere of a film often called the "greatest" in movie history, *Citizen Kane*, and musical icon Bob Dylan was born just three weeks later.

Another potent form of "clustering" on the mundane level occurs when two or more planets become stationary and change directions close to one another. As I discussed in my essay "Tectonic Triggers,"[1] station points aren't simply a matter of planets changing directions, but of the energies of those planets becoming exponentially amplified at such times, due to the "branding iron" effect of them being relatively motionless for so long.

One example of that took place in the Spring of 1967. The Beatles' album "Sgt. Pepper" is widely considered one of that decade's cultural milestones, and was formally released on May 26th of that year. On occasion I've seen astrologers trying to understand the significance of that album by erecting a horoscope for that single day. What that type of "snapshot" approach to historic events overlooks is the fact that this album came out in the midst of a triple station of Uranus, Pluto and Mars—the first two of those planets being widely regarded as those bodies most responsible for the revolutionary winds of change which swept that decade. Specifically, *Mars was stationing direct on May 27, Uranus on May 29, and Pluto on May 30.* Mundane astrologers often look to the exact conjunction of those last two bodies in 1965 and 1966 as the primary dates of their influence; but I'd suggest that the proximity of those stations in late May of 1967 essentially constitutes another "conjunction"—a "stationary conjunction" of sorts—exerting much the same effect. (It's also worth noting that musician Noel Gallagher was born on May 29th that year, and he went on to front the English rock group Oasis—a band hailed by some fans and critics at the time as the "musical heirs to the Beatles." A passing of the archetypal torch, perhaps?)

A more tragic example of clustered station points happened in July of 2014, when Saturn and Uranus changed directions within just 48 hours of one another: Saturn changed directions on July 20th, and Uranus two days later on July 22nd. Over the years I've found these two planets to be particularly involved with notable aviation disasters, including the deadliest one in all of history: the 1977 Tenerife disaster in the Canary Islands. That tragedy occurred when two passenger jets collided on a runway and 583 men, women, and children perished as a result—and it happened precisely as Saturn and Uranus were in an exact square. It all led me to wonder if we might also see some similar aviation problems in July of 2014, since these two planets would be amplified to an extraordinary degree then, this time by a stationary conjunction.

As it turned out, the few days surrounding that double station witnessed *several* aviation tragedies: Malaysia Airlines Flight 17 was shot down in eastern Ukraine, killing all 298 passengers; two Ukrainian fighter jets were shot down; a Taiwanese jet crashed; and an Algerian passenger jet went missing—four aviation disasters, all within just a few days. But that's not all: in addition, the Israeli/Palestinian conflict heated up dramatically at that point, and due to rising tensions between Russia and the U.S. some media commentators seriously began comparing the events of that week to those which ignited World War I. For me, one of the key takeaway from events like these is that joint stations can be interpreted in much the same way as conjunctions involving those same bodies.

An exceptionally powerful cluster occurred recently during the second week of January, 2020, when several powerful triggers converged close to one another. In addition to the epic Saturn/Pluto conjunction astrologers had been speculating about for years, there was a full Moon eclipse, a Uranus station, and even a station point of the dwarf planet Eris—all within just a 48 hour period. So what happened?

Keeping in mind that it's important to examine the weeks or even months surrounding any major cluster, there are quite a few things worth noting here. This period saw the heating up of Donald Trump's impeachment problems, with the formal Senate trial of the President beginning just over a week later on January 21ˢᵗ. This was also an exceptionally tense time for international relations, with America stepping close to the brink of world war after Trump assassinated Iranian general Soleimani on January 3rd, and Iran responding on January 8ᵗʰ by sending missiles against a U.S. military base in Iraq. Hours after that attack, a Ukrainian jet crashed shortly after takeoff from Tehran's main airport, killing all 176 passengers. During this period there were also major earthquakes in Puerto and Iran, as well as volcanic eruptions in the Philippines, Japan, and Mexico. In the days immediately leading up to this cluster the British royal family was rocked by news of Prince Harry and wife Megan Markle's decision to relinquish their royal duties to pursue a life of greater self-determination. While that one may be of little consequence to non-British subjects, it symbolically represented yet another break with the traditional order of things in terms of global affairs.

But perhaps most significant of all, in the weeks immediately following this cluster, media outlets started broadcasting news of a deadly strain of coronavirus out of Wuhan, China, which apparently began in December but only came to light globally in January and continued spreading in the months afterward. As I've pointed out in the past, the full effects of any major planetary pattern aren't often completely known until long after that pattern fires exactly. For instance, the last time Pluto and Saturn came together was back in 1982 and 1983, and its effects were felt throughout that entire decade, through such developments as the AIDS crisis and the so-called "Reagan Revolution" in the U.S, among others. The fact that this particular Saturn/Pluto conjunction was punctuated by several other celestial triggers would certainly seem to amplify the long-term influence it could hold for the world.

All of this naturally piques one's curiosity as to what celestial clusters might lie ahead for us. As of this writing (Summer of 2020), one of the more interesting of those is set to happen around December 21st of this year. Besides this being the date of the Winter solstice, it will also be when Saturn and Jupiter precisely conjunct for the first time in 20 years, in zero degrees of Aquarius this time (an elemental shift from their last conjunction in *earth* to a new domicile in *air*). In addition to that, this is precisely when Mars in Aries will be forming a tight square to that epic Saturn/Pluto conjunction from January of 2020 in 22 degrees of Capricorn, serving as a trigger to *that* pattern as well. The fact that three major triggers will occur so shortly after the U.S. Presidential election naturally leads one to wonder whether the impact of those celestial markers will somehow involve fallout from *that* political event—a "perfect storm" of political proportions, maybe? One way or another, it's not likely to be boring.

CHAPTER 21

THE POWER OF "STATIONING ASPECTS"

One of the many methods used by astrologers to examine the shifting planetary energies in one's life is to look at the effect of the transiting planets—especially the outer, slower-moving bodies—on one's natal planets and chart positions. Jupiter crossing over one's natal Sun shows one thing, Saturn squaring one's natal Mercury shows another, while Pluto crossing over the Ascendant means quite another, and so on.

But there are times when aspects like these seem to take on far greater power than normal. In the previous chapter, we looked at one of those instances, what I called the "cluster effect," when two or more powerhouse aspects fire close to each other. But another one involves something I call the "stationing aspect." That's when a transiting aspect takes place around the same time that the transiting planet also happens to be *stationing*. (For those new to astrology, a "station" is when a planet crawls to a stop before going backward forward, "retrograde" or "direct." In a word, it's *stationary*. See my chapter on station points in my book *Under a Sacred Sky*.)

For example, let's say your natal Mercury is at 5 degrees 30 minutes of Gemini, and transiting Jupiter comes along to cross over that point. Normally, the closest point of that approach will be felt most tangibly over the course of a week or two, during which time you'll undoubtedly experience a major activation of your thinking and communications. This could manifest any number of ways, such as through an unusual amount of talking or messaging, receiving important news, business dealings, travel experiences, writing projects, and still other possibilities.

But suppose that transiting Jupiter also happens to enter into a station point close to when that aspect to Mercury is exact. In other words, say that Jupiter will be stopping and changing directions at *5 Gemini 35 minutes*–just a few minutes of arc away from your natal Mercury. So instead of simply gliding past that degree of your natal Mercury, Jupiter will make its imprint onto that part of the zodiac—and in turn, that aspect to your natal planet—for a considerably longer time, which will cause that transiting aspect to be amplified exponentially. The "branding iron" effect of the station will cause that aspect to be energized far more than normal.

In my experience, stationary aspects like this can be hugely important triggers in people's lives—especially if there happens to be a connection between those two planets in the natal chart. In fact, even though the transiting aspect might not be technically exact until several weeks before or after the station itself, *the time of that stationary point will often be when that aspect manifests most dramatically.*

Here's another example. Suppose Uranus is crossing over someone's midheaven. With few exceptions, this is a once-in-a-lifetime transit that will be spread out over the course of a year or two, during which time it will reach exactitude (or become "partile") several different times. This could manifest through dramatic changes in that person's career, a rebellion against authority figures (landlords, parents, bosses, government, etc.), an impulse towards freedom, an involvement with media, an interest in astrology, and so on. Because it will simultaneously be opposing the 4th house cusp, this may also trigger changes in one's home environment or family relationships.)

But in some cases, it may happen that Uranus will actually become stationary close to—or even exactly on—that Midheaven degree. In that case, it will serve as an even more powerful trigger for that transit, taking all of those unfolding trends and bringing them to a dramatic head right at that point.

The Challenge of the Stationing "Hard" Aspect

Needless to say, this "transiting aspect" phenomenon cuts both ways, in terms of amplifying either constructive *or* destructive potentials in the chart. I'll use a personal example to illustrate this.

When I was born, my natal Mars was at 1 degree of Scorpio, and earlier this year transiting Saturn was stationing at 1 degree of Aquarius—thereby forming a tight square to my natal Mars. Now, I've watched Saturn form hard aspects to my Mars quite a few times over the course of my life, but this time would be different, I knew, since it would be the first time I could remember when Saturn would be actually stationing at the same degree as that square. Shown here is the transiting "hit-list" for that immediate period. As you can see, the square is *technically* exact on two dates, April 15th and June 5th, but right in the midst of that period, you'll notice that Saturn stands still and goes retrograde on *May 11th.* (underlined in the middle column):

♃ ☍ ♅	Jan 21	**Jan 25**	Jan 30
♀ △ AS	Jan 8	**Feb 7**	Mar 17
♃ □ ☽	Feb 6	**Feb 11**	Feb 16
♃ □ ♀	Feb 22	**Feb 27**	Mar 4
♃ △ AS	Mar 19	**Mar 26**	Apr 2
♄ □ ♂	Mar 28 **Apr 15**	<u>May 11</u>	Jun 25 **Jun 5**
♅ ☌ ♃	May 8	**May 26**	Jun 16
♃ △ AS	Jun 25	**Jul 4**	Jul 12
♀ △ AS	Jun 5	**Jul 20**	Sep 10
♃ □ ♀	Aug 1	**Aug 10**	Aug 22
♃ □ ♀	Oct 4	**Oct 16**	Oct 24
♅ ☌ ♃	Oct 17	**Nov 10**	Dec 8
♃ △ AS	Nov 11	**Nov 17**	Nov 22

Now, as Goswami Kriyananda often pointed out, the fact that a planet stands relatively still for so long creates a "branding iron" effect which amplifies the energy of that transiting planet—and in turn, *any aspects it's making*—considerably. As a result, I was careful to pay particular attention to that entire period, but with eye especially to the days right around that station point.

So what happened?

During the days from around May 8 to May 15th, I experienced some difficult health issues, which included extreme fatigue (a common expression of Saturn/Mars transits) as well as a mysterious skin condition that had me itching uncontrollably for several weeks where I felt like my skin was on fire (fire=Mars). I also had a very difficult confrontation with a friend over a misunderstanding, which wasn't just frustrating but forced me to exert extreme control (Saturn) over my anger and impulses (Mars). Synchronistically enough, it was also during those same days that I happened to be looking out my window and see the attendant in a nearby gas station do a running tackle on a teenager who had just tried to rob his mini-mart! (Talk about Saturn putting the brakes on Mars...) Most dangerous of all, that brief period also saw the brakes on my car start to fail while I was driving down a busy thoroughfare, forcing me to pull over quickly and call for a tow truck.

In the end, I survived it all, but it was easily one of the most difficult periods I've experienced in quite some time. Hard as it was, I have no doubt that knowing about those energies beforehand helped me cope better with what transpired, and possibly even avoid dangerous consequences. I had a rough idea of what to expect, so I went out of my way to be extra careful, not just in my personal interactions with others but in reacting to the car problems, which led me to pull over quickly rather than take the chance of making it all the way home and very likely getting into an accident.

Looking Ahead

If you choose to work with this concept more closely in your own life, you might begin by looking at the ephemeris to see what planetary stations are scheduled to occur over the coming year. I'd pay special attention to the outer planets, but even the stations of Mercury, Venus and Mars can be significant. Notice what degrees those planets are in when they station: do any of them resonate with the degrees of planets or horoscopic angles in your natal chart? If so, watch closely—and take special note of whether there are any aspects between those bodies in your natal chart, which could modify their expression considerably; you never know; they could turn out to be some of the most eventful triggers of your entire life.

CHAPTER 22

A TALE OF TWO ZODIACS: INTERPRETING 9/11 FROM BOTH THE TROPICAL AND SIDEREAL PERSPECTIVES

Of the myriad techniques and systems employed by astrologers around the world, few have been the source of as much heated debate within the community itself as the difference between the tropical and sidereal zodiacs.

Simply described, the tropical zodiac bases its understanding of the signs on the seasonal divisions of the year, taking the four solstice and equinoctial points and extrapolating these into twelve signs. Hence, the first day of Spring equates to zero degrees of Aries, while the first day of Summer equates to zero degrees Cancer, the first day of Autumn equates to zero degrees Libra, and the first day of Winter with zero degrees Capricorn.

On the other hand, the sidereal zodiac is based more closely upon the constellations and the fixed stars themselves. Notice I say "more closely," because in fact the average siderealist artificially divvies up their zodiac into 12 equal parts, something not found in nature herself. When a sidereal astrologer says that Venus is in Sagittarius, the implication is you can go outside and see that Venus is actually in the constellation of Sagittarius. However,

176

because those 30-degree divisions employed by most siderealists are artificial, there are times when Venus will actually be in a different constellation than the one their system shows it to be! But in the most general possible terms, the sidereal zodiac is indeed more star-based than the tropical zodiac is, with the latter's focus on seasonal points. [1]

So which of these systems is the more accurate and valid of the two?

Over time, I've discovered I'm in something of a minority amongst my colleagues in believing it's possible for more than one zodiacal system to work—much in the same way, perhaps, that Riemannian and Euclidian geometries can co-exist without either one disproving the other. As a result, while I prefer to work primarily with the tropical zodiac, I feel that both have their respective values.

And to my mind, one of the best examples of that is the tragedy of 9/11.

According to a majority of astrologers, the key planetary configuration underlying that event was the powerhouse opposition between Saturn and Pluto in effect roughly from 2000 to 2002. Without a doubt, there were other factors contributing to those events—for example, the lingering effects of the May 2000 Taurus stellium, or even the epic fixed Grand Cross eclipse in the Summer of 1999, among others. But it's clear that the Saturn–Pluto opposition played an especially pivotal role in that geopolitical drama, due to that planetary combo's pooled meanings of destruction, transformation, and turbulent emotions.

According to tropical astrologers, Pluto was in Sagittarius when 9/11 happened, while Saturn was in Gemini. In this writer's opinion, there have been few historic events that reflect the dynamics of zodiacal correspondences as clearly as that one: Pluto, the planet of power and willful extremism, was in the sign of religion and ideology, aggressively pitted against Saturn, the planet of structures, located in the sign of the Twins. Could there possibly be a more blatant expression of that duo than religious extremists causing the Twin Towers to crumble into the ground? (And almost like coming full circle, it's worth noting that the Twin Towers were constructed during the *previous* sojourn of Saturn through Gemini.)

As striking as that symbolism is, though, does that necessarily negate the role of the sidereal zodiac as a factor in that event? Not at all. Stop for a moment to consider the developments of that day from a more sidereal standpoint.

According to siderealists, Pluto was not in Sagittarius but *Scorpio* at the time, while Saturn was not in Gemini but in *Taurus*. (That's because there's an offset of roughly 23 degrees between these two systems, which places those two planets in the previous signs.) Applied to the events of 9/11, it's actually not hard to see how Scorpio could be related to the forces of death and transformation being brought to bear on the Taurean financial institutions of the time, which were indeed heavily impacted by the tragedy. Although the symbolism isn't quite as literal as it was when using the tropical signs, the correspondences still apply.

Now, as many already know, there are those who believe that the *mainstream* narrative surrounding the events of that day was really just a smokescreen for what actually took place behind the scenes. Yet, that very discrepancy between official and alternative accounts may actually provide a useful way to understand the relative importance and roles of these two zodiacs. Let me explain what I mean.

To begin with, consider that the mainstream theory claimed 19 Saudi terrorists hijacked commercial jets and flew them into the Twin Towers, and that this was ostensibly an act of religious fanaticism railing against the secular values of the West. But according to what's ironically described as the "conspiracy" viewpoint—ironic, since the mainstream narrative was itself a conspiracy theory citing 19 hijackers in collusion with Osama bin Laden—there were very different forces at work behind the scenes, variously attributed to oil industry interests (Google "911 + Middle East pipelines"), strategic military aims (Google "PNAC"), financial fraud cover-ups (Google "missing 2.3 trillion dollars"), Israeli involvement (Google "dancing Israeli art students"), designs for implementing restrictions on our civil rights (Google "the Patriot Act"), and probably others besides these.

Whatever your preferred alternative theory, if any, the possibility that there may have been secret motives behind the surface events of 9/11 actually fits in surprisingly well with the symbolism suggested by the *sidereal* signs occupied by Pluto and Saturn at the time. What do I mean? Simply, consider the fact that Scorpio is commonly associated with secretive actions or motives, while Taurus is associated with economic interests—and suddenly the sidereal signs appear to reflect the possibility of hidden economic agendas at work behind the tragedy. (And isn't it *always* about money, when it comes down to major geopolitical developments?)

So here we have an interesting example of how the two zodiacs may well co-exist and represent different levels of significance, both having their own validity but in different contexts. Because the tropical zodiac is more Earth-based and geocentric, some astrologers have suggested that it signifies the more obvious, surface level of events, while the sidereal zodiac, being more closely associated with the background star-field, may represent a deeper, possibly more esoteric or "karmic" level at work behind surface appearances.

In the case of 9/11, it's not hard to see how both of those could be at play. As a tropicalist, I don't see how any open-minded siderealist could examine the events of 9/11 and not be struck by how closely its symbolism coincides with that of tropical Sagittarius and Gemini; but by the same token, I also think it's clear how these same events can be interpreted to reflect the undercurrents of sidereal Scorpio and Taurus at work, too.

The Tropical/Sidereal Divide in Personal Horoscopes

But how might this dual perspective apply to individual horoscopes? I'd offer a simple example—two, actually. Singer Mick
Jagger of the Rolling Stones and actor Jason Momoa (*Aquaman,
Game of Thrones*) are two celebrities born with stelliums involving
four planets in tropical Leo, though by sidereal standards those
same planets are in Cancer. On the surface of things, both personalities could not seem more like classic Leos: in addition to their
overtly bold appearances, both figures are drawn to the spotlight,
extraverted in demeanor, and fun-loving. (A co-star of Momoa's
once described him as being "like a big kid" and "allergic to being
ignored.") At first glance, it's difficult to see the more retiring or
domestic influence of Cancer in either of their personalities.

Behind the scenes, however, it turns out that family plays a major
role in both of their lives. Momoa has been described as a devoted
father of two children, with actress Lisa Bonet; while Mick Jagger
is father to a whopping eight children, through various women,
and supposedly a good parent. So here as well, we can see how the
tropical zodiac seems to describe the more visible reality whereas
the sidereal zodiac reveals a more hidden, "behind the scenes"
level of experience.

In the end, I'm not suggesting that we necessarily try to use
both zodiacal frameworks in our readings, because while that may
be possible, in practical terms I believe it runs the risk of muddy-
ing the waters of our interpretations. As the old Chinese saying
goes, *Chase two rabbits, catch neither.* There is value to staying within
a given framework and exhausting its possibilities without trying
to mix in elements from other, quite different systems.

Rather, what I've tried to do here is simply provide a rationale
for how it's possible for two or more different systems to co-exist
and provide subtly different perspectives on events, whether they
be global or personal. Rather than dogmatically stake our claim on
one platform or another, I believe a more fruitful approach would

be to open our minds to the possibility that these systems simply differ in their relevance, and might even intersect in intriguing ways. [2]

This article first appeared in the February, 2017 issue of The Mountain Astrologer magazine.

CHAPTER 23

TURNING POINT: THE UNITED
STATES' PLUTO RETURN

(Author's note: The following piece about the coming Pluto return was published in late 2019, before the economic crash of 2020, the George Floyd murder, or the Covid-19 pandemic.)

Like individuals, nations experience "planetary returns," too, when celestial bodies make a complete circuit around the sky and return to the zodiacal position they once occupied. But the full return cycle of Pluto is an especially lengthy one, taking over 240 years to complete.

While individual life-spans obviously aren't long enough to experience one of these, nations and empires certainly can. Using July 4, 1776 as its birthdate, the United States is on the verge of experiencing its first Pluto return. While that's technically not set to occur until 2022, when Pluto reaches 27 Capricorn, for a planetary cycle as long-range as this it's necessary to allow for an orb of several years, if not a decade or more on either side.

So what will this mean for the United States?

One usually hears Pluto described in such general terms as transformation, death and regeneration, the pitfalls and potentials of power, confronting shadow issues, and so on. That's all true enough. But one way to begin understanding what to expect is by looking to historical examples of Pluto returns in other nations' horoscopes, since some of those nations have survived long enough over time to experience two, sometimes even three of them. While each of these nations' histories are distinct, they nonetheless offer some useful examples for us to draw upon

Pluto Returns in the Roman Empire

Using 27 BCE as the start of the Empire, Pluto's first return occurred during the period around the years 216-223 AD. This was, not surprisingly, a period of instability and change, associated with the Severan Dynasty. [1] The divisive and highly unpopular emperor Elagabalus reigned between 218 and 222 AD, and his rule became notorious for sex scandals, religious controversies, and various "outrageous" behaviors—including the infamous banquet where he allegedly smothered guests by flooding the room with rose petals. After he and his mother were dragged through the streets and assassinated by the Praetorian Guard, his reign was followed by that of Alexander Severus, who ruled from 222 to 235 AD. Though Severus restored some semblance of moderation to the Empire, he too fell out of favor with his troops and was assassinated along with his mother—thereby marking the end of the Severan Dynasty. His death in 235 AD is viewed as the pivotal event signaling the start of the "Crisis of the Third Century," where a succession of briefly-reigning military emperors, rebellious generals, and counter-claimants presided over governmental chaos, civil war, general instability and economic disruption.

The Empire's second Pluto return took place during the years around 461-468 AD, which was a period of turmoil during which the Empire found itself increasingly threatened by forces at its borders. Several years before, in 455 AD, the Vandals entered and sacked Rome itself, while at the Battle of Cap Bon in 468 AD the Vandals destroyed a combined Western and Roman invasion fleet. But it was several years later, during the reign of the barbarian

Flavius Odoacer from 476 to 493 AD, that the Roman Empire collapsed altogether.

In short, both of the general periods associated with the Empire's Pluto returns represented dramatic periods of change, power struggles, and political instability. But it's important to note it was only with the second of those returns that the Empire finally collapsed. In and of itself, in other words, a Pluto return doesn't necessarily portend the demise of a nation, although it does always seem to involve considerable upheaval.

Pluto Returns in the British Empire

In some ways, England offer an even better illustration of a nation's Pluto returns, since it survived three of them in all. Using the coronation of William the Conqueror on Dec. 25, 1066 as the birth of modern England, the first of those returns (allowing for both precession-adjusted and non-precession-corrected dates) occurred around the years 1311 to 1315; the second of those around the years ranging from 1555-1562; while the last of those unfolded around the years ranging from 1801-1810. (Note that I say "around the years" since it's important to also allow a wide orb for Pluto aspects, due to its exceptionally long orbital period.)

Regarding the first of those, the time-frame 1311-1315 was accompanied by serious environmental problems, most notably in the so-called "Great Famine" which began in 1315 and caused enormous social unrest for years to come and resulted in the death of millions. And, as my colleague Kenneth Bowser pointed out, 1314 saw the pivotal victory of Robert the Bruce at the Battle of Bannockburn, signaling the separation of the Scots from England.

The general period around England's second Pluto return, 1555-1562, was a key turning point in the Empire's history in various ways. In addition to a major insurrection in Kent in 1554 and the widespread persecution of Protestants in 1555, this period saw the ascension to the throne of Queen Mary I, who reigned from 1553 to her death in 1558—making her the very first, non-jointly ruling female monarch of England. That was followed by the ascension of Elizabeth I to the throne in 1558, which was a time of high drama for both her and the nation, bracketed on one end by the beheading of Elizabeth's mother, Anne Boleyn, and the famed stand-off between Elizabeth and Mary Queen of Scots on the other.

Perhaps most significant of all, though, this period signaled the inauguration of the so-called Elizabethan era, regarded now as a "golden age" in English history and literature, and characterized by such luminaries as William Shakespeare, Ben Jonson, Christopher Marlowe, and Edmund Spenser. (Elizabeth's reign was also associated with the famed astrologer, mathematician, and occultist John Dee—the individual credited with actually coining the term "British Empire.") In several respects, this period was indeed a Plutonian "rebirth" for England, insofar as Elizabeth took an essentially bankrupt economy and restored fiscal responsibility to it, while overseeing a great surge in global exploration and ushering in a period of relative stability and internal peace to the country. But underlying that relative peace and stability were serious problems, among them longstanding animosities between Catholics and Protestants that simmered below the surface and led to several assassination attempts on Elizabeth's life.

England's third Pluto return occurred in the period around 1801 to 1810. Aside from this being the general time frame associated with the Industrial Revolution, 1801 specifically saw the formal creation of the United Kingdom, when Great Britain (England, Wales, and Scotland) joined forces with Ireland—arguably as profound a transition point in English history as any. And whereas 1801 witnessed the end of England's commercial boom, 1809 saw a fiscal regeneration with the start of a new economic boom—a true Plutonian "rebirth" of sorts. During this general period England also found itself embroiled in various military conflicts in the effort to hold its Empire together, including the Battle of Trafalgar in 1805, the Napoleonic Wars from 1803 to 1815, the Peninsula War from 1808 to 1814, the Anglo-Russian War from 1807 to 1812, the Anglo-Swedish War in 1810, and the 1812 conflict with the newly independent United States. [1] This period also saw the British monarchy becoming increasingly unpopular, and even played host to the famed "madness of King George," when the head of the Empire was himself slipping in and out of dementia, having been formally recognized as "insane" in 1810. It's tempting to consider that the king's condition may well have symbolized a deeper imbalance festering within the Empire itself, perhaps reflecting the darker stirrings of Pluto.

But there is another development around this period of English history that's easily overlooked but which may be crucial toward understanding America's own Pluto return. To see that, though, we need to step back and look at something which began under England's *previous* Pluto return, and which came to an end under this third one. I'm referring here to the fact that during the earlier reign of Elizabeth I, the Empire saw *the formal inauguration of its slave trade*, under the direction of Sir John Hawkins—truly, the nefarious shadow side of that era's "golden age." Then, more than two centuries later, it officially came to its end during Pluto's *next* return, with the passing of the 'Abolition of the Slave Trade Act' in 1807—directly in the midst of England's third Pluto return.

It's not difficult to see the Plutonian character of this development, in both positive and negative respects. On the one hand, the slave trade showed England acting out the darkest impulses of human nature, with all its bigotry, cruelty and greed; then, the abolition of slavery during England's third Pluto return revealed England in a more redemptive and cathartic light, as the nation struggled coming to terms with that bloody institution. Pluto transits often involve contending with some unresolved darkness or transgression from the past, and if one truly confronts and resolves those issues, the effect can indeed be transformative; if not, though, those unresolved issues can consume and destroy from within. Fortunately, under that third Pluto return, England chose to confront and finally abandon that legacy.

The Implications for the United States

So what does all of this mean for America, in terms of what we can expect the years ahead? These are a few of the possibilities I'd suggest we watch for.

1. One effect of the Pluto return for America will almost certainly be economic. In doing research for this article, I thought it might be helpful to look back at what happened during America's *half-return* of Pluto during the mid-1930s, when it reached 27° Cancer, in hope that might provide some symbolic hints as to what the *full* Pluto return will bring. While that technically became exact in the mid-30s, its influence extended for a number of years on either side. The 1930s represented the very midst of the Great Depression, when Americans were facing privations and anxieties they'd rarely experienced before. While we may not experience anything quite on that scale again under the coming return, there are enough troublesome indicators already in play to believe it will be a turbulent time for the U.S. economy. (It's good to remember, though, not everyone was affected equally or in the same way by the Great Depression; in fact, some individuals actually became quite wealthy during that period—which simply goes to show that seemingly difficult planetary energies can manifest quite differently for different individuals.)

2. Based not only those earlier Pluto returns of both Rome and England but on what we *already* see happening in the U.S., it's also safe to say we can expect to see a growing

mood of social unrest in the country—possibly bordering on a civil war-type atmosphere. Notice I said "type." Do I personally believe that could result in an *actual* "civil war," with neighbors shooting and attacking each other? While even a few politicians have hinted at that possibility, I think that's highly unlikely. But there's little question there will be strong—and potentially violent—emotions bubbling up to the surface these next few years. What could possibly trigger such an extreme level of anger and unrest? Well, let me count the ways. In addition to hot-button issues like abortion, immigration, political corruption, and income inequality, it's likely that *whoever* wins the next presidential election will elicit a firestorm of reaction on the opposite side of the political divide. If Trump wins, that would trigger much frustration and anger among his detractors, while his loss certainly would not be taken well by his supporters either, to put it mildly.

3. As I pointed out, during its last Pluto return England was embroiled in a number of military conflicts in various parts of the world, and it's possible America could likewise find itself embroiled in one or more conflicts, too, whether that involve Iran, Korea, Venezuela, or another country. But considering the more covert, even underhanded side of Pluto, this could just as easily manifest through acts of sabotage, terrorism, or cyber-terrorism directed at the U.S. rather than conventional battlefield conflicts. We saw a striking example of Pluto at work in the events of 9/11, where the attack itself may have been out in the open but the perceived enemy seemed almost anonymous. Where was the terrorism being directed from exactly, and how could we respond? Americans felt a nearly paralyzing sense of powerlessness in their inability to get a clear grip on the situation, its perpetrators, or a possible resolution; in fact, that sense

of powerlessness is one of the key signatures of challenging Pluto aspects. While I hope the United States doesn't experience anything along those lines again, that possibility can't be entirely dismissed, and we even need to consider the possibility of a "false flag" attack in which a perceived act of "foreign" terrorism is actually orchestrated from within the U.S. itself to serve some homegrown political or militaristic purpose.

4. Falling as it does in Capricorn, the impending Pluto return strongly points to explosive scandals or falls from grace involving prominent individuals, be those politicians, celebrities, religious authorities, or business leaders. Previously hidden corruption, including sex crimes or possibly even treasonous activities, will be exposed to the light of day. Will that extend to the very highest political office of the land—i.e., the President? Impossible to know for sure, but it will undoubtedly be a challenging time for *whoever* is occupying the Oval Office at the time, whether they be Republican or Democrat.

5. Especially since the Pluto return is occurring in an earth sign, another likely impact will be *environmental* in nature, in terms of problems with the land and agriculture. Archetypally speaking, Pluto governs such things as toxins, refuse, and hazardous materials, so it's not unthinkable our country's problem with pollution could reach a tipping point, and that we'll be forced to come to grips with the poisons in our food that result from fertilizers, pesticides, and herbicides. Oil spills or problems with nuclear fuel sources are always a possibility, so that could be added to this mix. As before, I wondered whether we might find some useful clues from the earlier half-return of Pluto, and was struck by the fact that the mid-1930s also witnessed the infamous "Dust Bowl," which was a natural calamity affecting millions

of Americans but precipitated in large part by (hu)man-made agricultural practices. Interestingly, while that condition lasted throughout the entire decade, it climaxed almost precisely with the exact Pluto half-return. This is from a Wikipedia description about that time:

"Severe drought hit the Midwest and Southern Great Plains in 1930. Massive dust storms began in 1931. A series of drought years followed, further exacerbating the environmental disaster... By 1934, an estimated 35 million acres of formerly cultivated land had been rendered useless for farming, while another 125 million acres—an area roughly three-quarters the size of Texas—was rapidly losing its topsoil. Regular rainfall returned to the region by the end of 1939, bringing the Dust Bowl years to a close. The economic effects, however, persisted. Population declines in the worst-hit counties—where the agricultural value of the land failed to recover—continued well into the 1950s... *The worst dust storm occurred on April 14, 1935.* An Associated Press news report coined the term "Dust Bowl" after the Black Sunday dust storm." (Emphasis mine) [3]

While we may not actually experience another "Dust Bowl" exactly, it's a good possibility we'll be dealing with environmental problems that impact our farms and our food supply in the coming years. To some extent, of course, that's already happening, due to severe flooding and fires in large portions of the Midwestern and Western states, which has led some agricultural experts to predict food prices could skyrocket over the next few years. The effects of hurricanes on the southern and southeastern states are also a possibility to consider.

6. Another effect that strikes me as worth mentioning centers around the growing threat of *autocracy*. It's no secret Pluto can behave quite dictatorially at times, and we've already started seeing signs of that not only in Donald Trump's unabashedly forceful style but in the rise of various far-Right neo-fascist elements throughout the country. [4] (While it's true that we've been seeing the rise of "strongman"-type governments in several countries besides the U.S. in recent years, that's more likely due to the influence of the current Saturn-Pluto conjunction in Capricorn, along with the fact that transiting Pluto has been opposing its 1930 discovery point of 17° Cancer in recent years, too.)

Even here, I was surprised to find some intriguing parallels from that period of America's half-return of Pluto in the 1930s. Though now largely forgotten, America in the 1930s saw the rise of various pro-fascist groups around the country including the Silver Shirts, Black Legion, Khaki Shirts and Fascist League movements. While for the most part this trend remained outside the mainstream, it received support from no less prominent figures than Ezra Pound and Charles Lindbergh. And in 1934, the U.S. came perhaps the closest it's ever come to a true fascist *coup d'état,* when democracy was nearly subverted by a cabal of wealthy individuals and businessmen, but prevented by Major General Smedly Butler. As one article described it:

"Fascism had reared its head in Europe, and the world had yet to make up its mind what it thought about it—that would come later, in World War II. *Many thought that the best way to pull America out of the Great Depression was to install a dictator*—even the New York Herald-Tribune ran a headline called 'For Dictatorship If Necessary.' Although the newspaper's article was in support of FDR, a group of wealthy financiers believed that America should indeed have a dictator...

So, they began to plot a *coup d'état* that would later come to be known as the Business Plot, or the Wall Street Putsch." (Emphasis mine} [5]

It's startling now to realize that had it not been for General Butler, America could have gone in a dramatically different direction during the 1930s, similar to Germany. So with Pluto now coming up to its first full return, does this mean that an elected candidate—Trump or otherwise—will try to exert even greater control over our country's government? A related possibility could be that Trump loses the election but simply refuses to abdicate the Oval Office, thus creating a constitutional crisis. Or could it be simply mean that wealthy plutocrats will consolidate their already formidable control over the country, such as through more corporate-friendly legislative measures and judicial appointments?

7. The last possibility I want to touch on harkens back to what happened with England during the early 19th century. What "darkness" from our own past will we be contending with these next few years? It seems clear that, on one level anyway, it's similar to that of England during the early 1800s—namely, *the legacy of slavery*. America was built upon it, the nation's economy thrived because of it, and while the institution itself was officially discontinued, we're still coming to terms with its legacy and all it implied—racism, bigotry, greed. Slavery and racism have long been a stain on the nation's soul, and though we've tried hard to deny that history, it's becoming increasingly hard to avoid. There's even been talk in the U.S. these last couple of years about the feasibility of *reparations*, and making amends to America's black population for slavery. While I think that's unlikely to happen, strictly from a legislative standpoint, the timing is certainly fitting in light of Pluto returning to its founding degree.

As usual, I often look to cinema for symbolic clues into the shifting "zeitgeist," and in that spirit I was especially struck by the block-buster horror film *Us!* released in March of this year (2019). To my mind, the movie presented an uncanny illustration of America's impending Pluto return in terms of contending with that legacy of racism. Aside from the fact that its writer/director was himself black, along with most of the film's actors, the movie focuses on America coming face-to-face with that underworldly "shadow" side, and with the hidden darkness that's been simmering beneath our nation's sunny surfaces for too long. I don't want to give too much away about the plot for those who haven't watched it yet, but for those who would like to see a more imaginative depiction of America's Pluto return, I highly recommend watching it with an astrologer's perspective in mind. (Also, note how one of the "shadow" children in the movie is even named "Pluto"!) [6]

Nor is this impending challenge solely about America's black population. The Pluto return also seems related to our national discussion around minorities in general, and our culture's uneasy relationship with Muslims, Native Americans, Asian Americans, Latinos, and the LGBTQ community. Previously repressed elements of our population (including women) now seem poised to make their voices heard in ways like never before, something which became especially evident in the latest U.S. mid-term elections. The influence of Pluto is also apparent in our national debate over immigration and the ongoing crisis involving Mexican and Central American refugees at our southern border. Here, too, there are fascinating parallels with what unfolded in America during the 1930s. While researching this article, I was surprised to learn about the following controversy from that earlier time.

"Most Americans are familiar with the forced relocation in 1942 of 112,000 Japanese Americans from the West Coast to internment camps. Far fewer are aware that during the Great Depression, the Federal Bureau of Immigration (after 1933, called the Immigration and Naturalization Service) along with local authorities rounded up Mexican immigrants and naturalized Mexican American citizens and shipped them to Mexico to reduce relief roles. In a shameful episode, more than 400,000 repatriodos, many of them citizens of the United States by birth, were sent across the US-Mexico border from Arizona, California, and Texas. *Texas' Mexican-born population was reduced by a third. Los Angeles also lost a third of its Mexican population...*" (Emphasis mine) [7]

On an archetypal level, much of this anxiety over immigrants and minorities seems rooted in a deeper fear or even hatred of the "other," and a disdain for all those existing outside our own familiar tribe. One of Pluto's painful secrets seems to be just this: the hatred we direct towards others is actually *self*-hatred, projected outward. Once we become conscious of that dynamic, it becomes possible to transmute those emotions, and the result is genuine transformation and rebirth. But that takes considerable self-awareness, courage, and intelligence—qualities that seem to be in short supply amongst many Americans these days. [8]

Some Timing Considerations

As for when these dynamics can be expected to start manifesting, the Pluto return is technically set to fire exactly on February 22nd of 2022 (and by precession-adjusted standards, in February of 2024). As I hinted at the outset, though, a long-term cycle like Pluto return requires an exceptionally wide orb of influence on either side, so as with both Rome and England the long-range effects of this cycle necessarily extend for many years before and after that window of exactitude; indeed, I don't think would be excessive to speak of the entire 2020s as representing the peak period of America's Pluto return.

In terms of its early influence, it's therefore clear to me that it's already being felt—and has been for quite some time, actually. I'd even suggest that we were permitted an early sneak preview into that influence when Pluto first ingressed into Capricorn back in 2008. Did anything of importance happen then which correlates to what we've been talking about thus far? Well, besides a major tremor in America's economy that year, the United States elected its first black American president, Barack Hussein Obama. He was elected in November of 2008 but assumed office in January of 2009. I can hardly think of a clearer symbol of America's having to come face-to-face with its legacy of racism and slavery, and general uneasiness towards the "other," than the election of a black president with a Muslim-sounding name. I also believe that the Saturn/ Pluto conjunction which will become exact in January of 2020 will likewise serve as an early trigger for the U.S. Pluto return, and that much of what we're already seeing in the country in terms of unrest over Trump, immigration policies, abortion, partisan loyalties, and racism, is directly intertwined with that larger Pluto-return cycle.

But as noted, the U.S. Pluto return will technically not be *exact* until February of 2022. It's important to remember that alignments like this are similar to New Moons in that they represent the initiation of new cycles, and as such "plant seeds" that continue developing long afterwards. So while its possible there could be some important symbolic "seed-events" happening around that month, the full effects of America's Pluto return will probably not reveal themselves for years, possibly even decades afterwards, in the various areas explored here.

Coda

On a final note, it's important to note that while the U.S. Pluto return will likely prove challenging in various ways, a configuration like this presents powerful opportunities as well. In that regard it's good to remember that despite the problems which attended England's second Pluto return, that period eventually became one of its culturally richest. In turn, England's *third* Pluto return witnessed both a decline and a rebounding of its economy. As for the tangle of issues we already see coming to a boil in the U.S., one could think of it in much the same way that health practitioners talk about the "detox crises" a body goes through after a long build-up of poisons before it can become well again. We've been seeing just such a toxic build-up of America's social, political, economic, and environmental issues these last few years, and that could all intensify these next few years. Will we confront and resolve those problems, and emerge from this period a newly reinvigorated and healed society, having survived the death/rebirth dynamic of Pluto?

One way or another, we'll be finding out soon enough.

This essay first appeared in the December/January 2019/2020 issue of The Mountain Astrologer magazine.

CHAPTER 24

A MYSTIC LOOKS AT ASTROLOGY:
CONVERSATIONS WITH SHELLY TRIMMER

*I*n the late 1970s and early 1980s, I conducted a series of interviews
with a little-known mystic and occultist by the name of Shelly Trimmer
(1917-1996). Raised in the magical traditions of Pennsylvania Dutch culture, Trimmer studied for several years with the famed yogi Paramahansa
Yogananda in California. But unlike the far more public Yogananda,
Trimmer chose to remain comparatively reclusive, largely due to Yogananda's
encouragement, later settling with his family in the woods of Minnesota
and finally near the Gulf Coast of Florida. Throughout his life he chose
to teach students primarily in a one-on-one fashion rather than through
public lectures or publications.

In my own interactions with him, he struck me as extremely knowl-
edgeable on a wide variety of topics. But I was especially interested in his
understanding of astrology, on both practical and esoteric levels, and his
ideas formed the basis for much of my own writings through the years.
The following exchanges are excerpted and adapted from my book An
Infinity of Gods: Conversations with an Unconventional Mystic -
the Teachings of Shelly Trimmer.

—RG

Ray Grasse: What is astrology?

Shelly Trimmer: Astrology is the language of the soul. Astrology is nothing more or less than a symbolic interpretation of astronomy. You're taking the sum total of all the factors in the solar system and translating these events symbolically. That's all. When an event happens, there are two possible interpretations: the literal interpretation, which is what obviously happens as the ordinary person sees it, like the Sun rising in the morning, and the *symbolic* interpretation, which is looking at the Sun more as a spiritual or symbolic principle. Which is how astrologers use it. You have to know when the literal meaning of the event is more important, and when the symbolic meaning is more important.

Perhaps more clearly than any other system of symbolism, astrology can tell us about our relationship to everything that's ever been, everything that will be, and everything we are aware of now.

RG: Can a person really transcend the difficult aspects in their horoscope?

ST: I'll explain it like this. Yogananda's secretary was a good astrologer, and she wrote for astrology magazines. But Yogananda told her she was too enslaved by it. So he said to her, "Pick out the worst possible aspect for me to do something, and I will do it just to show you that I can transcend the planetary energies." So she gave him just such a time. He wanted to bring a church made out of redwood that he liked down to Hollywood. This was a big project, and he needed money to do it, so he put out fliers to everybody, and the money came in.

They moved the church from its original spot; but a telegram came in saying that the trailer had broken loose and crashed into some farmer's yard. That led to legal problems, as well as damage to the crops. As a result, Yogananda needed more money, and sent out another flier. He had hoped to get the church into place by Easter, and he did so—but by the skin of his teeth. He finally had it set up so that people could go into it. And by then, all the adverse aspects had finally passed. He said, "You see, you can transcend your horoscope...but not without difficulty!" (laughs)

Here's another example. I knew a man who had Mars square Mercury, and he wanted to be an auto mechanic. Boy, he learned the hard way. But he kept at it, and eventually he became a very good auto mechanic. In other words, you'd say that this individual, through a lot of effort and perseverance, "trined his square." And so in his next incarnation, he might have a Mars trine Mercury, rather than a Mars square Mercury.

RG: So you can resolve difficult aspects so that in a future life those difficult energies will be softened or eradicated?

ST: Oh, yes, even in this life, you can. Like this young man I knew. By the time he became an excellent auto mechanic he was about thirty-six years of age, but he started before he was twenty. And the reason they put up with him was because the owner of the garage was his relative! When he started out, he was a nuisance, he did everything wrong; he hurt himself, he cut himself—with Mars there, you can see that. He made bad decisions. But he kept at it, he kept at it, and he kept at it. Naturally, that was one of the strong desires of his nature. He wanted to keep at it, see? And eventually he learned what he could and couldn't do, all through hard knocks and hard experience.

RG: What about a horoscope with lots of trines?

ST: Trines produce dreams. Trines make life easy. And they can be just as difficult as squares, but in a different way. Take the person whose chart consists solely of trines. They tend to think the world owes them a living. They dream away. They can even become a parasite, and take everything away from you they can get. If someone has a whole bunch of trines in their chart, be extremely careful going into business with them! That individual thinks the world owes them a living; he'll dream away and take everything from you he can get. And a grand trine can be the aspect of dreamers, very definitely. They need a square—or something—to get them out of their dreaming, to do something about it. You see, *a square indicates a problem that has to be solved.* And it takes effort to solve the problem, it takes a measure of control. That couples well with the opportunity provided by the trine.

This much I do know about astrology, that it's the *science of balance.* If things are too favorable, it's just as bad as if they're too unfavorable; too many good aspects can have the same exact effect on the individual as so-called bad aspects. The ideal is to have both a harmonious and an inharmonious aspect to each planet—say, an adverse aspect to Jupiter will stimulate it, and a good aspect will give it something worthwhile to do, and some luck. But if there's too many good aspects to Jupiter...you see, Jupiter by itself only gives you dreams, it becomes more Neptunian than anything else.

Besides its philosophical importance, there are very real practical values to astrology. Remember, forearmed is forewarned. If you know something about the future, you have a chance to do something about it. But if you don't, you don't have a chance to do anything about it.

Or say that a person comes into your life. You can mark down the exact moment that happens, and then move your horoscope to that exact moment. For instance, let's say the Ascendant right then is ten degrees of Taurus. Move your own chart around so that ten degrees of Taurus is on the Ascendant. Now you can tell what this person means to you.

RG: Let me see if I understand that. You check the time when you meet the person, and see what the degree of the Ascendant is at that moment?

ST: Yes. If you see ten degrees Taurus on the ascendant at that particular time, then spin your own horoscope so that degree now becomes the Ascendant, find ten degrees of Taurus in your chart and spin that around, and see where your own planets fall within that new framework. This then gives you the meaning of that person to you, or for that matter of any event that transpires in your life, in relation to your own chart.

For instance, say you have a progressed Mercury trine natal Jupiter in your chart happening. Your progressed Mercury has moved to five degrees of Gemini, and your natal Jupiter is in five degrees of Libra; that is the aspect firing in your chart at a particular time. So suppose that a man comes into your life right when five degrees Gemini is on the horizon, and says "I've got a new project for you." Listen to him!

But let's say Mars is square Saturn in your natal chart, and Mars is in Taurus at two degrees. Suppose that same person came into your life when two degrees of Taurus was on the horizon. That would trigger your Mars square Saturn, see? You'd need to be very cautious of that person. Don't go along with them, since they could cause you trouble.

Now remember, you can have a good friend, and he might be emotionally very favorable to you, but he can have a whole bunch of screwy ideas which you wouldn't want to go along with on other levels! For example, I had a very good friend, and just on a friendship level, he was an ideal friend. But it also said, in my chart, don't get involved with him in a business way, because he's a screwball as far as business is concerned. As a result I never got involved with any kind of business proposition with him, and we remained very good friends. So you've got to know the individual, you've got to know his or her nature. After all, not all of us are good at everything. In other words, a man might be extremely good in one thing, and real bad at something else. We all have the same planets, but they're all in different aspects. And somebody might have a trine in one thing and a square in another. Avoid his square influence as much as possible, (laughs) but enjoy his trine influence!

RG: What's the most important thing towards really understanding any chart?

ST: As far as interpreting any chart goes, the main thing is to *feel* it. For example, when you say Mars, you must *feel* Mars. When you say Jupiter, you must *feel* what Jupiter is, not *think* what it is, but *feel* it. So when you see it, you *really* see it. You clear you mind with meditation, which is like clearing your circuits, and now you let the feeling flow around it, you let it read itself.

RG: The art of interpretation …

ST: That's the art. And it involves intuition. Astrology is one way to develop good psychic ability.

RG: It is?

ST: Oh, yes. Even reading the Tarot cards is one good way to developing your psychic ability. Or even reading the tea leaves. What does it matter which modality you use? You can throw sticks up in the air, if you know the technique, and read how they come down. But whatever your system, *you must know the science first.* And you must know it to the best of your ability, and when you've digested it, convert it into feeling, and like a poet you let it write itself, you let it tell its own story. You no longer do it consciously or laboriously.

RG: I was wondering whether the chart can tell one about past lives?

ST: Yes, with the chart there are ways of telling what you were in the past—what you did and how you did it, things of this sort. I pay little attention to these things, because this incarnation now is the highest incarnation, as far as your spiritual unfoldment is concerned. In any of the others you weren't as highly evolved spiritually as you are now. Now, socially, you have been *all kinds* of things in the past, from a peasant to a king. But regardless of what you were in the past, this is the highest spiritual incarnation you have ever had.

RG: Isn't there some value to knowing about one's past experience, though? For example, there are some astrologers who do past-life readings in hope of helping people understand why they have the karmas they do, to help clarify a lot of the vagueness they have about their current challenges. Is there some value in knowing these things?

ST: If God thought that was so important or necessary, you *would* be remembering those things.

RG: I *could* remember if I had the psychic abilities!

ST: If it was so important to you, you *would* have the psychic abilities, you *would* be remembering. I've found that most people go into their past lives to find out if they were somebody important back then, because they don't feel very important in this life. And I've heard them say, "I may not be so-and-so now, but boy, in the past life I was really important!"

For instance, in this house were two good friends of mine, both men. Each one thought that in his past he was Quetzacoatl in Mexico, the man in that culture who was like Christ. When one left my house, the other said, "Boy, he sure thinks he was something, doesn't he? Why, *I* was Quetzacoatl!" (laughs) So each one was convinced he was that particular being. Yet they didn't have the inner qualities to indicate they were any such being in the past. We're now dealing with spiritual characteristics, see? And this shows up from one incarnation to another.

RG: How, exactly?

ST: Your emotional pattern is almost identical to what it was in your past incarnation, and so your response to stimuli is almost the same. You may not remember the intellectual things which you carry on from one incarnation to another, but emotionally you do. So your emotional pattern slowly changes. In order to see a great deal of change in your emotional pattern over lifetimes, it takes about three to four incarnations. If I take a picture of you now, and a picture of you at the same age in your past incarnation, and I put them together here, you would say it's the same person. Everyone would recognize you. But after about three incarnations, no, they wouldn't recognize you anymore. And after seven incarnations, there would be a tremendous difference.

The horoscope can tell you things about the nature of your karmas, but it will not tell you what the *intensity* of your past karmas were. It merely tells you which adverse seeds you have sown, or the favorable seeds you have sown. Cosmic law says, "As ye sow, so shall ye reap"—and astrology is the proof that karmic justice does exist. And it not only tells you what karma is due and payable but when it's due and payable. But it doesn't tell you what its intensity is.

RG: But wouldn't the intensity be shown by how close the aspects were, by degree and minute?

ST: Oh, no, no. Here's a case that is well-known among astrologers. In Great Britain a king (George VI) was born at the same time a commoner was born. When the commoner rose and opened up his own store, the other man became king. They both reached the same relative position of elevation, but one was much higher than the other. A cow can be born at the same time you are, and the cow will go up and down in the scale of events like you. But the cow is still a cow. Astrology in that respect just tells you the cycle of what is going up and down in the different houses.

RG: But doesn't the horoscope show the intensity of the karmas, in a way that's proportional to each being?

ST: Yes, but you don't know how *great* that intensity is. It didn't say the commoner was going to be a king too. In other words, if I merely take 10th house matters as the point of reference, all the chart shows is that the 10th house matters of each individual were going to rise. But it didn't say how far. No one could tell from Hitler's chart that he was going to rule Germany. There was undoubtedly a cow born at the same time Hitler was, but that cow wasn't going to rule Germany.

So for instance, here's a woman, and she was born with Saturn square Mars. In a past life maybe she hurt her husband, perhaps even physically, and knocked him out. So that karma comes up for her in this lifetime, and what does her husband do? He blackens her eye a couple of times, maybe. But that's the extent of it. But now take a man who is born at the same time and under the same aspect, and in his past life he worked in a torture chamber and tortured to death many people. So he's got a progressed Mars square Saturn coming up—and woe unto him...Look what happens to him when that aspect begins to fire. He's not going to get hit and simply have his eye blackened by someone; he's really in for it. You see, the symbolism is the same for both, but one has a much greater intensity. And you can't tell that from the chart. The woman and the man may have been born at exactly the same time, both of their karmas are due at the same time, and one gets a tremendous wallop from the aspect, the other gets a black eye. There's a huge difference.

RG: Do you place any importance on the nodes?

ST: Sometimes the node of a planet can cause an awful lot of activity when it's in a certain position of a sign or the chart. But very few people use nodes. The Moon's nodes can cause an enormous effect, but look at what the other planets can produce, too.

RG: Are there any others in particular?

ST: Yes, Mars nodes would be rather important. But I think any of the planetary nodes would be important.

RG: Why is it that some mystics or magicians refuse to reveal their horoscopes? Is there a reason for someone keeping that information under wraps?

ST: If you know someone's chart, you actually have a tremendous advantage over them. Not only in terms of timing factors, but in

terms of working magic on their horoscope. Some say that is the reason Adolf Hitler put several different dates or times out for his horoscope, so that his enemies wouldn't know exactly when he was born.

**RG: As far as what the horoscope shows about relationships, are
we automatically drawn to the type of individuals who will manifest the karmas in our horoscope? Or can we choose differently
than what our karma suggests?**

ST: Well, for instance, let's take the chart of an astrologer I knew.
I'll give you his aspects: Saturn ruled his 7th house, it was squared
to Venus in the 4th house, and it was squared to Jupiter in the
10th house, and naturally Jupiter was in opposition to Venus. In
other words, he had a T-square to Saturn in the 7th house. So this
individual married a woman who he thought was beneath his station, and the reason he claimed he married her was to "uplift her
spiritually." You see, he thought he was himself quite evolved spiritually! And after he'd lived his life with her, he said it had been a
waste of time, because he wasn't able to lift her even one step up,
spiritually. They fought all their life together, and he was always
trying to leave her for some other woman.

But you could say it was his destiny to live with a woman he'd
fight with all his life, because he wouldn't have felt normal being
married to any other kind of woman, see? He had a tendency to
want to be with a woman who would harass him and generally be
difficult. This is what his chart said he wanted; he actually wanted
to be browbeaten by a woman, and that's what he got. If it were any
other kind of woman, he wouldn't have felt satisfied. At a deeper
level, you see, he felt he had "sins"—which his chart said he probably
did have, in terms of some difficult karmas—and this was his time
to pay the piper. And the time had come, so this is what unfolded.

*An essential key to the more esoteric side of Shelly's teachings about astrology
centered around its relation to the doctrine of the chakras. While it's beyond*

the scope of this chapter to summarize the full scope of those teachings, I'll distill a few of the essential points he made here. In particular, he taught that the seven traditional planets relate to the chakras in this ascending order: Saturn relates to the root chakra (Muladhara), Jupiter to the second chakra (Svadisthana), Mars to the third chakra (Manipura), Venus to the heart chakra (Anahata), Mercury to the throat chakra (Visshudha), the Sun to the third eye (Ajna), and the Moon to a chakra in the back of the head, called Chandra. The solar system outside us is a reflection of the inner "solar system," in other words.

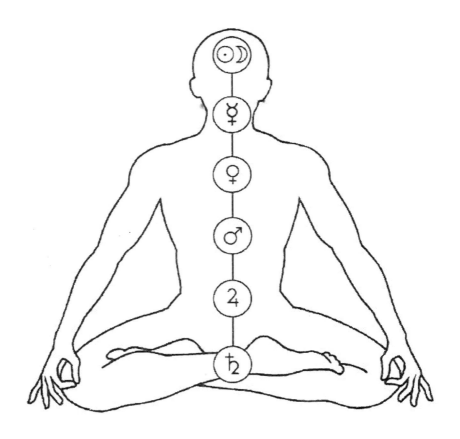

A critical point Shelly emphasized was that *each of the chakras has three distinctly different expressions.* This in turn relates to the yogic doctrine of the three vertical "nadis," or spinal currents that weave in and around the spine: *Pingala, Ida, and Sushumna.* These relate to the three realms of waking, sleeping, and spiritual consciousness, respectively. Shelly said: "In their *purest* form, the chakras are located within Sushumna, within the *very center* of the middle channel. But they have expressions in both Ida and Pingala as well, and the mode of consciousness each chakra expresses is different in each of these three realms, with Sushumna being the truest essence of that chakra, in its balanced form."

For example, in its most masculine (or extraverted) expression in Pingala, the root chakra (Saturn) manifests as Aquarius; in its feminine (or introverted) expression in Ida it manifests as Capricorn. ("By day," Shelly remarked, "Saturn rules Aquarius and by night it rules Capricorn.")

In its more extraverted expression in Pingala, the second (Jupiter) chakra is known as Sagittarius, while its more introverted expression within Ida it's known as Pisces.

For the third or Martian chakra, Aries represents its more extraverted, Pingalic expression, while Scorpio symbolizes its more feminine or Idic expression.

For the heart or Venusian chakra, its extraverted expression to the one side is Libra, while its more introverted expression to the other side is Taurus.

For the throat or Mercury chakra, it's extraverted expression in Pingala is known as Gemini, while its more introverted expression in Ida is Virgo.

Importantly, there are two chakra centers at the level of the fore head—the Ajna chakra (or "third eye") in front, which is symbolically ruled by the Sun; while its counterpart in the back of the head is known as the Chandra chakra, or what Yogananda referred to as the "mouth of God," and this relates to the Moon. These two centers are unique in that each relates to a single zodiacal sign by itself: Leo for the Ajna chakra, and Cancer for the Chandra chakra. (The spiritual center at the top of the head, Sahasrara, or the "1000-petaled lotus," represents a point of contact with the Divine beyond the personal self, and has no precise planetary or zodiacal correlate. It can also be thought of as the balancing or perfection of the two centers directly below it, Ajna and Chandra, like the peak of a triangle.) As for the outer three planets—Uranus, Neptune, and Pluto—these can be thought of as "harmonics" of the lower three chakras, and are associated with Aquarius, Pisces and Scorpio, respectively. They fit within the chakric scheme, in other words, but in a subtler and more indirect way.

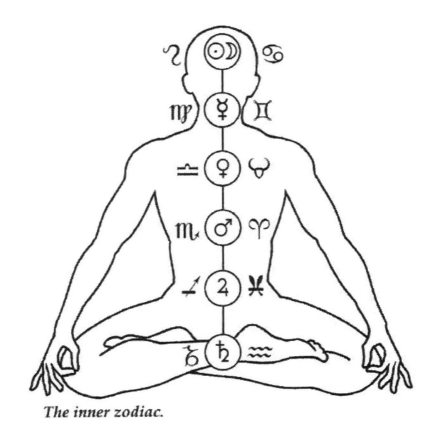

The inner zodiac.

In short, *the horoscope is a reflection of the various energies within one's different chakric levels.* According to Shelly, we're primarily aware of the chakras almost entirely in their Idic or Pingalic states, and relatively unaware of how they manifest in a more balanced way, within that central channel of Sushumna.

Shelly often referred to the dual influence of Ida and Pingala on the right and left sides of the spine as "the wheel," since that represents the domain of karma and of phenomenal experience, akin to the "wheel of rebirth" described by Buddhists. As Shelly put it, "These three states are what you're normally consciously aware of. If we are in a state of balance, within Sushumna, the 'wheel' ceases to exist, it comes to a stationary position, so all that is written upon it cannot function. So long as the wheel is moving and you are on the wheel, you're in Ida and Pingala, and you're bound by the law of what is written (in the horoscope)."

The horoscope says nothing about that central channel and one's level of awareness there. I asked Shelly, "Is it possible to tell how spiritual developed someone is from their horoscope?" "No," he replied. "There are two things you can't see in the horoscope. You cannot tell how highly evolved a saint is, nor can you see how deeply someone is in love, just from looking at the horoscope. Because what causes real love, and what causes a saint to be a saint, is not on the wheel, but it's in that central channel of Sushumna."

These, then, are some glimpses into Shelly Trimmer's teachings on astrology. For those wishing to know more, I encourage you to check out my book of conversations with Shelly, *An Infinity of Gods.*

CHAPTER 25

THE CHALLENGE OF SCORPIO: ANGER, POWER AND TRANSFORMATION

(co-written with Linda Puffer)

"Still Waters Run Deep"

—Traditional saying

Within the twelve signs of the zodiac, some signs have been considered more desirable than others and too often Scorpio has borne the brunt of some of the more negative associations.

One reason for that might be the way many of the realities within Scorpio's domain are associated with deep-seated, powerful psychic energies—so powerful, in fact, that the potential for destructive expression is equal to that of its more constructive expressions. Said another way, the same intensity that redeems Scorpio can just as often be its undoing.

Twentieth-century astrology has helped us re-vision our attitudes toward the signs and their energies. It is particularly helpful to view these energies in terms of polarities that exist not only within our psyches but as universal principles operating at all times and in all manners of manifestation. Every sign has its positive and negative aspects, all dependent on whether one expresses those energies with conscious awareness. Unconscious expression leaves room for more negative consequences.

If we accept that the psyche of every individual contains all the signs and their corresponding polarities, we quickly realize that, regardless of whether we have a planet overtly "marking the spot" for us, *everyone* has Scorpionic energy. That is, we *all* must come to terms with the challenges inherent in Scorpio, particularly as expressed through anger and its shadow, resentment.

Scorpio within the Chakra System

One way to better understand the varied expressions of Scorpio is through a consideration of the esoteric nature of Scorpio suggested by the yogic chakra system, such as we've considered in the previous chapters. The chakras are sometimes described as an archetypal hierarchy of psycho-spiritual potentials, ranging from the more earthy concerns of the root chakra at the base of the spine to the more spiritualized concerns of the energy centers within the head. And as we pointed out, each chakra has *three distinct* modes of expression: to the one side, masculine (externalized); to the other side, feminine (internalized); and within each chakra's center, a more neutral (balanced) expression.

The third chakra within this symbolic ladder of consciousness is called, in Sanskrit, *Manipura*, and is associated with the element of fire and the planet Mars. The struggles of will, forcefulness, and power are experienced most intensely at this level. This chakra represents the level of the "inner warrior," who must achieve balance of the fiery energies to truly experience spiritual mastery of the psyche's powers. This level also relates to the development of ego-awareness, and so it is here that we clarify personal boundaries and forge our own unique definition of *self* versus *other.*

This chakra has its defensive side as well, for along with the awakened sense of *me* comes the fear of *other*—and the consequent realization that *me* can be destroyed. Said another way, *with eros comes thanatos:* with life comes the awareness of death. Martian energy is therefore crucial, both for the awakening of awareness and the activation of self-protection through assertiveness, by establishing walls or boundaries. This also includes the extreme aggressiveness associated with unhealthy territoriality.

Feminine Fire/Masculine Fire

The deeper significance of both Scorpio and Aries is thus closely linked to the psychological meaning of the third chakra and the fiery energies of awakened ego-consciousness that accompany this level. Off to one side of this chakra is Aries, the externalization of Martian energy represented by assertiveness, aggression, and drive, as well as a more explosive, direct form of anger. It is a visible kind of energy that is projected outward in a manner that might be symbolized by a spear or sword.

On the other side of this chakra is Scorpio, representing a more internalized expression of that Martian energy. Whereas the Aries side concerns the directing of force outward into the world, the Scorpio side reflects a more compressed, concentric channeling of energies that can be envisioned as the spiraling power of a whirlpool or vortex pulling energy inward. For some esotericists, the subtle contrast between the Arian and Scorpionic expression of Martian energy is aptly symbolized by the male and female genitalia: the male genitalia thrusting outward and the female energy drawing inward. For this reason, Scorpio may be thought of as the "feminine Mars," in contrast to the more "masculine Mars" symbolized by Aries.

Of these two, Scorpio's power is at least equal to what is expressed outwardly by Aries, but with compression it may become even more forceful. One need only think of the way that pressing down on a metallic spring increases its power to understand how dynamic the forces of compression can truly be. Indeed, the coiled symbol astrologers use to depict Scorpio itself calls to mind something of that compressive, spring-like process. It is this very aspect of Scorpio, as the internally compressed and directed Martian force, that makes it so powerful and, for many, so potentially problematic.

At its most constructive, Scorpio possesses the discipline and investigative single-mindedness to explore the inner planes and manipulate the inner forces that it understands so well. Esoterically, Scorpio is the zodiacal principle associated with the "magical will" (especially when Scorpio is accompanied by aspects to Leo in the horoscope). It is therefore the energy of mystics, occultism, and magic. Those with strong Scorpios have an incredible will and can move mountains when they put their mind—or, more precisely, *emotions*—to the task. Many years ago I came across an older astrology text that offered the seemingly odd notion that among the various symbols associated with Scorpio was the camel. Why? This was because of that animal's ability to travel across the desert—i.e., the *desert of life*—for long stretches of time sustained solely by the water contained within it—a pithy illustration of the principle of "fixed water" and the great tenacity and drive that accompany Scorpio's ability to contain emotional energy.

Scorpio's capacity for penetrating beneath surface appearances is what gives it its detective-like ability to investigate any mystery, unlock any truth. Leaving no stone unturned, Scorpionic probing can pierce to the heart of any matter and unveil that which has been concealed—whether this be a metaphysical enigma, a buried archeological treasure, or some politician's dirty laundry!

At its most destructive, however, this same compressed Martian energy can turn back on itself in a destructive way. Thus we have the symbol of the scorpion stinging itself with its own tail, making it the only zodiacal animal that can actually kill itself. Here, the Martian force can fester, become infected, and pick at its own wounds so compulsively that they never quite heal. [1]

Nor is it simply anger that becomes problematic with the Scorpionic process, since *any* emotion or thought, when compressed or repressed, assumes added power at a subterranean level that can sooner or later erupt into consciousness. Those of us who have played the game of trying *not* to think of something, be it a white elephant, a monkey, or any other nonsensical item, know only too well the power of repression and compression. The mere fact of holding in too much, whether that be childhood-based traumas, sexual energy, or any carefully concealed secret about one's life, can take a serious toll on one's mental or physical well-being. As one popular saying expresses it: "You are only as healthy as the secrets you keep."

This is the great tightrope of Scorpio: if one works with these powerful energies in a healthy way, they can be utilized to bring about personal transformation and rebirth, or confer remarkable powers of healing. Conversely, if one is unable to direct them in a healthy and positive way, they can be destructive, not only to themselves but to everyone around them. Scorpios and Scorpionic energy can be either distorted, manifesting as the scorpion, or spiritualized to become the eagle, where those potentially lethal energies are utilized in a devotional manner toward self-actualization and the appropriate expression of great power.

Resentment - the Scorpion's Poisonous Sting
At their most intense, both Aries and Scorpio relate to the experience of emotions in uniquely opposite ways. Take sex, for example. Whereas Aries charges outward like the ram to conquer the object

of its desire, Scorpio's approach is more "feminine" and inwardly directed, seductively alluring the other toward it as if using what *Star Trek* movies called a "tractor beam." This recalls the old romantic saw: "He chased her and chased her—until she finally caught him!" The "he" here is the proverbial Aries, thrusting forward, while the "she" is akin to the seductive Scorpio, drawing the other toward it in its wake.

Yet, of all the emotions they deal with, it's that struggle with anger which most often reappears in Scorpios' own accounts of their recurring life-challenges. One way of better understanding this is through the idea that every sign has its own addiction or "drug of choice," with spiritual growth having much to do with controlling, transmuting, or breaking free from those compulsive patterns of behavior and learning to master the energies of that sign. For example, the "addiction" of heavily Geminian charts will tend to involve *ideas*, or perhaps excessive communication; for Taurus, it might be material security; for Capricorn, status or overachievement; and so on as we go through each sign.

For Scorpio it can be argued that the drug of choice is *resentment*, which is basically anger that's been repressed. Resentment feeds on itself in much the same way that heroin addicts must feed their addiction. We've all known individuals who repeatedly put themselves in situations they can feel angry about, because of the perverse (i.e., irrational and likely unconscious) "pleasure" they derive from bathing in the toxic juices of resentment they've conjured up for a fix. While one can argue that anger has a potentially constructive side, such as when mustering up energy in order to combat a social injustice, resentment is much more insidious and therefore more damaging. One would be hard-pressed to describe any rationale for resentment being "good"—ever. The English poet William Blake expressed something of this problem in his poem, "A Poison Tree":

A Poison Tree

I was angry with my friend:
I told my wrath, my wrath did end.
I was angry with my foe:
I told it not, my wrath did grow.

And I water'd it in fears,
Night & morning with my tears;
And I sunned it with smiles,
And with soft deceitful wiles.

And it grew both day and night,
Till it bore an apple bright;
And my foe beheld it shine,
And he knew that it was mine

And into my garden stole,
When the night had veil'd the pole:
In the morning glad I see
My foe outstretch'd beneath the tree. [2]

To be sure, not all Scorpios indulge in this behavior, any more than all Geminis gossip or all Aries engage in fistfights. Yet such extreme examples can serve as useful reminders of the subtler challenges facing those who encounter these energies. In fact, because we each contain all the signs and planets within us, we are *all* subject to both the challenges and strengths of Scorpio. Depending on where Scorpionic energy is tucked into our own horoscopes or psyches, we all will deal with this issue in varying degrees, depending upon how well-aspected or afflicted Mars and Pluto are, and how obscure or obvious the house and sign placements are.

A case in point concerns one of this article's co-authors, who has Scorpio on the cusp of the 12th house, with no planets in that sign. During the writing of this article the author realized that a concurrent Pluto square to a stellium of personal planets was forcing an unexpected confrontation with long-buried anger and resentment hitherto considered resolved or even non-existent. The synchronicity of this could not have been more timely nor less profound, and the author has definitely begun to work with Scorpio from a new (and humbled) perspective.

Transforming Anger and Resentment

How, then, does one begin to lift the energies to their highest potentials, to transform the scorpion into the eagle? Perhaps the most fundamental psychological step involves a deeper understanding of what truly lies behind the more defensive manifestations of this energy. At their most irrational, both Aries and Scorpio center around the psychological factors of *insecurity* and *fear.* One fears or resents those who awaken one's own insecurities. As pointed out, with the awakening of self-awareness at the third chakra also comes the awakening of vulnerability and defensiveness. Anger is a normal reaction when one's boundaries have been transgressed. What happens to that anger, in terms of how it is expressed and ultimately processed, leads to our consideration of three possible ways to work with the more troublesome energies of Scorpio.

The first of these methods is that of *forgiveness.* If resentment represents Scorpio's primary Achilles' Heel, then the key lesson of this sign is sometimes about *letting go,* of loosening the grip of long-nurtured hurts on one's soul. Forgiveness can mean many different things, and for most of us it may very well be an unexamined concept first instilled through religious tenets or strictly defined by our families and cultures of origin. On an occult level, however, forgiveness is often described as the powerful neutralizing of negative force fields within the chakric system, a literal clearing away of parasitical thought forms that weigh on the subtle body like barnacles on the hull of a ship. With this in mind, it is useful to consider several different ways of working with forgiveness, although these are not the only ways.

First, forgiveness can be a way to deal with anger through visualizations and guided imagery that help us to let go of the heaviness that comes with anger held onto far past the point of its "shelf life." In *The Egyptian Book of the Dead*, there is the moment when the soul reaches the underworld and must face the judgment of Thoth who determines what its final disposition will be in the afterlife. This determination is made by weighing the heart against a feather on a balancing scale. If the heart is "too heavy" the soul cannot proceed; whatever is being held onto within that heart is an impediment to any further evolution of that soul. If the heart is lighter than the feather, it is a heart without sin and worthy of redemption. In terms of one's own experience, one might reflect on all those individuals who have ever been a source of resentment, or even hatred, throughout one's life. Then one might spend time in meditation pouring forgiveness and compassion toward each of these personalities until one feels the emotional "charge" associated with each of these figures gradually lessen in intensity. (An especially helpful forgiveness exercise can be found in Stephen Levine's excellent book, *Guided Meditations and Visualizations.*[3])

Yet some would argue that forgiveness, in and of itself, may not necessarily uproot the source of deep-seated angers or resentments. This brings us to the second of our methods for transforming the shadow energies of Scorpio. This approach centers around the view that transformation truly comes about only as a result of a deeper experiential understanding, or "unlocking," of those turbulent emotions at their energetic roots. The intent is to investigate the emotional problem in an honest and open manner, probing into the true source of the feelings underlying the psychological states. In so doing, we defuse their obsessive or addictive qualities. *This is not about analyzing an emotion.* Rather, one allows oneself to truly experience the "felt" sense of one's anger and resentment at their core while remaining the conscious witness. Though this process can be undertaken with the guidance of an experienced therapist, it is also possible to engage in this investigation by oneself. Perhaps the most powerful method along this line is the widely-acclaimed "focusing" technique pioneered by Eugene Gendlin, which distills many of the most effective elements of classic therapeutic methods into a simple, step-by-step approach. (For those interested in learning more about this uncanny therapeutic approach, the best book is still Gendlin's own work on the subject, appropriately titled *Focusing.*)

A third approach for dealing with the anger and resentment of Scorpio is that of "transmutation." Here, the emphasis shifts to taking the essential energies of the Scorpio experience and channeling them into alternative and more constructive modes of expression. On a more mundane level, for instance, some astrologers find it helpful suggesting to clients with an abundance of Scorpio energies (natally or by transit) the usefulness of finding outlets for those energies through some form of vigorous exercise, lest those energies bottle up and pose greater problems. On a more mystical level, some have used rituals or visualizations for transmuting these same energies into higher, more spiritualized states of awareness.

A case in point: One young Scorpio of our acquaintance described a mini-enlightenment he once had during a nearly overwhelming bout of resentment. Having lain in bed for hours one night, seething over a spiteful comment directed at him by his girlfriend, he finally decided to try using a powerful meditative visualization learned while studying Tibetan Buddhism the previous year. In essence, this involved channeling his intense feelings into a focused meditation on a particular "wrathful" deity, which served to redirect those feelings without suppressing them.

After several minutes he suddenly found himself awakening to a profound realization of the inherent sacredness and luminosity of all phenomena—even those very angry emotions he was beset by. In other words, the very intensity of his troubling emotions provided the very fuel necessary to reach "escape velocity" into a more transcendental perspective on his condition. Needless to say, techniques of this sort should probably be undertaken under the supervision of an experienced teacher, therapist, or meditation instructor, rather than strictly on one's own.

Ultimately, the core of any effort to harmonize the powerful energies of Scorpio lies in the compassionate acceptance of one's own emotional nature. From a healing perspective, forgiveness is about integration. We cannot integrate what remains unconscious. Furthermore, when there is polarization, we need to find a way to hold *both* positives and negatives consciously until we recognize what it is we need to integrate in order to heal, to become whole. When we can bring conscious awareness to what is being obscured or distorted by anger, we contact the essential authentic self's feelings of fear, hurt, and vulnerability that have previously not been acknowledged. With this acknowledgment—witnessing—arises the possibility of releasing those feelings, of transforming anger and resentment.

The enlightenment and self-growth that are revealed when one seeks to generate self-acceptance rather than self-rejection are some of the most profoundly soul-making gifts of Scorpio. When we reject another, we are rejecting our own self. The fruits of Scorpio grow from the deepest sources rooted in the psyche. What we nurture those fruits upon, be it unexpressed bitterness and secret resentment, or sincere openness and compassion for ourselves and others, determines the way in which we meet the challenge of Scorpio to not succumb to the fruit of the poison tree.

This article first appeared in the February, 1999 issue of The Mountain Astrologer magazine.

CHAPTER 26

IS MODERN ASTROLOGY
REALLY MORE "VAGUE"?

It won't come as a surprise to anyone who's followed the astrological field in recent years that there's something of a divide between those who adhere to more traditional methods and those practicing so-called "modern astrology" (also sometimes referred to as "psychological astrology"—but more on that in just a bit).

To briefly sum up these two approaches, traditional astrologers, whether East or West, tend to be more "event-oriented," more reliant on relatively precise formulas and rules, while also subscribing to a comparatively deterministic attitude towards fate. On the other hand, modern-day astrologers tend, as a group, to focus more on the inner, psychological experience of clients, while subscribing to a more malleable attitude towards fate and the vagaries of circumstance. Said another way, for the modern astrologer what's "good" or "bad" in life tends to hinge more on a person's subjective attitude and reaction than the external event itself.

One of the common criticisms leveled at the modern approach, especially in its more psychological variants, has been its supposed tendency toward vagueness in both natal and predictive interpretations. Some of the terms I've seen used to describe the modern approach have been "wishy-washy," "overly focused on the subjective responses of clients," or even "sloppy." As an extreme example, imagine a client coming into the astrologer's office just as transiting Saturn is about to square their Sun, and the astrologer tells them something along the lines of, "You have a great growth opportunity ahead of you!" Or, "This will be an ideal time to learn about your limiting attitudes toward success and your own ego patterns!" While comments like that might be encouraging in their own way, such an approach actually says more about a particular counseling style than it does about the real-world problems the client is about to face, and would certainly leave that client with little practical understanding of what's about to transpire in their life.

In contrast, it's sometimes said that classical techniques are not only more precise but less reliant on the subjective responses of clients to the vagaries of fate, with a greater tendency to speak more plainly and concisely to actual events. As one writer put it:

> "Classical techniques assume you are a mere mortal whose hopes and fears and very body is subject to the sorts of slings and arrows that positive thinking and the law of attraction can't do a thing about. *Classical techniques describe those sorts of experiences better and more reliably than modern ones ever could.* In classical astrology those slings and arrows suddenly get really clear. They're no longer a statement of how you perceive the world about you, they describe that world in bright, vivid, unflinching detail." (Emphasis mine) [1]

To some extent, I actually agree with these criticisms of modern/psychological astrology—at least, as they apply to the more extreme examples of that approach. The hypothetical case I proposed above—of an astrologer's response to the client undergoing a Saturn square—represents something of a caricature of the modern approach and can't properly be compared with how one finds this style expressed through the works of figures like Stephen Arroyo, Liz Greene, or the late Howard Sasportas, for starters.

But I'd also like to point out that there are some ways in which the advent of modern astrology has actually *increased* the specificity of our readings, rather than diminished it. The problem here lies in the unfortunate tendency to mischaracterize "modern astrology" strictly as *psychological* astrology, when in fact the two aren't necessarily the same. That's because there is an entirely different dimension involved with the evolution of modern astrology besides just that of psychology, and it has to do with *the inclusion of the trans-Saturnian planets: Uranus, Neptune, and Pluto.*

Although these three planetary outers can indeed be incorporated in any purely psychological approach to astrology, that isn't by any means necessary, since they can easily be employed in a completely event-oriented, non-psychological way as well. As such, I'd argue that they've provided us with the possibility of discerning details in horoscopes that would be completely missing in any pre-modern system of interpretation, whether that be Vedic, Medieval, Hellenistic, or otherwise. (To be clear, there are practitioners of traditional astrological systems who *do* incorporate the outer planets in their methods, but that is not universally the case.) I'll offer four concrete examples of what I mean.

I had a client come to me who had just survived a devastating year in a failed relationship, when it turned out the man she fell deeply in love with was a drug addict, and had also been cheating on her. One year before coming to me, she had gone to a respected Vedic astrologer who didn't incorporate the outer planets, and who predicted nothing problematic on the horizon for her in matters of the heart. When I drew up her horoscope, however, I immediately saw that Neptune had been squaring her Venus throughout that entire year—with that square first becoming exact the same week she met the man (in a tavern, no less).

There was no real need for me to discuss the inner, psychological dynamics of the Neptune–Venus energy at all (although I could easily have done so, had I thought it would be helpful); it was quite enough to describe the outer misfortunes that customarily result from such a transit. My point here is, including that aspect in my reading gave a real-world precision to my consult that would have been lacking in one that didn't incorporate that outer planet.

Here's another example. A woman in her thirties came to me just as transiting Uranus was about to cross over her 4th-house cusp. While I did touch on some of the psychological implications of that transit, I also pointed out that there could be major changes or possibly even disruptions in her home life, which might even involve a move. However, because of the fact that her natal Uranus was reasonably well-aspected at birth (it was conjunct Jupiter), I sensed that these changes could ultimately prove more positive than negative. As it turned out, that is exactly what transpired. When the transit fired one month later, she had an unexpected job offer from out of state, which involved working for a major information technology firm (Uranus-ruled) and that required her to relocate. (*Note:* Any planet that affects a horoscopic angle will simultaneously affect the opposite angle, so it's not surprising that a major conjunction with the 4th-house cusp would also involve her 10th-house career in some way.) Again, here was a level of specificity using the outer planets that would have been absent without them.

Another Uranian example concerns a writer friend whose progressed Sun was coming up in several months to trine his Uranus. Since he was a somewhat public figure, I told him he might experience some unexpected media exposure around the time that aspect climaxed, due to Uranus's concern with media and technology. As it turned out, certain statements he posted online unexpectedly drew widespread attention and he found himself the subject of discussion in media outlets around the entire world—all of this climaxing within just days of when his progressed Uranus aspect became exact. I was nearly as surprised by this turn as events as he was, not just because of the magnitude of what unfolded but due to how closely it coincided with the astrological aspect involved.

On a whim, I decided to see if my friend's brush with media fame could have been detected using more traditional methods, so I approached a colleague conversant in Vedic methods to see what his system of interpretation indicated about that period. I was careful not to explain what happened and simply gave him my friend's birth data, and asked if he saw anything unusual about that period in question. He described that general period as being a positive one, but said nothing about the worldwide fame, electronic media, nor pinpoint anything about the specific week in question. Yet again, the outer planets afforded extreme specificity rather than vagueness.

Now, two examples from natal astrology. The first of those involves a client who came to me with a nearly exact natal Mars-Pluto opposition between her 2nd and 8th houses. (Though I personally prefer to use Placidus, I should note that this aspect remained consistent in other house systems, including Whole Sign.) My experience has shown that any oppositions to Pluto in the 8th house nearly always point to conflicts or control issues with partners over money or shared resources, and can even involve problems of theft and/or betrayal. Indeed, this turned out to be probably the single most vexing problem in this woman's entire life, having endured three marriages, all of which ended in contentious divorces over money and alimony settlements. This client had previously consulted a traditional astrologer—in this case, a respected Hellenistic practitioner (one who chose not to incorporate the outer planets)—who failed to note any of the turbulent struggles she experienced over money in relationships, as clearly shown by her natal Mars-Pluto opposition. [2]

Lastly, I had a client whose chart displayed an extraordinary natal configuration involving Jupiter in a very tight conjunction with Uranus in her 5th house, forming an equally tight trine to her Moon in Leo on the Ascendant. Even if Uranus hadn't been involved in that pattern, I knew that this pattern could show a flair for creativity and performing, and her coming before the public in some way. But with Uranus added to the mix, I knew that technology and media could easily play a big role as well. I told her that, and added that her career could easily see her becoming involved with TV, radio, the Internet, and so on. She informed me that she actually owned her own media production company at one point, and appeared on camera for many of the videos it produced. My point here is that while Jupiter in the 5th trining her Moon on the Ascendant could by itself point to creativity and being in the spotlight, the involvement of Uranus specifically suggested technology and the media could easily play a major role in that. As a result, adding that outer planet to the mix allowed me to be considerably less vague about her horoscope than I would have been otherwise.

In short, while modern astrology has certainly suffered from its ignorance of classical techniques, it's important to appreciate how astrology has benefited from modern developments, too. Rather than see the two approaches as separated by a vast gulf, astrologers would benefit from exploring all the ways these two paths can illumine one another. By failing to do so we run the risk of overlooking important insights in our interpretation of horoscopes, whether personal or sociopolitical in scope.

This article first appeared in the June/July, 2018 issue of The Mountain Astrologer magazine.

CHAPTER 27

RETHINKING TRADITIONAL CONCEPTS
OF DIGNITIES AND DEBILITIES

O n more than one occasion I've had a student or client come to me and say something along the lines of, "I have my Venus in Virgo. I've heard that this is the worst placement for Venus. Is that true?"

I find comments like that sad, because they reflect a basic misunderstanding of horoscopes and the nature of astrology generally. As I've been suggesting throughout this book, we have to be careful in placing rigid value judgments on our astrological interpretations. But comments like the one above at least serve to shed light on the divide between the modern and traditional approaches to this ancient discipline.

Among the key points of disagreement between older and newer systems is the use of terms like "malefic" or "benefic." For example, whereas many older texts tend to describe horoscopic patterns in comparatively black or white terms, even to the extent of using terms like "good" or "evil," modern schools tend to be more ambiguous, with less inclination to make stronger value judgments. As we saw in our previous chapter, that can become so extreme at times that modern-day astrologers open themselves to criticisms of being too vague, with little clear awareness of the real-world problems posed by certain placements.

Enter the Neo-Traditionalists

In recent decades, a growing number of practitioners in the traditionalist camps—particularly of the Hellenistic school—have gone to considerable lengths to bring greater nuance to the older terminologies and how we think about them. For instance, some have pointed out that terms like "malefic" actually serve a useful function in describing the subjective experience of challenging placements. As a result, saying that a transiting Saturn/Mars square is negative or malefic indeed holds a certain validity in terms of accurately describing how the individual him or herself may be experiencing it, emotionally. A similar point has been made about the so-called "dignities" assigned to the planets in their various zodiacal placements, with terms like "fall" or "detriment" traditionally seen as having a more negative connotation, while terms like "exaltation" and "rulership" (or "domicile") are traditionally accorded more positive connotations.

Table of Traditional Dignities (Abbreviated)

Sun
Exaltation: Aries
Rulership: Leo
Detriment: Aquarius
Fall: Libra

Mars
Exaltation: Capricorn
Rulership: Aries, Scorpio
Detriment: Libra
Fall: Cancer

Moon
Exaltation: Taurus,
Rulership: Cancer
Detriment: Capricorn
Fall: Scorpio

Jupiter
Exaltation: Cancer
Rulership: Sagittarius, Pisces
Detriment: Gemini
Fall: Capricorn

Mercury
Exaltation: Virgo
Rulership: Gemini
Detriment: Sagittarius
Fall: Pisces

Saturn
Exaltation: Libra
Rulership: Capricorn, Aquarius
Detriment: Cancer
Fall: Aries

Venus
Exaltation: Pisces
Rulership: Libra, Taurus
Detriment: Scorpio
Fall: Virgo

Some modern practitioners are careful to avoid interpreting these concepts in the more extreme, black-or-white terms of older times, instead suggesting they simply relate to "how effectively can a planet convey its virtue." [1] From this standpoint, a zodiacal placement like Venus in Pisces—the sign of that planet's exaltation—would thus be seen as having an easier time expressing its inherent virtues, whereas in the sign of its fall, Virgo, it would have a harder time expressing those virtues.

Likewise, in the sign of Capricorn the planet Mars would feel more comfortable and "at home," and have an easier time expressing its inherent virtues; whereas in the sign of its fall, Cancer, it would have a harder time effectively expressing those virtues. To put it a little differently, its sometimes been said that a planet in its fall is relatively weakened, whereas in the sign of its exaltation it is comparatively strengthened.

Lingering Concerns

While I believe these terms have a certain value, especially when employed in traditional contexts (and with techniques such as horary), I still believe they can be problematic, even misleading at times. Let me give some examples of what I mean.

Consider my opening example of Venus in Virgo, which is traditionally the sign of this planet's fall. According to the traditional Hellenistic perspective, that means that this planet should be less capable there of expressing its inherent virtues, less "at home" or less comfortable becoming what it is truly capable of. In some ways, it's easy to see how the otherwise loving, aesthetic, romantic, and "flowing" instincts of Venus might indeed feel stymied when channeled through the largely analytical, discriminatory, and dissecting lens of Virgo.

But while doing research on famous musicians several years ago, I was struck by the startling number of brilliant or notable singer/songwriters born with this particular placement: John Lennon, Mick Jagger, Sting, Joni Mitchell, John Mayer, Leonard Cohen, John Mellencamp, Eminem, PJ Harvey, Chrissie Hynde, Roger Waters, and Jack White. In short, some of the most creative songwriters of the last few generations were born with this planet in the sign of its supposed "fall."

What are we to make of that? Clearly, most astrologers would agree that one of the "inherent virtues" of Venus is artistic expression or the appreciation of beauty. So if indeed Venus in this sign is supposedly "weakened" somehow, in the sense of having a harder time expressing its inherent virtues, how do we explain the fact that so many successful artists with this placement produced such notable (not to mention lucrative) works of art? Rather than being weakened or in some way debilitated, it seems that this planet's potential qualities are actually *enhanced* by being in this sign—in certain contexts anyway.

Ahh—*in certain contexts...* Therein lies the rub. That's because it's entirely possible that in some contexts the qualities of Venus might well be *hindered* by being in Virgo, but in other contexts those inherent virtues might actually be *enhanced*. That's because it *all depends on what one is trying to do.*

What do I mean? Well, suppose your primary goal in life is to have a perfectly contented love life where you feel totally satisfied with your romantic partner. In that case, I think this placement might indeed be problematic for some, since it can be so analytical and discriminating that one might have difficulty extending or even receiving unconditional love, or simply feeling content in relationships. Like I say—*for some people.*

However, what if your primary life-dream is to channel your artistic impulses through writing lyrics and music to songs, say, like our aforementioned singer-songwriters? In that case, it could actually be the *best* possible placement.

Let me say it a little differently: *there is no sign placement for any planet that isn't beneficial for some things and problematic for others.* Simply making a blanket statement about how "planet x is weakened in this sign and strengthened in that sign" strikes me as an overly simplistic way to approach dignities, since it doesn't sufficiently take into account the many nuances of those placements, or the subtleties of context. I'll give a few more examples of my point.

Take Mercury in Pisces, which is considered to be the zodiacal place of its "fall." It's safe to say this could well be problematic for someone working a job requiring an eye for precise details and material facts, such as a proofreader, bank teller, or an accountant. But what if someone's lifelong ambition is to be a poet, singer, a novelist, or even a mystic? In that case, having this placement might be the best possible placement—as it was for Dane Rudhyar, Eckhart Tolle, Edgar Cayce, Victor Hugo, and the famed yogi Ramakrishna.

Or take the example of Saturn in Aries, considered by traditionalists to be the place of this planet's "fall," and thus where Saturn's inner virtues are supposedly weakened or debilitated. How then how do we explain someone like my earlier example of George Washington, who was born with this planetary placement and became one of history's most celebrated military leaders? The explanation is simple, really. For someone who came here to exercise discipline, structure and authority in matters of war, aggression or competition, Saturn in Aries could well be the best possible placement for someone—although there might admittedly be a steep learning curve in realizing and cultivating that potential. (Indeed, it's possible those very difficulties with in positions of "fall" or "detriment" are precisely what leads to the constructive potentials inherent in those placements, through an arduous process of refinement born of trial-and-error.)

What I'm saying here applies in the other direction, too, in terms of the so-called "exalted" zodiacal placements, traditionally considered the most intrinsically positive and favorable positions for planets. A good example of that is Venus in Pisces, where this body is supposedly strengthened and more able to express its inherent virtues. But here as well, that only gives one side of the story. How many individuals have I seen with this placement who had difficulties balancing their checkbooks, or who didn't use sufficient discrimination when selecting partners and friends (unlike Venus in Virgo, which can sometimes be a bit *too* discriminating in such matters)? In some contexts, Venus in Pisces is indeed an extraordinary asset, while in other areas it's much more problematic.

As I said, it's all a matter of context.

The View from 30,000 Feet

I should point out that my own perspective on this stems from a philosophical view I've long subscribed to with horoscopes, which I'd sum up this way: *Every person has exactly the horoscope they need to accomplish what they came here to do.* In other words, I believe that we take on the lives and the horoscopes we do in order to serve some purpose in our spiritual growth. If that's true, then there is nothing in the horoscope that's inherently or exclusively "wrong," "evil" or "bad." Difficult, challenging, or problematic? Absolutely. But *inherently* or *exclusively* negative? No.

As a result, even the most seemingly difficult pattern in a person's chart can be seen as somehow suited to that person's destiny, and as such harbors a potentially constructive expression or outlet *somewhere*. This in no way denies the potentially problems of those placements, but simply aims to provide a fuller sense of their potentials. The challenge then becomes one of finding the best possible outlet for those energies.

As I've touched on earlier, this applies to planetary aspects as well as zodiacal placements. Take a difficult pattern like Saturn-opposition-Mars, an energy that often indicates considerable frustration, repressed anger, problems with authority figures, thwarted ambitions, and so on. But what if someone came here to discipline and control their aggressive impulses, like the famed martial artist Bruce Lee? Then it might be—and in Lee's case, was—the best possible aspect.

Or take a pattern like Neptune-square-Venus, an aspect which sometimes shows disillusion in romance, carelessness with money, addictive tendencies, or other problems. But what if someone's innermost desire is to be a musician or singer—like Whitney Houston, Madonna, Frederick Chopin, Joan Baez, or Tina Turner? In that case, that aspect might be just what the doctor ordered, despite whatever other life-challenges might come along with it. But even in areas of romance, it could wind up being an extremely favorable aspect—once one has dealt with the more challenging tendencies it presents, that is.

In the end, I'm suggesting the need for greater caution in our use of some familiar terms and perspectives when reading charts. It's not that the classical dignities and debilities are wrong, or that there aren't certain values to concepts like "fall," "detriment," "malefic" or benefic." In fact, I believe a good argument can be made that certain zodiacal placements are subjectively felt as more *pleasant* or *unpleasant* than others—such as the Moon in Sagittarius versus the Moon in Capricorn or Scorpio. But that's a very different story than talking about the full range of potentials inherent in those placements, be those constructive or destructive. To my mind, this difference in approaches is akin to the difference between seeing in black-or-white or in technicolor. Using the "technicolor" approach to sign placements and aspects, one has access to a wider palette of possibilities to draw on.

For me, then, it all comes down to finding the right context and expression for our myriad energies. I'd suggest that we approach every element of the horoscope with that in mind, because anything less than that fails to honor the true complexity of either horoscopes or of human experience.

This article first appeared in The Astrological Journal, March/April 2020

CHAPTER 28

SCORPIO, PISCES, AND AQUARIUS: OLD RULERSHIPS OR NEW?

W hen fellow astrologers tell me they prefer to use the traditional rulers for Scorpio, Pisces, and Aquarius—the planets Mars, Jupiter, and Saturn, accordingly—I respect that, since there's genuine value in staying within a consistent system, such as the traditional approach offers. Besides, I've come to believe that many modern-day astrologers miss out on important subtleties by ignoring the old rulers for those three signs, not to mention the systems which incorporate them.

But as someone who uses both the old *and* new rulers, I respectfully differ with those who claim there's no value *at all* to using the modern bodies as either rulers or co-rulers—or who suggest there isn't even a discernible relationship between the outer planets and those three signs (as one colleague recently said to me). All right, let's examine that last claim more carefully, and from there we'll consider a few other related issues.

Exploring the Commonalities
Let's start with the basic question: Is there even a close correlation between the outer three planets and those three signs modern astrologers have assigned to them?

Take Aries and Scorpio. No doubt about it, Mars seems to play a role in the rulership of both signs. But what are we to make of the possibility that Pluto might also have a compelling resonance with Scorpio? I've known many Scorpios and Aries throughout my life, probably more than any other zodiacal signs, in fact, since some have been family members. Both zodiacal signs are assertive, intense, and power-packed.

But I couldn't help but notice that they express that energy and assertiveness in *diametrically opposite* ways. To illustrate that, I've sometimes pointed to the difference between the James Caan and Al Pacino characters in the first *Godfather* film: The James Caan personality ("Sonny" Corleone) embodies a textbook Aries at its most extreme—expressive, in-your-face, with fiery displays of anger. On the other hand, Al Pacino's character (Michael Corleone) is more of a classic Scorpio—secretive, powerful but considerably more indirect in expressing anger, playing his cards close to his vest, etc.

Look closely at Mars and Pluto, and you'll find *precisely* the exact same contrast in play. Both planets are powerful and assertive, but whereas Mars is very direct and in-your-face, Pluto is more subterranean and indirect. In no way can Mars really be called covert or indirect, and in no way can Pluto be called overt or direct. If you've ever studied the horoscopes of individuals with hard Sun–Mars aspects versus those with hard Sun–Pluto aspects, you'll know what I mean. Case in point, the famous and flamboyant mobster Al Capone was born with Sun opposing Mars, whereas Vice President Dick "power behind the throne" Cheney was born with his Sun opposing Pluto. So it's one thing to say you choose not to use Pluto as the ruler of Scorpio, but another matter to say it bears no resonance with that sign at all. It does—and with a vengeance (so to speak).

Let's move on now to Sagittarius and Pisces, where we encounter much the same situation vis-a-vis those signs and the planets

Jupiter and Neptune. Both of these zodiacal signs deal with matters of idealism, inspiration, faith, and belief. But whereas Sagittarius is more outgoing and expressive in these areas, Pisces is decidedly more introverted, reserved and reflective. And we find exactly that same difference at play between Jupiter and Neptune. Whereas the former is more outgoing and expressive in matters of faith and idealism, Neptune is far more introverted and subdued in its approach. To use an analogy, it's like the difference between a Bible-thumper out on the street corner preaching the gospel and a monk off in his monastery cell engaged in contemplation. We also see that difference in how these two signs and their rulers deal with their more extreme escapist tendencies. Both Sagittarius and Jupiter tend to express their escapism more externally and overtly, as for example by wandering off to some foreign country, while Pisces and Neptune tend to express their escapism more emotionally and internally, such as through dreamy fantasies or substance-fueled reveries.

It's when we come to the sign Aquarius that we tend to find the greatest difference of opinion regarding the old vs. new rulerships, because of the purported "great differences" between Aquarius and Uranus. First of all, regarding the traditional rulership of both Capricorn and Aquarius by Saturn, it's clear to me the ringed planet has a big hand in *both* signs, since even Aquarius has its more conservative side (think Ronald Reagan, Sarah Palin, or Dick Cheney). Yet, as for the claim that Aquarius has nothing "Uranian" about it at all, due primarily to its "fixed" nature—really?

Consider just a few of the famous Aquarians from history who were notably progressive or even rebellious in their impact or temperament: Thomas Edison, Abraham Lincoln, Charles Darwin, Francis Bacon, Thomas Paine, James Joyce, Jules Verne, Charles Lindbergh, William Burroughs, Huey Newton, Saul Alinsky, punk rocker Johnny Rotten and, last but not least, James "Rebel Without a Cause" Dean. It seems fairly clear to me that there are more Uranian influences at work in these cases than conservative, Saturnian ones. That's not to say there is *no* Saturnian influence in these personalities—after all, anyone who feels called on to challenge or transform "the establishment" likely possesses quite a bit of that establishment inside them, which they've projected outward as an external "other" they're compelled to overturn. Yet the predominant influence in all those lives seems demonstrably more Uranian than Saturnian.

(In fact, this strikes me as part of the fascinating complexity and paradoxical nature of Aquarius, insofar as it's a sign that embodies the *interplay* of those differences between Saturn and Uranus—conservative vs. progressive, individual versus collective, structure versus anarchy, whole system versus part, and so on. There's an inherent tension of extremes within Aquarius, which is perfectly reflected in that joint rulership of Saturn and Uranus. This may also shed light on the supposed contradiction some point to between Aquarius and the planet Uranus, specifically in the fact that Aquarius is a "fixed" sign while Uranus is more associated with qualities of suddenness and unpredictability. But if we accept that *both* Saturn and Uranus play a role as co-rulers, that seeming discrepancy is largely resolved, with this sign now being seen as a *dance between* those extremes. So while we do find some Aquarians who embody Saturnian conservatism, like Dick Cheney and Ronald Reagan, we can just as easily find individuals who embody qualities of suddenness and unpredictability, like Johnny Rotten or Huey Newton. For that matter, note how the otherwise strictly conservative Dick Cheney advocated an extremely Uranian case for gay rights after his daughter Mary came out as a lesbian, while Ronald Reagan completely changed course in mid-career, morphing from a union-supporting Democrat to a union-busting Republican. So even in very conservative cases like these we can detect the influence of both Saturn *and* Uranus.)

Approaching it slightly differently, I could point up the resonance between the outer planets and these three signs even more simply. For example, Moon conjunct Neptune in a natal horo-scope is extremely similar in influence to the Moon in Pisces, in terms of the extreme sensitivity involved. Likewise, Venus conjunct Pluto is very similar in influence to Venus in Scorpio is like, in terms of the depth of passion, romantic intensity, and extremism involved. And Mercury conjunct Uranus is surprisingly similar to Mercury in Aquarius, in terms of the intellectual brilliance and unconventional thought patterns involved. In other words, the fact that these three signs correlate so closely with those outer planets in their influence further underscores a deep connection between them.

The Case Against "Affinity"

But there are some who suggest that even if there is a close *affinity* between the outer planets and these three signs, that's something very different from saying these planets play a role in *ruling* those signs. This argument takes several different forms, and while some of those are too involved to simply explain here, I'll try to distill a few of the basic points they raise.

One of those arguments was summed up simply by the pioneering astrologer Rob Hand, who said, "... affinity is not the basis of traditional sign rulership. Traditional sign rulership has more to do with *how the signs reinforce, positively or negatively, the essence of a planet*—hence, the term *essential dignity*." (Emphasis mine.) [1] Or, as astrologer J. Lee Lehman put it:

"In brief, the 'modern' rulerships were assigned after the true meaning of 'rulership' was lost. In the modern sense, 'rulership' is associated with analogy or likeness: Aries is believed to be 'like' Mars. *In the true traditional sense, 'rulership' meant 'strength'...* So if you ask people what is their criterion (for the modern rulerships), and you can see this clearly in the astrological literature of the 30's and 40's after Pluto was discovered, what everybody talked about was, 'well, now

I think Pluto is *most like...*' and the sign that most fit that list is Scorpio. So the modern definition of what a planetary ruler is, is which sign most resembles the perceived quality of that planet. *What I have been talking about has nothing to do with that idea! What I have been talking about is what sign is a planet strong in, and what is the quality of that strength. That is a completely different question than the modern one of what it's like.* (Emphasis mine) [2]

The point raised by both Hand and Lehman is an interesting one, and suggests that the traditional basis for assigning rulership of planets to specific signs has more to do with where (and how) those planet's qualities are most accentuated than they do with what signs those planets are "most similar" to.

To my mind, that creates unnecessary dichotomy, since these two perspectives—the traditional and the modern—aren't necessarily at odds. That's because claiming that a given planet rules a given sign because it has "a deep affinity" with it may not actually be all that different from saying what sign that planet is "strong" in, or which sign modifies its strength. After all, most modern astrologers believe that Uranus has greater strength in the sign Aquarius, while Neptune has greater strength in Pisces, and Pluto has greater strength in Scorpio—with some astrologers extending this out even further to suggest various places of *exaltation, detriment* and *fall* for each of those newly discovered bodies. As a result, suggesting that these newer bodies don't involve factors of "strength" or "power" isn't really accurate.

But the roots of that disagreement actually go much deeper, since this also connects to a broader philosophy involving how the planets fit into a particular model of the cosmos. As my friend Jon Parks expressed it to me, the pattern of traditional rulerships represents a metaphysical sense of cosmic symmetry and balance in the world. Planets aren't given rulership in just any random way;

the whole ancient idea of a cosmos is that it is fundamentally a system of beautiful order, and if we are to treat them as rulers, we need to have a good metaphysical foundation for doing so, not just out of a sense of 'likeness' to a sign." Or, as astrologer Demetra George put it,

> "The rationale for the traditional system of rulerships was based upon a geometrical substructure depicted by the *thema mundi*, the symbolic chart of the creation of the world, rather than upon the modern principle of affinities between planet and sign." [3]

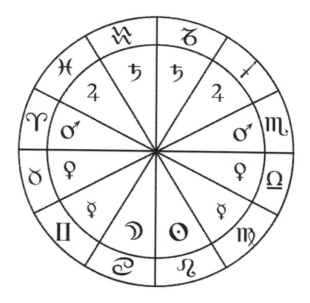

In short, the *thema mundi* is a symbolic model traditionally related to the mythic "birth of the world" (sometimes displayed with Cancer in the Ascendant position, at other times depicted like above, with Taurus on the Ascendant and Aquarius/Capricorn positioned at the top). Accordingly, the Sun and Moon are shown in connection with Leo and Cancer, with the traditional visible planets shown fanning out upward along the wheel in their classical zodiacal rulership positions. The rationale for this particular arrangement is explained in various ways, such as in connection with the relative speeds of the planets, or in terms of their relative distances from the Sun. The bottom line is, this model is regarded as reflecting a cosmic, archetypal order, and the planets occupy their zodiacal places and rulerships precisely because of their role and status within that divine order.

But as readers familiar with the chakric/zodiacal model we discussed in chapter 24 know, there is a striking similarity between the chakric model and the *thema mundi* proposed by traditionalists—the main difference being that in the yogic/chakric system, the zodiac is inverted so that Cancer and Leo are instead positioned at the top (an arrangement I personally find much more appealing, metaphysically). Not unlike traditional Hellenistic astrologers with their *thema mundi,* those subscribing to the chakric/zodiacal model likewise believe that it, too, holds an archetypal importance rooted in the nature of the cosmos itself.

As a result, if we use the chakric model as our symbolic frame of reference instead, we discover that the outer bodies *do* fit into this cosmic rationale very closely, as co-rulers of those lower three levels. (To briefly recap Shelly Trimmer's description, each chakra actually has *three distinct* expressions. On the one side, there is an extraverted manifestation off in the channel of *Pingala;* on the left side, there is a more introverted side within the channel of *Ida;* while the chakra has its most balanced expression smack dab in the middle of the spine, in the channel known as *Sushumna.* As a result, Uranus relates to the more masculine, extraverted side of the root chakra, Neptune resonates more to the feminine, introverted side of the second chakra, while Pluto connects with the more feminine introverted side of the third, or Martian chakra. [4])

In other words, by using this scheme we see that the outer planets work as zodiacal co-rulers not simply because of some perceived "affinity" or "likeness" with those three signs—although that's true, too—but because they, too, fit within the profound cosmic order represented by the zodiac.

The True Essence of "Rulership"

But there is one more point worth bringing up here. To suggest that traditional notions of rulership *solely* involve "how signs reinforce the essence of a planet," or how they fit into the "geometrical substructure depicted by the *thema mundi*," is misleading, because while that's certainly *part* of the picture it's not the whole picture.

I say that because even if there are philosophical differences in how ancient astrologers *derived* their "rulerships" as compared with modern astrologers, when it comes down to how they were *actually used*, the principle of rulership was in most cases *exactly the same* for ancients as it is now for moderns. That's something I can illustrate with a simple example which I suspect even an ancient scholar like Vettius Valens would have found acceptable, and it goes something like this.

Suppose a client comes to you and wants to know about the general state of their finances. Most astrologers would look to the condition of the 2nd house (or what traditional Hellenistic astrologers might call the "2nd Place"). A standard approach would then be to examine the condition of the planet which "rules" the sign situated on that house. Suppose that person has Cancer on their 2nd house; for both the traditional and modern astrologer, the primary ruler of this sign would be the Moon. Let's further suppose that their Moon is located up in that person's 9th house, which among other things might indicate that their finances are somehow connected to faraway places, institutions of higher learning, publishing, or possibly even religion.

Now, look at what we've just done there. Regardless of the underlying rationale for *why* we presume a connection between the Moon and Cancer, both the modern and traditional astrologer assume that rulership entails a mysterious thread of connection linking the Moon in one part of the chart with the zodiacal sign Cancer somewhere else in the chart. Those two factors are in completely separate parts of the chart, yet we see them as somehow intimately connected. So what does that invisible thread of connection consist of exactly, and what is the mechanism involved? Is it String Theory? Gravity? Or electromagnetism?

No, it's something commonly known in esoteric and magical circles as "correspondence," the classic notion that subtle resonances exist between diverse phenomena based on qualities of symbolism, analogy, and inner meaning—otherwise known as *affinity*. After all, affinity isn't simply a matter of *obvious* resemblances or likenesses as you might find with a typical voodoo doll constructed to resemble its intended victim. Rather, it has to do with a deeper *vibrational* or *symbolic* connection.

For example, when we say that the Moon "rules" water, women, the mother, dairy products, breasts, or receptacles of any kind, it's not because of any *obvious*, tangible connection or "affinity" between these things—after all, the physical Moon floating out there in space bears no obvious likeness to any Earthbound women or water, let alone to anyone's mother! Rather, the connection is more akin to what Carl Jung called *synchronicity*—an acausal connection, yes, but an acausal connection based on symbolism and meaning. And that holds true for the relationship of the Moon to the zodiacal sign Cancer as well. They're connected by a factor of "likeness," but a likeness of *meaning*. Likeness, affinity, correspondence, analogy, rulership—*a rose by any other name...*

So suggesting that the traditional understanding of rulership is completely different from how it's used by modern astrologers is simply untrue. Whether one is working from the traditional or modern perspectives, the actual, boots-on-the-ground usage of "rulership" when interpreting horoscopes is identical in terms of both involving a subtle link or affinity between planets and zodiacal signs, which is in turn based on a similarity of *meaning*. To use a simple analogy, strike a tuning fork in one room, a tuning fork in another room will resonate in sympathy. That, in a certain sense, is "rulership."

Which brings me back to the argument I mentioned at the beginning of this piece. If indeed there's a close vibrational affinity between the outer planets and those three signs, as I think my earlier examples demonstrated, how could there *not* be a powerful connection between what happens to those planets and the affairs of the houses those signs are found on, in the manner of our proverbial tuning forks?

Suppose an eclipse comes along and forms a close aspect to Pluto in one part of the chart; how could that *not* resonate back to the sign Scorpio somewhere else in the chart, in sympathetic resonance? Likewise, if Jupiter were to come along and trigger someone's natal Uranus in one part of the chart, how could that *not* have some effect on the affairs of whatever house Aquarius is sitting on? Simply in terms of fundamental occult logic, it's not hard to understand how one would have some resonant impact on the other. [5]

Final Thoughts

As I mentioned at the outset, I personally use *both* the traditional and modern planetary rulers when interpreting charts—not just one or the other. To be clear, I'm not suggesting that traditionally-based astrologers should start using these bodies as zodiacal (co) rulers, since their system was designed to be used without them. Rather, I'm simply pointing out their potential value for astrologers working in more contemporary contexts. Whether or not the newly discovered planets fit in every conceivable way to the interpretive and philosophical frameworks of the ancients—to be sure, they don't—the fundamental question we're left with is simply whether they actually *do* work, as co-rulers—and my experience over several decades has demonstrated that they do. I'll close with a simple, real-life example of how the old and new rulers can operate, side-by-side, using the case of a client who was born with Pisces on her 7th-house cusp, whose main concern was her marriage.

With Pisces on her house of partnerships, I naturally paid close attention to any aspects being formed to either her Neptune and her Jupiter. As it turned out, precisely when transiting Saturn crossed over that woman's natal Neptune, she discovered a long-standing deception on the part of her spouse—a pitch-perfect expression of that transit relative to the house of partnerships, and a classic expression of disillusionment. Then, a year or so later, when Saturn continued moving forward and crossed over her natal Jupiter, the classical ruler of Pisces, she wound up going to court over that earlier deception and filing for divorce from her partner—yet another near-perfect expression of that transit in relation to that horoscopic house, especially considering Jupiter governs judicial matters. In short, *transits to both the new and old rulers of Pisces triggered 7th house matters, in closely related yet subtly different ways.* Now, we can debate whether one of those planetary rulers, new or old, should take priority over the other—but that's a different discussion. For me, there was little doubt that *both* planets played a role in the affairs of that house.

So that's been my experience, and I'd simply suggest that readers who are interested in exploring this idea further take some time to experiment with both sets of rulers to see what they come up with. I'll be curious to see what you come up with.

CHAPTER 29

WHEN WORLDS COLLIDE: THE DYNAMICS OF THE SHIFTING GREAT AGES

When European explorers first arrived on the shores of North America and encountered the indigenous peoples of the new world, the gulf separating these two groups, both geographically and culturally, made for a challenging experience on both sides of the divide. Their respective attitudes towards many areas stemmed from fundamentally different worldviews, and posed a series of both problems *and* opportunities for these cultures as they attempted to adjust to each other's lives.

Whenever civilizations separated by geography first come into contact, it's an especially sensitive time when the possibilities for either triumph or tragedy are heightened and can be tipped by the smallest of variables. But that same double-edged potential exists for encounters between cultures separated not just by space but by *time*. Let me explain.

The Turning of the Ages

For many astrologers, the grand sweep of world history can be understood in part through the doctrine of the "Great Ages."

According to this theory, roughly every 2,100 years global culture experiences a seismic shift in its attitudes and beliefs. As the Vernal Point—that point in the sky where the Sun resides on the first day of spring—slowly moves backward and shifts its position against the zodiacal backdrop, a corresponding change takes place in the collective psyche, in turn reflecting itself in society's myths, symbols, and customs.

As I've suggested elsewhere, the transition between Great Ages likely doesn't occur on a single day or year, but evolves very slowly over many years, perhaps even centuries. [1] I've likened it to the incoming tide, which arrives in waves rather than all at once. In turn, those historical waves can be punctuated by certain key astrological alignments like those between Uranus and Pluto, or Pluto with Neptune, to cite just two examples. So even though an emerging Great Age may not make its presence fully felt for several centuries, it's possible for its influence to start surfacing into global consciousness long beforehand.

The essential point is this: When paradigms associated with different Ages come into contact, that encounter can take different forms and unfold through a wide range of dynamics. Not unlike citizens of separate civilizations meeting for the first time, the encounter between denizens of different Ages can be peaceful and constructive, or be turbulent and destructive. In this article, I'd like to propose *four primary dynamics* associated with this age-shifting process, and the transformation of cultural mythologies. Understand these dynamics can not only help us better identify key historical trends and themes across millennia of time, but help us make better sense of epochal developments taking place in the world right now, as we find ourselves perched on the threshold between the Piscean and the Aquarian ages.

Dynamic 1: *The Old Order Resists the New*
At the threshold between Great Ages, the encounter between different worldviews is not unlike tectonic plates butting up against

one another, with the resulting friction sending faint rumblings throughout society. At first, those early subtle vibrations are noticed almost exclusively by society's "living antennae"—artists, mystics, and philosophers who express their intuitions through books, artworks, or teachings—while the larger population barely notices the impending transformations underfoot. But as the differences between contrasting worldviews evolve and become even more pronounced, defenders of the old regime often set out to repress or even destroy those heralds of the incoming one.

In some ways, the Roman Empire can be seen an embodiment and dramatic culmination of the Arian Age (which lasted roughly 2100 BCE to 1 AD). When the first shoots of Piscean Christianity began appearing two millennia ago, Rome shifted from a policy of uneasy tolerance toward the followers of the fish *(ichthys)* to eventually one of persecution. Over time, of course, the Piscean mythos itself became the dominant order of Rome, as well as much of the world—at which point denizens of the Piscean order eventually began setting their sights on those vanguards of the next zodiacal epoch, the Aquarian Age.

In its very earliest stages, that began with the persecution of pioneering figures like Giordano Bruno and Galileo, for espousing ideas that promoted the secular and scientific values of the Aquarian mythos. But it erupted with a special vengeance during the mid-19th century when Charles Darwin proposed his theory of evolution, which reverberates even today in the views of conservative politicians and religious figures who continue to express skepticism about the findings of science. But a similar tension is also visible in the ongoing debate over abortion, with Christian pro-life advocates on the one side espousing a distinctly Piscean sympathy for the unborn, while pro-choice advocates on the other side reflect a distinct Aquarian concern for personal freedom and independence.

Robert Zemeckis's film, *Contact*, based on the Carl Sagan novel of the same name, features a subplot involving religious fanatics upset over a high-tech NASA mission to send an astronaut into deep space. Determined to thwart the mission, they set out to destroy the experimental craft scientists designed to whisk its occupant (played by Jodie Foster) to a far-off world. [2] It's a succinct cinematic expression of that resistance to modernity, which is fundamentally archetypal in nature and born of a clash between radically different paradigms—the Piscean versus the Aquarian. Nor is this just a Western or Christian phenomenon. In areas like Afghanistan and Saudi Arabia, we've seen Islamic fundamentalists working to prevent women from seeking rights long enjoyed by men. Such is the ferocity of individuals still rooted in Piscean religious ideologies, who find it hard adapting to the values of a newer and more secular order. Remember, Pisces, like its sibling sign Sagittarius (both under the co-rulership of Jupiter), has a dark side that includes dogmatism and an inflexible attachment to belief systems and religious ideals—and that's a way of thinking that refuses to take the liberal sentiments of the Aquarian revolution lying down.

Dynamic 2: *The New Order Resists the Old*

The resistance of one Great Age to another can move in the other direction as well, when the new order rejects the forms and beliefs of the older one. A classic example of that is the Biblical story of Moses rejecting the golden calf, which has often been interpreted by esoteric commentators as heralding the shift from the Age of Taurus (the bull) to that of Aries (the ram). Then, with the ushering in of the next Great Age of Pisces, we saw much the same dynamic playing out with Christians engaged in destroying and defacing earlier so-called "pagan" temples and statues, and in their persecution of Jews.

A literary example of this dynamic from more recent times is Herman Melville's great novel, *Moby Dick*. Like Moses and the golden calf, Ahab's efforts to find and destroy the great whale symbolized the violent rejection of Piscean Age values by the incoming Aquarian Age. On a different level, it's tempting to also see Melville's tale as a telling portent of the great cataclysm that was about to shake America to its core a decade later—the Civil War. There as well, we see the clash between Ages being played out, with the Union forces ostensibly representing the values of freedom, led by Aquarian Abraham Lincoln (born on the same day as evolutionist Charles Darwin), who were seeking to overturn the slavery-based Piscean values of the South. And just as the whale ultimately took down Ahab, so Lincoln's battle with the Confederacy ultimately proved his own undoing as well, via the South's avenger, John Wilkes Booth. [3]

Archetypally, the same essential dynamic was at work over a century later in the tragic story of government agents destroying David Koresh's religious compound in Waco, Texas in 1993. Whatever one's opinions about the attack and its justification, or lack of, the esoteric symbolism is clear enough: a secular government imposing limits on a fundamentalist religious community—i.e., Aquarius rejecting Pisces. The fact that the attack took place precisely as the planetary rulers of the two signs associated with these Ages moved into alignment, when Uranus conjoined Neptune in 1993, succinctly underscores the archetypal significance of that event.

However, this particular dynamic doesn't always take a violent form, and can simply manifest as a peaceful disengagement of the new order from the old one. Case in point, the biggest box office hit of the 1960s was Robert Wise's film *The Sound of Music*, which premiered in 1965—the same year as the epic Uranus/ Pluto conjunction which defined that decade. Consider the film's central story about a young woman named Maria (played by Julie Andrews) who lives in a Catholic convent and aspires to become a nun. But she eventually gives up that dream to pursue a more secular, pleasure-filled life as the wife of Captain Georg von Trapp (played by Christopher Plummer). They eventually fall in love, and after much soul-searching, Maria decides to leave her life of religious service completely behind and pursue a life of romantic happiness in marriage. [4] Viewed symbolically, this break from the Church symbolizes the shift from the religious orientation of the Pisces/Virgo Age, geared as it is toward self-sacrifice and other-worldly ideals, to that of the Aquarian/Leo axis, with its emphasis on secular values and concerns like "life, liberty, and the pursuit of happiness." In fact, it's much the same symbolism as we find in the earlier film, *The Jazz Singer*. Known primarily as the first feature-length film to utilize fully synchronized sound, the film likewise depicts a character struggling with that decision to leave a life of religious service behind to pursue a more secular calling in the world—specifically performing that most Aquarian of all musical forms, *jazz*.

Dynamic 3: *The Old Order Embraces the New*
As I said, the encounter between Great Ages isn't always negative or violent, as demonstrated from the other side of the divide by instances where we see an older Age not only tolerating the incoming one's traditions and values, but embracing them for itself.

For example, after leading a campaign of persecution against devotees of the newly formed Piscean Christian faith, Roman authorities under Constantine wound up adopting Christianity and making it the state religion for the Empire. The result was a curious hybrid of Arian and Piscean energies, as reflected in the underlying militarism that characterized the emerging Roman Catholic faith. *Onward Christian soldiers*, indeed!

In our own time, we find similar expressions of that hybridization in the form of movements like the Christian Science church, a 19th-century offshoot of Christianity spearheaded by Mary Baker Eddy (born on July 16, 1821 under a conjunction of Uranus and Neptune). It retained the essential principles of Piscean Christianity but refashioned for modern tastes;, even to the extent of including the word "science" in its name. While the Piscean era was based more fully on an ethos of self-denial and a reliance on external saviors, the emerging Aquarian Age was introducing a different mindset, geared more toward an ethos of personal empowerment and taking responsibility for one's own "salvation." Consciously or not, movements like Christian Science and New Thought draw on Aquarian impulses in their rejection of notions like Hell or "atonement," while emphasizing the power of each individual to improve or even heal themselves through the proper use of the mind, and allowing for a more democratic approach to leadership.

Another clear example of an older tradition incorporating the values of an emerging one is apparent in modern-day "televangelism," where we see traditional churches incorporating modern media technologies to preach the gospel to their audiences. A more ironic expression of that same alliance between old and new is visible in the way some Islamic fundamentalists have adopted high-tech tools like cell phones, text-messaging, and video technologies in their faith, in no small part to combat the evils of Aquarian secularism and modernity!

In the 1960s, pop music took an unexpected turn when a Belgian religious sister by the name of Jeanine Deckers (born October 17, 1933) scored an international hit with the French-language song, "Dominique." She became widely known as the "Singing Nun," and her step from the convent into the high-tech entertainment field likewise reflected a shift from the Piscean world to the secular and technological Aquarian Age. Similar symbolism was visible in another prominent icon of the '60s, Sally Field's "Flying Nun" character from the television series of the same name. As we saw earlier in this book, aviation is a distinctly Aquarian activity, so the surreal image of a Christian nun becoming airborne spoke to yet another metamorphosis of Piscean religiosity into one of Aquarian freedom, not much different from that expressed by the Julie Andrews' character in *The Sound of Music.*

Dynamic 4: *The New Order Embraces the Old*

In contrast with tales like Moses' rejection of the golden calf or Ahab attacking the White Whale, there are times when individuals or organizations associated with an emerging Great Age don't simply strive to reject the legacies of earlier ones, but actually find ways of drawing upon their forms and values.

A simple example from contemporary pop culture is the music of groups like Enigma, which reinterpreted Piscean-era Gregorian chants in a distinctly Aquarian "techno" context. This merging of new and old shows itself in political and economic contexts as well. For instance, forms of socialism and communism like those seen in 20th Century Russia and China harken back to Piscean Age values in the way they involve a sharing ownership of personal wealth with the greater community. By contrast, capitalism draws on a decidedly more Aquarian values in being based on principles of independence and freedom, allowing individuals to acquire personal savings and self-determine their own futures.

On the other hand, the surge in popularity of "democratic socialism" in recent years reflects an intriguing blend of both Piscean and Aquarian principles, by respecting personal wealth and entrepreneurial ambition but also providing safety nets for the elderly, the sick, and victims of natural disasters—a balancing act between Great Ages, as it were. It's a tightrope walk that the United States has been struggling to perfect since its inception, actually, and likely will continue struggling with for years to come.

A cinematic expression of that economic interface between Great Ages was portrayed in Steven Spielberg's film *Schindler's List*, released in late 1993 (precisely as Uranus and Neptune moved into conjunction). Set in Nazi-governed Germany, the film is based on the true story of a successful entrepreneur who used his business skills to protect scores of otherwise doomed prisoners in a brutal concentration camp. This offers a good example of how the sometimes cold-blooded machinations of Aquarian capitalism can be employed toward the common good, when tempered by the compassion of Piscean values.

The ability of one Great Age to mine the archetypal ore of an earlier one sometimes takes a more mythological turn, as when an emerging era appropriates the religious stories and symbols of earlier times and re-clothes them for more contemporary audiences. That practice has been occurring since time immemorial, of course, such as when Christianity recast the resurrection saga of Osiris as the story of Jesus, or when the Hebrew scribes refashioned the flood story of the Babylonians for their own religious ends. But this tradition of putting "old wine in new skins" persists into the present day, especially in the realm of popular entertainment, where we see modern media blending the symbols of Aquarius and Pisces in interesting new ways.

As an example, consider the original 1951 film version of *The Day the Earth Stood Still*, which revolved around the tale of a Christ-like alien who comes down to Earth in a spaceship, is then "crucified," resurrected, and finally ascends back up into the heavens—Jesus refashioned as a spaceman, in other words (similar to the comic book hero, Superman, in fact). Years ago, I attended a lecture in Chicago by the film's director, Robert Wise, and during the following Q&A session I asked whether the striking parallels between his movie and the life of Jesus were intentional, since they seemed so obvious. He answered that, surprisingly, they never really considered that until others began pointing it out after the movie had been released. Much the same thing is visible in the blockbuster film *The Matrix,* with Keanu Reeves' character Neo reinventing the mythic motif of the dead-and-resurrected hero as a modern-day cyber-superman. It simply goes to illustrate something what mythologist Joseph Campbell often pointed out, how creative individuals sometimes tap into universal themes from the collective unconscious, whether they realize it or not.

When Paradigms Meet: Conflict or Cooperation?

The four dynamics described above are but a few of the possible ways that the encounter between any two Great Ages can unfold, and serve to illustrate both the perils and potentials that can occur when dramatically different paradigms come into contact. To a certain extent, conflict may be unavoidable, but as we also saw, the outcome isn't necessarily a negative or violent one. There is ample room for creative interaction to occur in that encounter between paradigms, if individuals are mature enough to approach the problems they pose in a constructive way.

For me, one image that beautifully illustrates that harmonious bridging of old and new can be seen in the 2002 film, *Whale Rider*. The movie's central character, a young girl from New Zealand's Maori tribe, is shown struggling to reconcile her burgeoning independence with the more restrictive ways of her traditional community. Initially, there is an element of friction in that meeting of old and new, but it slowly comes to a resolution. An iconic sequence in the film, which symbolically embodies that marriage of paradigms, centers around her learning to ride atop a great whale in the ocean—an image that expresses a dramatically different symbolism from that envisioned by Herman Melville in *Moby Dick*.

By depicting her as harmonizing peacefully with the whale, that sequence symbolizes the possibility of drawing on the gifts and legacies of a passing era, rather than simply rejecting them wholesale. The movie shows the young woman and her community working to balance tradition and modernity, instead of a single-minded insistence on one side or the other. A dramatic high point of the film comes when the young woman delivers a heartfelt speech to her community where she utters these strikingly Aquarian words, illustrating the intersection of the old and the new:

> "But we can learn, and if the knowledge is given to every-one, then we have lots of leaders, and then soon everyone will be strong, not just the ones that have been chosen."

CHAPTER 30

THE PROBLEM OF THE YUGAS

While a great many Western astrologers subscribe to the doctrine of the "Great Ages," along with such related concepts as the "Age of Pisces" and the "Age of Aquarius," for astrologers in the Vedic tradition of India a more familiar method of understanding history has been in connection with the doctrine of the *Yugas.*

Unlike the 12-fold approach of the Great Ages, this doctrine sees history as comprised of four primary stages, referred to as *Satya Yuga, Treta Yuga, Dvapara Yuga,* and *Kali Yuga.* Each of these stages has its own characteristics and quality, ranging from the most spiritually-elevated level of *Satya* to the least spiritual and most materialistic level in *Kali.* According to many adherents of this model, we now find ourselves immersed in *Kali Yuga,* widely considered an era of darkness and greed.

Like some others, I've struggled hard to reconcile the doctrine of the Yugas with that of the Great Ages, since they seem so different on their surfaces. It led me to wonder, are these two models simply different ways of slicing up the same proverbial pie—or are they based on completely different archetypal dynamics, never to be fully reconciled?

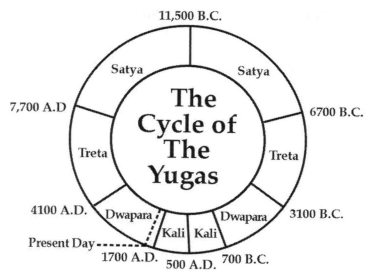

The cycle of the Yugas (according to Sri Yukteswar's formulation)

Even more controversially, is it possible that one of them might be valid while the other is not?

Over the years I've had numerous discussions with proponents of the Yugic model, and I'm intrigued by their explanations as to how this model explains certain aspects of world history. But I continue being troubled by a few vexing problems that the system raises. The first of these involves the fact that there is massive disagreement even amongst Vedic astrologers as to how long the larger Yugic cycle really is. For instance, while some Vedic astrologers see the overall cycle lasting over 4 million years, the Kriya Yoga teacher Sri Yukteswar saw the great Yugic arc as being much shorter in duration, and associated more closely with the precessional cycle of 24,000 years. (That number of his is slightly shorter than what most other astrologers and astronomers have come up with for the precessional cycle, which is closer to 25,800 years—although there are some modern researchers who do support Sri Yukteswar's view. In his book *Lost Star of Myth and Time*, independent researcher Walter Cruttenden makes a case for the 24,000 years figure based on an interesting theory about how our solar system may be influenced by a binary star companion. [1]) That's a huge difference of opinion amongst Vedic astrologers! So which version should we go with—the ultra-long duration proposed by the ancients, or the much shorter version suggested by Yukteswar? And what would be the basis for preferring one version over the other? It's true, there are disagreements even amongst proponents of the Great Ages model, too, but those differences are generally much smaller in comparison to what we find in the Vedic community regarding the Yugas.

But the second problem I have with the Vedic model relates to the length of the individual *sub-Ages*. According to all versions (including Yukteswar's), these stages aren't based on visible astronomical phenomena so much as on numerological principles—specifically, *the ratio of 4:3:2:1*. That is, the "Golden Age" of *Satya Yuga* is four times longer than *Kali Yuga*, three times longer than *Dwapara Yuga*, and two times longer than *Treta Yuga*. By contrast, when most of us talk about the Age of Pisces, the Age of Aquarius, and so on, we're talking about something comparatively tangible in the sky which astronomers can actually study—namely, the Vernal Point moving backwards through the constellations at the rate of a degree every 72 years. But according to the Yuga model, the length of each Age isn't based on astronomy but rather a mathematical abstraction, specifically those proportions of 4:3:2:1.

Does the fact that the Vedic approach involves a purely symbolic division like that invalidate it? Not necessarily; after all, we do that sort of thing in Western astrology at times, too. Take our division of the chart into 12 houses or "places." Those are purely mathematical, symbolic divisions not based on anything observable in the sky. (You can't look up in the sky and see someone's 11th house, for instance.) So it's possible that the 4:3:2:1 division of sub-ages holds an archetypal value beyond any purely astronomical basis. But is clearly puts the doctrine of the Yugas on a very different footing from that of the Great Ages, with that system's basis in the Vernal Point moving through the sky.

While these problems frankly leave me with concerns about the Yugic system, I keep an open mind about it. If nothing else, issues like these I've mentioned point up the fact that there is still work left to do establishing a consistent theory of the Yugas we can apply in any practical or precise way. I look forward to seeing what that might look like.

CHAPTER 31

ASTROLOGY AND THE COVID-19 PANDEMIC

On May 9, 2020, the New York Times published an article by Haley Phelan titled "Will Coronavirus Kill Astrology? The Pandemic affected all of us. Who saw it coming?" [1]

To sum up simply, the article questioned not only why astrologers (supposedly) didn't foresee the horrors of the pandemic, but why so many people would continue to take astrology seriously after such seeming lapses in predictive accuracy.

It's an understandable attitude. Unfortunately, it's also a wrong one.

While most astrologers didn't specifically predict there would be a lethal virus coming from Wuhan, China and killing untold numbers of people around the world, many of us *did* in fact foretell something of world-changing consequences coming down the pike in 2020, due to the planetary "pile-up" I hinted at in an earlier chapter. On December 17th of 2019, I posted the following prediction on several different Facebook pages, involving energies that would be igniting in January of 2020:

During the second week of January we'll be seeing a rather unusual celestial phenomenon. No, I'm not just talking about the Saturn/Pluto conjunction (which last occurred in the early 1980s)—though that's part of it. Rather, I'm talking about what might be called a 'cluster' effect, which is when two or more major planetary triggers come together at the same time, within a day or two (or three) of each other. Whenever these sorts of patterns occur, they tend to trigger significant developments in the news, for better or worse (sometimes both). That could include such things as political upheavals, earth changes, scientific or creative breakthroughs, tragedies for some while triumphs for others, etc. The cluster happening this January involves at least three astrological events, all of which involve fairly 'powerhouse' energies:

1. *A full Moon eclipse on January 10th*
2. *On that same day Uranus will be changing directions*
3. *That will be followed roughly 48 hours later on January 12th by the Saturn/Pluto conjunction.*

Mind you, each of those has an influence that extends considerably beyond those specific days—those are simply the exact partile points. In fact, the whole month should be pretty active, but the ripple effects of those few days could extend for months or even years into the future. Clusters like this represent a kind of "seeding" time, when we see the entering wedge of change setting in, rather than its full culmination.

Because those three celestial triggers are so different in tone from one another, it's hard to predict specifically what to expect—or even whether the net effect will be positive or negative (probably a good deal of both)—but at the very least I think we can expect quite a host of turbulent emotions being stirred up, possibly including some seismic shifts in the world's socio-political hotspots, such as India, Paris, Hong Kong, Israel and of course Washington D.C. (See my blog post from June of 2019 for my predictions about how the Saturn/Pluto could be triggering Donald Trump's horoscope specifically. [2])

While it's true I didn't specifically predict a pandemic, it was obvious due to the clustering of significators, as well as from a study of previous alignments between Saturn and Pluto, that we were entering into an extremely challenging period, one with potentially long-lasting consequences.

Also, take a look at Richard Tarnas's epic work, *Cosmos and Psyche: Intimations of a New World View* (pages 209-288). While he addressed the historical implications of Saturn/Pluto alignments over time in broad terms, anyone who read his work carefully prior to the pandemic wouldn't have been the slightest surprised by what happened across the world in 2020. In one particularly relevant passage where he spoke about several Saturn/Pluto alignments through history, he wrote:

"Another such defining [Saturn-Pluto] conjunction was that of 1348-51 that coincided with the eruption and spread of the Black Death, which similarly devastated Europe and set in motion cultural and economic shifts that permanently transformed European life in the late medieval period. The Black Death, or bubonic plague, began in China in 1333 in coincidence with the preceding Saturn-Pluto opposition and reached a climax in Europe in the 1348-51 period during the conjunction. A comparable pattern can be discerned in the AIDS epidemic, which first widely emerged and was identified during the Saturn-Pluto conjunction of 1981-84, and which reached pandemic proportions worldwide, especially in Africa, during the following Saturn-Pluto opposition of 2000-04." [3]

Then there is what the late French astrologer Andre Barbault wrote, in which he specifically cited the possibility of a pandemic in the 2020-2021 period. Utilizing a unique system he devised known as the "Cyclic Index," he carefully charted how the closeness or separateness of the planets from Jupiter all the way out to Pluto over time coincided with major world events, including wars, epidemics and natural catastrophes. In an article for the French magazine *L'astrologue* in 2011, he wrote:

"Going back to the pandemics and going back to the past century, the four crises of 1918, 1954, 1968 and 1982 are obvious, the two considerable being the first, the famous "Spanish flu" which is said to have claimed 25 million lives, and the last one in which AIDS, which is even more devastating and continues to be deadly. Since then, there has also been a small influenza surge in 2009, against the last lowest cyclical index (2010). *We may well be in serious danger of a new pandemic at the 2020-2021 mark*, at the lowest peak of the cyclical index of the 21st century, with the quintet of outer planets gathered over a hundred degrees, a conjunction Jupiter-Saturn-Pluto can more specifically, and even specifically, lend itself to the "tissue" of this imbalance. Nevertheless, this configuration can also transfer its core of dissonances to the terrain of geophysical disasters, without ultimately sparing the international affairs scene, Nature and Society being indiscriminately affected. (Emphasis mine.) " [4]

Commenting on Barbault's novel contribution, astrologer Roy Gillett remarked, "Andre's basic point is that when the outer planets are close together, the impetus for change is strong. But change can be either beneficial or unbeneficial—it depends on from where you are looking at it. What's good for an ant infestation may not be good for my kitchen. The present corona virus is a good example. From the point of view of global warming, biodiversity, excessive activity and travel, uncontrolled consumption, the quality of the environment, and closer family relationships, the present situation is far more beneficial than anything that could be decided and implemented by human decision. We are being forced into rethinking and being controlled as we come out of it. From the planet's perception and most creatures on it, this controlling of human activity is beneficial," he added. "Barbault's work stands as a remarkable testament to the value of astrology. Had he been listened to the 2008 financial crash might have been largely avoided. And we could have been better prepared for the corona virus pandemic." [5]

In short, astrology is an interpretive art, and as such is only as precise as the astrologer utilizing it. But the fact that there always exists a margin of error with it is no reason to discard it entirely. By analogy, one's local weatherperson may not be able to pinpoint weeks in advance the moment an approaching storm will hit, or the exact locale that will be affected, yet that doesn't cause us forego his or her services entirely. Astrology is an extraordinary tool; let's work towards making our grasp of it just as extraordinary.

CHAPTER 32

THE CROWD WITHIN: MULTIPLE PERSONALITY DISORDER AND TRADITIONAL ESOTERIC PSYCHOLOGIES

There has been a longstanding debate over the phenomenon of "multiple personality disorder" (more commonly referred to now as "dissociative identity disorder," or DID), including whether it even qualifies as a legitimate clinical condition. That's a debate that's continued since I first published this essay in 1992. Disagreements aside, though, the essential point I made here remains a valid one, I believe—namely, that consciousness is essentially multiplistic in nature, whether we understand that through models like MPD/DID or traditional esoteric systems of consciousness like astrology or the chakras.—RG

"One of the most harmful illusions that can beguile us is probably the belief that we are an indivisible, immutable, totally consistent being... Each of us is a crowd. There can be the rebel and the intellectual, the seducer and the housewife, the saboteur and the aesthete, the organizer and the *bon vivant*—each with its own mythology, and all more or less comfortably crowded into one single person."

—Piero Ferrucci, *What We May Be*

In his novel *Dr. Jeckyll and Mr. Hyde,* Robert Louis Stevenson tells the tale of a man who behaves as if possessed of two separate personalities: at one moment, he's the refined and mild-mannered Dr. Jekyll, in another moment, the brutal Mr. Hyde, capable of murderous behaviors. While intended on one level as a literary allegory for the dualities that characterize all of our lives, Stevenson may just as well have been describing a condition that has been gaining increasing attention in recent years among doctors and scientists—known as Multiple Personality Disorder (or MPD). Individuals with this condition have been known to display up to as many as several hundred distinct sub-personalities. While there are still many questions about the nature and treatment of this condition, what researchers have already learned could profoundly affect our understanding of both the human body and mind. In this article we will briefly review some of these findings and explore how they may be compared with models of the psyche found in more traditional systems of esoteric thought.

The Causes

While some believe the phenomenon of MPD has likely existed throughout history, it is only in recent decades that researchers have begun gaining their first clear clues into its probable dynamics and causes. In a great majority of cases, it's believed that MPD-prone individuals share a history of extreme childhood trauma or abuse, either of an emotional or physical nature. Researchers theorize that in response to the overload of disturbing emotions generated by those early traumatic events, the conscious ego defensively splinters off (or "dissociates") into various *sub*-personalities through which the buried emotions can then be acted out—usually without the knowledge of the central, organizing ego. Each of these sub-personalities may in turn develop elaborate personal histories, sometimes even forming complex relationships with other of the "alters."

In the book *The Minds of Billy Milligan*, we find one individual's intriguing account of how the various sub-personalities may co-exist as active potentials within an individual's awareness:

"It's a big white spotlight. Everybody stands around it, watching or sleeping in their beds. And whoever steps on the spot is out in the world... Whoever is on the spot holds the consciousness." [1]

In recent years researchers such as Dr. Richard Kluft have begun suggesting the need for a more complex view of MPD and its causes. Without dismissing the potential importance of childhood trauma as a contributing factor, Kluft argues that the MPD condition be seen as a complex *combination* of influences, including such factors as genetic predisposition and suggestibility (or "hypnotizability"), as well as various environmental and sociocultural influences. Kluft theorizes that it is when several factors come together within the experience of one individual that we're most likely to encounter the extreme dissociative characteristics associated with true MPD. [2]

MPD and the Mind/Body Connection
Among the more startling results of modern MPD research has been the way it's forced us to reexamine the relationship between the mind and body. The well-known "placebo effect" aside, modern science has remained largely skeptical of claims linking the state of someone's thoughts or feelings with the condition of their health. Yet in many cases of MPD, researchers have found dramatic evidence suggesting that individuals can exhibit radically different bodily symptoms in different sub-personalities.

For example, a person with severe allergies in their normal conscious state may, on shifting into one of their many "alters," suddenly exhibit *no signs at all* of those same allergies. [3] Aside from providing tentative validation for the reality of MPD itself, examples like this raise the obvious question as to how a seemingly lifelong health condition can appear or disappear simply on the basis of a personality shift, unless the body-state was not indeed directly linked to that of the mind/brain. Equally provocative have been those instances in which MPD-prone individuals have shown a capacity to heal bodily injuries more quickly than other, non-MPD individuals. [4]

MPD and Psychology

The findings of MPD research are raising important questions in the field of psychology as well. Could it be, for instance, that the extreme form of splintering that we see in multiples actually reflect a more exaggerated form of a multiplicity that exists in all of us? In other words, is it possible that *each* of us is a "crowd," with an inner "cast of characters" that interact to provide the illusion of a single, unified personality? By this model, the chief difference between a "normal" individual and someone with MPD would be that for the "normal" person, the wide array of potential sub-personalities are integrated into a relatively harmonious whole, under the control of a centrally overseeing ego (or "executive"). By contrast, within the extreme dissociative state of an MPD individual each of these different state shifts is magnified and experienced as a separate, autonomous personality.

By way of illustration, the various potential state-shifts might be likened to the "roles" donned by an actor stepping onto a stage. Whereas for the average, healthy individual there usually remains an underlying sense of distinction between the actor and the role being played, for the MPD individual it would be as if the actor fully became the role at hand each time, with little or no sense of distinction between pretending and reality.

For some, however, the possibility of inner multiplicity holds nothing less than the transforming power of revelation. In his book *Avalanche*, W. Brugh Joy writes:

"One of the most powerful renovations of my consciousness occurred when I entertained the almost taboo consideration that there may simply be no such thing as a single self, a single soul in a body. [This realization has come to] include the possibility that the basis of the human psyche... may be a collective of selves, independent and autonomous yet interrelating with one another, and mostly unknown to the outer awareness...The idea that unknown to the outer mind, many selves utilize the same eyes and the same ears in each body is an awesome creative thought that has profoundly changed how I perceive myself and others." [5]

The "multiple" model of human nature suggested by MPD research naturally invites comparison with the theories of such thinkers as psychologist James Hillman. In contrast with more conventional psychological models where the personality is often described in terms of an all-important central ego around which other facets of our nature are seen as subordinate, Hillman argues for a psychology that acknowledges *all* the facets of psyche as important and integral to our psychic well-being. In that sense Western psychology has largely tended to be "monotheistic" with its emphasis on rational ego-awareness, whereas Hillman has suggested the need for a more "polytheistic" view of personality, one that might draw fruitfully from the pantheon of ancient mythology for a more fitting representation of psyche's diversity and needs. [6]

Those considerations aside, the findings of MPD research raise important practical questions. For instance, if we are indeed an inner "crowd," to what extent can such diverse facets of our personality be accessed or controlled at will? Consider the case of Billy Milligan, for whom the emergence of different sub-personalities was directly related to the needs of the moment. In situations of danger, a particularly strong alter named Ragen became dominant, while in more secure situations a sophisticated and intelligent alter named Arthur would emerge into consciousness. Although for most multiples that accessibility to inner potentials is a largely involuntary affair, it's not difficult to imagine the benefits that voluntary control over inner multiples would provide.

As to *how* an individual can develop such skills, a possible starting point would be to explore those psychological systems which purport to help provide mastery over our inner potentials and "selves." A partial list of these would include such techniques as visualization, the NLP method of "modeling," and techniques found in Roberto Assagioli's system of "psychosynthesis" whereby individuals learn to access the assorted facets of their personality by conceptualizing them as "sub-personalities." Whether or not the philosophy behind each of these systems corroborates the more radical implications of MPD theory, it's still worth considering what they may have to offer in any deeper understanding of our inner multiplicity and its mastery.

MPD and the Paranormal

By far the most controversial aspect of MPD research involves its potential application to the study of paranormal experiences. In such wide-ranging areas as "channeling," past-life recall, possession, or even accounts of alien abduction, the theory of MPD has already been invoked as a possible explanation for phenomena that have long baffled scientists and psychologists. For instance, could it be that individuals who sincerely claim to be channeling information from discarnate entities are actually accessing nothing more than sub-personalities in themselves? Or, could an individual who claims to have been abducted by aliens actually have experienced a dissociative "splitting" in which fragmented aspects of the personality were misperceived as creatures external to themselves?

While explanations like that may indeed shed light on some otherwise mysterious phenomena, they have their limitations. That problem becomes even more apparent in those instances where the evidence itself flies in the face of existing materialistic theories. How, for instance, can we fall back on notions of "dissociative disorder" or "multiplicity" to understand substantiated cases of *xenoglossy*, where individuals are allegedly able to speak languages they couldn't have learned during their present lifetimes? [7][8] Likewise, conventional theories strain to explain cases where an MPD-prone individual exhibits knowledge or skills absent in their normal conscious state. [9] While still largely anecdotal in nature, such cases would, with further substantiation, revolutionize not just our current theories about multiplicity but human nature itself.

The "Inner Self Helper"

Of the many types of sub-personalities exhibited in MPD cases, there is one in particular that has gained increasing attention for its potentially constructive potential. Termed the "Inner Self Helper" (or ISH for short) by Ralph Allison, this is a unique form of alter which appears to possess the characteristics of a spiritual, even transcendent observer. [10] In contrast with most conventional sub-personalities, which generally possess elaborate personal histories and distinct ages, the ISH is frequently ageless, and often serves as a guide to both the MPD individual and the therapist working with them. This has even led to speculation by some researchers that the ISH might be synonymous with the "Higher Self" or "Inner Guru" described in many esoteric traditions.

Other researchers remain skeptical, wondering whether the ISH phenomenon ever appears in clinical settings besides just those in which the therapist already believes in its existence, as if to suggest the possible role of subtle "cues" by the therapist in co-creating the ISH experience. Along a different line, some researchers question whether we can definitively say the ISH is a healthy expression of higher psycho-spiritual potentials or merely another expression of the multiple's pathology, disguised as a detached, "spiritual" observer.

MPD and Traditional Esoteric Views of Psyche

Finally, let's briefly consider some possible connections between MPD research and models of human psychology found in more ancient systems of thought. In fact, the notion of inner multiplicity is intrinsic to many traditional systems, of which astrology is perhaps the most well-known. The horoscope is not defined solely by the Sun, of course (even though most non-astrologers tend to think of it that way due to the popularity of "Sun-sign" astrology). Rather, the chart is a map which includes all the major celestial bodies of our solar system as if to suggest that the human psyche is as complex and multiplistic as the cosmos itself.

But there are other traditional systems besides astrology which express that sense of multiplicity, of which two in particular stand out: the Hindu yogic doctrine of the *chakras,* and the Hebrew system of the *Kabbalah.*

Within the yogic system of the "chakras" the human psyche is depicted as a complex system of psychic energy centers located along the length of the spine, each with its own psychological quality and concern. Together, these form a hierarchy of values, needs, desires, and emotional dispositions ranging from the most primitive drive towards survival to the highest expressions of spiritual awareness. Interestingly, as I've written about elsewhere in this volume, some schools of thought suggest there is a close correlation between these chakric centers and the planetary bodies of our solar system, suggesting that each of us houses an inner solar system mirroring the outer one.

Whereas in the yogic system it's generally believed that there are seven or eight primary centers within the subtle body, in the Kabbalistic "Tree of Life," consciousness is viewed as being comprised of *ten* primary centers of energy, termed "Sephiroth, which are located throughout the subtle body. As different as these two systems are superficially, there are actually striking similarities between them, such as the fact that each of them divvies consciousness (and the cosmos) into three vertical channels. In the yogic system, these are called *Ida, Pingala, and Sushumna*, while in the Kabbalistic system they are known as the *Pillar of Mercy*, the *Pillar of Severity*, and the *Pillar of Balance*, respectively.

In both of these systems, it's possible to describe each of these centers in terms of "personifications" appropriate to that center. For instance, in the Yogic system, the fourth, heart chakra (termed *Anahata* in Sanskrit), might be described as the "inner lover" or "inner artist"; whereas the third chakra (termed *Manipura*) might be personified as the "inner warrior"; while the fifth, throat chakra (termed *Vishuddha*) might be described as the "inner communicator" or "inner teacher." Different individuals in turn express differing degrees of emphasis on different chakras or sephiroths. Genghis Khan, for example, would express a greater activation of the third chakra, because of his warrior nature, whereas a great intellectual like Aristotle might express an amplified throat center.

However, the vast majority of individuals should be viewed as a reflecting a complex *blend* of different chakras, with those various centers coalescing to comprise the overall state of their personality. Rather than simply being a static pattern, this network of chakric or sephirotic centers can be thought of a constantly changing in accord with one's varying moods and thoughts.

But to my mind, what's most interesting about these systems is simply the fact that they depict human nature as *multiple* in nature, as a *constellation* of different sub-states in relation to one another. Could it be that within these ancient philosophical models we're encountering early intuitions into the complexities of personality that modern investigators have only recently been rediscovering? Moreover, if we take the further step of accepting such systems indeed describe actual energy centers in our subtle being, then it's also worth considering that the various sub-personalities exhibited by MPD individuals—indeed, by all of us in our varied moods and states—might well reflect different activations of these subtle chakras or siphiroths.

It's also worth considering what insights these traditional systems might offer concerning the deeper mastery and control of our inner potentials. Within both the Yogic and Kabbalistic schools of thought, for example, great importance is placed on the ability to consciously access these various energy centers at will, and towards that end each employs a wide range of techniques. In Yogic chakric psychology, we find complex associations and symbolisms associated with each chakra, which can be used to activate the chakras in intended ways. For instance, if one wanted to activate one's third chakra, the locus of one's "inner warrior," one could meditate on the various images, sounds, or gestures associated with that chakra, or perform certain rituals designed to act upon that center. In this way, one could learn to activate one's chakric sub-personalities in increasingly complex and interrelated ways, with a degree of skill not unlike that of a concert pianist eliciting melodies from a keyboard.

Yet another potentially fruitful area of comparison between these perspectives is their relative views of psychological health and well-being. Whereas Western psychology has classically described this growth process as hinging on the development of an increasingly strong central ego (or "executive"), for the yogi, the Kabbalist, and some MPD theorists, a healthy personality is seen as one in which all of an individual's sub-personalities (or energy centers) are harmoniously integrated within a balanced whole.

Ultimately, what this comparison of modern research with more traditional models may reveal to us is a glimpse of our inner potentials, but *at different levels of consciousness*. In other words, while the majority of sub-personalities displayed by MPD individuals reflect psychological potentials that are more pathological in nature, and therefore located at the lower end of our inner "ladder of selves" (to use Colin Wilson's apt phrase), in more traditional systems like Yoga or the Kabbalah we encounter the possibility of experiences that extend upwards into much higher levels on that same ladder of consciousness. Indeed, how we as individuals evolve beyond our current stage of development may eventually hinge not only on our understanding of these myriad levels, but on our ability to control or re-direct the energies they contain at will.

This article first appeared in Quest magazine, Autumn 1992.

CHAPTER 33

ONE SMALL STEP FOR MAN:
ASTROLOGICAL REFLECTIONS ON
THE FIRST LUNAR LANDING

T *his essay was written on the 50ᵗʰ anniversary of humanity's first walk on the surface of the Moon, which took place on July 20th, 1969.*

One could likely fill an entire book with all the astrological implications of the first lunar landing—which happened 50 years ago today, the date of this writing. (And yes, the landing really did happen. If you doubt that, simply explain why NASA would go through the effort of faking not just one lunar mission but *nine*, with six of those missions involving actual landings and strolls across the lunar surface. Surely one faked mission would have sufficed to fool the public, so why bother faking so many more and increase the risk of being exposed? I rest my case.)

Among those astrological factors was the fact that exactly when JFK made his famous speech first announcing the goal to put a man on the Moon, Jupiter was turning direct in the futuristic sign Aquarius; or the fact there was a tight Uranus/Jupiter conjunction at the time of that first lunar landing; or when Neil Armstrong was born, his Moon in Sagittarius was conjuncting the Galactic Axis;

or the fact that the first landing occurred on the Uranus opposition point from Charles Lindbergh's solo flight across the Atlantic, 42 years earlier—and on it goes. [1]

But a somewhat different approach would be to view the mission in the context of the shifting Great Ages. After all, this was the first time humans had ever set foot on a celestial body beyond Earth, so this was clearly a watershed moment, both historically and symbolically—and one that might even hold archetypal significance as a key toward understanding the coming era. Because even if the Aquarian Age won't be in full force for quite some time yet, it should be obvious we're already seeing early harbingers of it in play, through developments like the Internet, space travel, and democracy, all of which are decidedly *not* Piscean Age manifestations!

I remember years ago hearing a radio interview with the late author Stephen Levine where he spoke about the live television broadcast of Neil Armstrong's walk on the Moon in 1969. He mentioned hearing it suggested that the emerging Great Age would begin "with the one-pointed consciousness of the whole world on a single happenstance." No doubt, that ties in closely with one key aspect of Aquarian symbolism—namely, *the linking up of many minds across the planet.* It's fairly miraculous when you stop to think about it, really, the possibility of billions of people tuning into the exact same thought at the exact same moment, by means of technologies like TV, radio, or the internet.

But that's a decidedly double-edged sword, since that "one-pointed consciousness of the whole world" could just as easily be in service of a totalitarian "hive mind" society as it could be for the uniting of people in more creative or spiritual ways. It's good to remember Hitler was the first major politician to utilize the medium of television, when he inaugurated the opening of the Berlin Olympics in 1936 (a fact exploited to good effect in Carl Sagan's novel *Contact*). So there's no guarantee which way that collective mental link-up will go, whether for good or ill. Either way, though, the underlying archetype at work seems to be a decidedly Aquarian one.

But then we need to look at Neil Armstrong's first comment on setting foot on the lunar surface: *"That's one small step for man, that's one giant leap for mankind."* While it seems clear he botched that line (almost certainly intending to insert "a" before "man"), the comment still conveys a distinctly Aquarian message, and one that expands on Stephen Levine's point: *the interconnectedness of life, and how what one being does affects the all.* That, too, is a decidedly double-edged Aquarian sword, since a single person with nefarious intentions can exploit that interconnectedness to burn down the world as much as to heal and unite it.

What came as a special surprise for me, though, was learning (thanks to my colleague Larry Ely) that Neil Armstrong *himself* read astrological implications into that first lunar landing. Here is an actual excerpt from the Congressional record from a talk he delivered to the United States Congress in the wake of that first mission, where he puts the lunar landing into the context of the shift from Pisces to Aquarius:

"We came in peace for all mankind whose nineteen hundred and sixty-nine years had constituted the majority of the age of Pisces—a twelfth of the Great Year that is measured by the thousand generations the precession of the earth's axis requires to scribe a giant circle in the heavens. In the next twenty centuries, the age of Aquarius of the Great Year, the age for which our young people have such high hopes, humanity may begin to understand its most baffling mystery—*where are we going?"* [2]

(For years it was nearly impossible to obtain a video recording of that talk, but it's finally been posted online, fortunately, with Armstrong's astrological comment coming in at around the 17 minute mark: https://www.youtube.com/watch?v=O8Fx7BC11qw)

I find it fascinating to think one of the most famous figures in modern history chose to use this occasion to speak before a group of secular-minded politicians and scientists about an unabashedly astrological view of history. But did Neil really understand the deeper astrological import of what he was saying? We may never know, since no one seems to have uncovered any other statements from him on the topic. I hope those turn up some day.

Whether he did or not, I believe his setting foot on the lunar surface in 1969 nevertheless offers a useful point of contemplation for helping us better understand where we are in the great arc of history, and maybe even help to solve that mystery he referred to in his address—namely, *where are we going?*

CHAPTER 34

THE CHALLENGE OF EXO-ASTROLOGY: OR, HOW WOULD WE CONSTRUCT HOROSCOPES ON OTHER PLANETS?

Since I first became involved with astrology during the 1970s, I've often pondered the question of how astrology might operate on planetary bodies other than the Earth. Part of that was simply for the fun of it, since it stretched my imagination in interesting ways. But on another level, it also provided a way to think about what really underlies our own Earthbound forms of astrology.

For instance, how much of what we use and assume in erecting horoscopes here is truly universal, applicable anywhere in the universe, and how much is strictly cultural or local, not exportable anywhere beyond the confines of our own little pocket of space and time? Was there an archetypal basis to astrology that could be applied anywhere, and if so, what does that consist of? And if not, what might exotic forms of astrology in other locales look like or involve?

So when my colleague Thomas Gazis approached me recently with the idea of partaking in an online roundtable discussion about "exo-astrology"—the practice of astrology on celestial bodies other than the Earth—it prompted me to go back over several decades' worth of notes and assemble my thoughts on the subject, which I've distilled here. As you'll see, I have more questions than answers to offer, but hopefully these might serve to stimulate some further thoughts and discussions around this intriguing topic.

(1) Different Skies, Different Astrologies

Probably the most fundamental challenge facing anyone trying to erect a horoscope for someone born on another planet or body would involve how to make sense of the different celestial patterns in play there. Those might encompass such factors as the presence of very different day/night/year cycles, such as we see on Venus, where the days are actually longer than the years (due to its reverse axial rotation); the lack of a tropical zodiac due to the absence of a tilt in a planet's axis (which would also negate the possibility of any "Great Ages" historical model like our own, based as it is on the seasons and the vernal point); the presence of more than one moon, as on Mars, or no moons at all, as on Venus—and other such differences.

That challenge is naturally amplified when we start talking about horoscopes in completely different solar systems beyond our own. Here on Earth, we have a pretty good idea of what the various planets in our horoscopes mean, as in the case of Mars, Venus, Jupiter, Uranus, etc. But let's say we land on a planet in a faraway solar system; how would we go about determining what the bodies in *that* system mean or symbolize? Trial and error over decades or centuries of examining charts? Pure intuition? Divinatory techniques? Remote viewing? Kinesiology, or muscle-testing?

I also wondered whether the planets there have similar meanings to those in our system. That is, do other solar systems have their own versions of "Saturn" (representing a principle of limitation), their own versions of "Jupiter" (representing expansion), their own "Mercury" (representing mind and communication), and so on? Do planets in different systems naturally fall into a universal order like notes in the musical scale or colors in the visual spectrum? Or would there be a dramatically different set of archetypal principles at work? In addition, the constellations in a faraway solar system would naturally be very different from our own; so what would that mean for any horoscopes drawn up there? And would the seemingly archetypal 12-fold division we use to divvy up our own sky apply there as well?

(2) Uniquely Different Suns

What about the meaning of different suns in different solar systems? We tend to think of our own sun as being somehow neutral, a principle of pure awareness almost like a colorless light. But there are trillions of suns in the cosmos, many of them dramatically different from our own in size, chemical composition, or internal structure, and every one undoubtedly has its own distinct "character"—just like everything and everyone else in the cosmos does. So how do we determine the meaning of a sun in the chart of a completely different solar system? Would we go by the symbolism of its color, such as a blue sun versus a yellow or red sun? It's age? Chemical composition? Its size? (Our own Sun is truly miniscule compared to some.) Those might give us clues, but how would we really determine its core meaning?

Incidentally, the notion that different suns might hold different meanings may seem like a novel idea to some, but it actually isn't. I'm referring here to the considerable body of teachings devoted to the *fixed stars*, which holds that each star has its own unique symbolism or "flavor." In that way, Alderbaran is believed to possess a more violent or conflicted vibration, whereas Spica is felt to convey a more benefic flavor, while Regulus is associated with energies of great power but also sudden downfalls, similar to a blend of Jupiter and Mars, and so on. It naturally raises the question: How might astrologers on a planet in another solar system characterize the qualities of *our* sun when placed in *their* horoscopes? (Think for a moment how you would react if you learned that our sun was considered to possess a more violent nature—or, conversely, a highly spiritual and peace-loving one?)

And what would it mean if there were *two* suns in a horoscope (like depicted on Luke Skywalker's home planet Tattooine in the movie *Star Wars*), so that someone could be born with one sun in a given house or sign, and another sun in another part of the chart? For that matter, what would the presence of more than one sun say about the consciousness or ego of someone born in that system? Would it signal a dual identity of sorts somehow—or something else?

(3) The Qualities of Different Solar Systems

Along similar lines, it's astro-logical to assume that *each solar system as a whole* must possess its own character and matrix of meanings. That is, just as a person's horoscope on Earth involves more than just the Sun, a solar system is actually a complex of energies involving *all* the planets, moons, and tertiary bodies in that system, operating as a whole. As a result, a solar system in the Alpha Centauri region would likely be different in meaning from one in the Sirius system, the Orion region, or the Pleiades—exactly as any two individual personalities or psychologies would be different from one another.

In turn, solar systems close to the center of our galaxy would likely have different meanings from those nestled at its outermost fringes—just as having millions of stars visible in one's night sky would surely be different from having a mere three or four thousand, like we have. Sentient beings born in each or any of these distant systems would almost certainly differ in some way from one another—and these are all subtleties and shadings that wouldn't be learned simply by drawing up a horoscope for a child on a specific planet in one particular system. So just how would we go about determining the meaning of any given *system?*

Likewise, what would it mean to be born in a solar system with just three planets orbiting the sun, versus one with twenty planets? Would the number of planets tell us something about the complexity or simplicity of the psychologies of those born there? And what would it mean if a solar system consisted solely of solid bodies (like Mercury, Venus, Earth, or Pluto), versus one strictly comprised of gas giants (like Jupiter and Saturn), or one consisting solely of "ice giants" (like Uranus and Neptune)? Would variations like these make any difference in the meanings of that system as a whole, or the horoscopes erected there? (Our solar system has all three of those, by the way.)

(4) What Does the Earth "Mean"?

There's another aspect to this discussion which strikes me as important, though it's subtle and not easily explained. When we erect a chart here on Earth, we talk about the meaning of the various planets in the chart but we never think about the meaning of perhaps the most important body in the chart, since it's the very ground upon which we stand—namely, *the Earth.*

We are, first and foremost, Earthlings. While we take that for granted, this is by far and away the dominant influence on the consciousness of every being born on this planet, and it determines the context for all of our celestial interpretations here, whether we realize it or not. Yet strangely enough, we don't really know what "the Earth" *means*, undoubtedly because we're so close to it, similar to how we can't really know what our voice sounds like to others or how our personality really strikes others. But surely, aliens visiting our planet over an extended period of time would see that all Earthlings exhibit certain fundamental traits and qualities unique to this particular body, probably similar to how we now see Italians as being different from Norwegians, Brazilians, or the Chinese. Said another way, an Earthling is fundamentally different from a Martian, a Martian is fundamentally different from a Venusian, and so on.

My point is simply that if a child was born on Mars, it wouldn't really be enough to just look at the *celestial patterns in the sky around them* when they were born; we'd need to figure out what it means *that they are a "Martian."* Now, that might not be quite so difficult in the case of someone born on Mars or Venus, since we already have a fairly good sense of what those bodies mean, astrologically speaking. But what if a child was born on a distant planet in another solar system? It would be critical to understand the archetypal meaning of that specific body they were born on, not just of the orbiting bodies in their sky.

As I mentioned, this even poses a challenge when it comes to our own planet, Earth, because of how close we are to it. What does it really mean that we are "Earthlings"? The irony here is, it may wind up to be that only by moving off-planet we'll finally learn exactly what the "Earth" means, as an astrological principle. How? Suppose we were doing horoscopes on Mars, and carefully watched as the Earth transited over someone's midheaven; or watched every time Saturn squared the natal Earth in their chart; or every time Jupiter conjuncted that same degree. Over time, we'd surely start to get a feel for what the "Earth" means as a working, astrological principle. (Personally, I suspect we'll discover that it's closely resonant in nature with the zodiacal sign Taurus. Thinking about this in terms of zodiacal rulerships, the ultra-hot planet Venus seems more resonant to me with the "hot/dry" sign Libra, whereas the largely watery planet Earth seems more fitting to the "moist" sign Taurus.)

(5) The Astrological Dimensions of Space Travel

I also need to mention a very different angle on this subject, and that involves the experiences of space travelers to other bodies. In other words, exo-astrology isn't just about constructing birth charts for beings born on or planets or bodies; it's also about constructing and studying the horoscopes of *individuals traveling to other celestial bodies.*

For example, what does it mean when an astronaut goes to another planet and sets foot on it, in terms of how that action either activates or reflects their own Earth-based horoscope? If I travel to Mars, would my consciousness somehow become more "Martianized" in the process? And would doing that somehow activate the Mars in my birth horoscope? In turn, would that hinge on the condition of my natal Mars? In other words, if I have a natal t-square to my Mars, would my experience going to that planet be vastly different than if I were born with a Grand Trine to my Mars?

Or, transit-wise, if I traveled to Mars when transiting Jupiter was conjuncting my natal Mars, would that turn out differently if Uranus had been squaring my Mars at that time instead? (It could make for an interesting study to examine the charts of the NASA astronauts who actually set foot on the Moon to see if their experiences varied in relation to their own natal Moons, and to see what transits or progressions were active in their charts at the time.) Or let's say an astronaut sometime in our future were drawn towards the Orion region in particular. Would that some-how relate back to those corresponding degrees in his or her horoscope?

(6) Children Born on Spaceships or in Satellite Colonies

What about the horoscopes of an infant born on a spaceship out in space, either between the planets or even between solar systems, rather than on any celestial body? Needless to say, there would be no tropical zodiac, since that's a geocentric framework based solely on planetary seasons and a planet's tilt; and there likely would be no house system to use, since that's based on a horizon line across the surface of a planet (although it's been argued by astrologer Ed Kahout that the trajectory of the spaceship might give some frame of reference in that regard). So what factors would be used to con-structs a horoscope in such a situation?

(7) The Art of Reading Life-Symbols

Last but not least—and this comes from a decidedly more philosophical and esoteric viewpoint—I recall a conversation I had in the late 70s with the yogi and mystic Shelly Trimmer. We conversed at one point about the challenges of erecting horoscopes on different planets, even on the Sun (which he naturally suggested would require a heliocentric horoscope). (Yes, I know people can't be born on the Sun, but hey, it's a thought experiment.) But then he added a very interesting occult observation.

He often spoke about the importance of reading the symbols and signs in life—which I've come to believe is truly the basis of astrology, more than any matter of tangible "causes" or material energies somehow streaming down to people. (I elaborate on this point more in my book *The Waking Dream*). He related all of this to something he called "the laws of Self-conscious awareness," which I'd simply explain as having to do with our world being based on the essential patterns of consciousness. It's through knowing this symbolic language that one can discover "where one is at" in the cosmic scheme of things, within the framework of all that was, is, or yet shall be.

I'll have to paraphrase at this point, since this part of our conversation wasn't entirely recorded, but he said, in essence: "If someone knows how to read symbols, you could put them down anywhere in the cosmos, on any planet in any solar system, or for that matter on any plane of existence, and they'd be able to figure out 'where they are.' Since the outer reflects the inner, by understanding the symbolic language of the world you can also determine where you're at in terms of your own inner states and levels of consciousness." This wasn't just a matter of looking to planets, moons and stars, by the way, but rather of looking to *all* the phenomena of one's experience—colors, shapes, landscapes, sentient beings, sounds, thoughts, feeling states, etc.—for clues. Like a mariner on the ocean knowing how to read not only the stars but the patterns of the wind, the waves, the behaviors of birds and fishes, and even temperature changes in the air, a skilled occultist can navigate through the straights of existence by means of their knowledge of symbols. That ability would naturally enable someone to also construct a form of astrology pretty much anywhere in the universe, if so desired, whether that be on some distant planet, moon, or even spaceship.

Conclusion

All in all, it seems likely we'll be able to construct horoscopes for those born on other celestial bodies, although it might require some dramatic rethinking about astrology as normally practiced here on Earth. But there are other implications besides that. The existence of different planetary and solar systems beyond Earth also seems to suggest the existence of different forms of consciousness and psychology than we're familiar with here. That naturally opens the door to other interesting, far-reaching questions.

For instance, if we eventually make open contact with beings from other solar systems, just how different would their psychologies be from ours? And what might we learn about those psychologies from studying the structures of their skies? For that matter, would those distant societies have their own versions of astrology, similar to or different from our own? And what about the possibility of beings even from other *dimensions*, rather than just from other regions of space? How would astrology apply in cases like these, if at all?

Hopefully someday we'll actually have the answers to questions like those.

CHAPTER 35

THE INVISIBLE LANDSCAPE: SEEING OUR WORLD THROUGH THE EYES OF A DIFFERENT TIME

E very now and then I come across a thought experiment posted somewhere which goes something like this: *If you could go back in in time and describe life in our modern world to a medieval peasant, what would most surprise them about it?*

I've reflected on that a great deal over the years, because I think it's actually an enlightening exercise in some ways. To explain why, I'd point to the familiar tale of the frog in the pail of boiling water. Plop the frog down into the hot water, the story goes, and it will jump out quickly. But raise the water slowly to a boil, and the change is so gradual that the frog becomes accustomed to the heat and is eventually boiled to death.

Societal change is quite a bit like that, though not always with that sort of dire conclusion, fortunately. Our world has changed in extraordinary ways over the last few centuries, but much of that change has been so gradual that it can be hard seeing just how profound it's been in the context of any one lifetime. Not only have our external institutions, fashions, and technologies transformed radically over the centuries, but our inner attitudes and hidden assumptions about the world have as well. Together, these hidden assumptions comprise what I call the "invisible landscape" of our lives, since they can be as difficult to perceive as water is to the fish swimming in it. Yet these hidden assumptions shape our behaviors and thinking in a multitude of ways both great and small, whether we realize it or not.

So how exactly can we go about making that "invisible land-scape" visible? How can we better see our current situation and our hidden assumptions about it more clearly? Short of flying off to spend several months living with a remote Amazonian tribe and returning to modern society with fresh eyes, my opening thought experiment offers a simple way of doing just that, more or less. By trying to imagine how someone from a distant historical era might perceive our modern world, we can begin to get a simple sense of the profound changes that have taken place over the centuries. Like that proverbial frog which experiences temperature changes more rapidly instead of slowly, seeing the contrast between eras in a more stark way like that draws out those differences more clearly, and allows us to better grasp where we stand in the broad arc of history.

Which, for astrologers, naturally leads us back to the doctrine we've been touching on throughout this book—namely, the concept of the "Great Ages," and the seismic shifts associated with the transition between the Piscean and Aquarian eras. This exercise helps shed light on that too. With that in mind, let's begin by considering the most obvious of these historic changes—namely, our technologies.

Newfound "Magical" Powers

For the average medieval villager living in their own time, the available technologies of the era were simple and few. Men and women may have had the capacity to start a fire, till a field, prepare food, sometimes even work with heated metals, but not much more than that. True, there were specialists possessing more advanced skills and tools—just think of cathedral builders, as the prime example—but for ordinary citizens the technologies of the period consisted primarily of things like weapons for hunting or protection, wheeled carts, cooking implements, fabric-making, and so on.

So try to imagine describing for that villager the array of conveniences casually enjoyed by the average man or woman today. Picture telling them how we can now produce both light and heat (or cold) at will in our homes, or climb inside of gigantic metallic containers that can take us high into the sky—in some cases, even to the Moon! That villager would also be astonished to discover citizens now possess flat boxes on the walls of their homes which allow them to see, as if by magic, events and people happening far away, or that even happened years or decades earlier. In turn, you might explain how all these machines in our modern world are powered by something we call "electricity," which is essentially the powers of lightning brought under human control. Even more surprising, that power can now be accessed by anyone through tiny holes in the walls of their homes, allowing the average person access to one of nature's mightiest powers, literally at their fingertips.

But if you could somehow transport that medieval villager into the present time, none of those things would prepare them for the shock of simply walking through a modern major city, where they'd find some buildings taller than the greatest cathedrals of their time, lined up in rows for miles on end. Along our streets and avenues they'd also see metallic vehicles moving at terrifying speeds, all taken totally for granted by pedestrians scurrying about their business, many of them talking into small objects held up to their ears which allow them to communicate with people far away, possibly even on the other side of the world. ("The *other* side of the world"?!) If our time-traveling villager asked how such long-distance communication was even possible, you might explain that those images and sounds are transmitted through invisible forces that soar through the air at inconceivable speeds and can even pierce solid walls and barriers. (Well, you could *try* explaining that, at any rate.)

An Explosion of Knowledge

Over the course of his or her life, the medieval villager would have been exposed to an extremely limited range of information, since education was meager at best and literacy confined mainly to the clergy or nobility. A person's daily routine in those days largely consisted of basic activities like eating, working, and child-raising, along with certain religious or communal activities, but with limited opportunities for novel experiencing or information-gathering. The church taught modestly about ancient times and foreign cultures, invariably in connection with Biblical stories, but for the most part knowledge about history and the world at large was limited and general at best.

By comparison, the amount of data an ordinary person consumes during a lifetime now is relatively (and in some cases actually is) astronomical. Literacy is widespread, and by the time they've graduated from school the average student has gathered at least a rudimentary knowledge of math, grammar, science, history, and geography. Though most of us now take it for granted, a modern citizen's exposure to TV, movies, and The Internet will have exposed them to vast amounts of information about other cultures and places. By the end of his or her life, the average man or woman now will have seen countless TV shows on subjects both real and imaginary, learned about the existence of previous epochs in history from the medieval to the Jurassic, and encountered artworks or music from all over the world. In fact, we even have the ability to hear musical compositions without the performers or composers being present, since we have mechanical devices for preserving those performances so they can be listened to years or decades later. An average man or woman now could likely regale our medieval counterpart with at least a cursory knowledge about a wide array of matters extending far beyond local conditions or time-frames.

In fact, this body of knowledge we moderns now have at our fingertips also includes what we know about the universe *over our heads.* As seen through our medieval villager's eyes, the night sky would have seemed vast just in terms of the 3000-plus stars they could themselves could spot with their naked eyes on the clearest of nights. But nowadays, we know that most of those visible points of light speckling the blackened dome of heaven are actually suns just like our own, which together form part of a larger group now called a "galaxy." Not only that, there are many more such galaxies or "island universes" in existence out there, more numerous than the number of stars visible on the clearest of nights. And whereas that villager might have seen planets simply as those wandering stars which mysteriously move through the sky, even the average citizen nowadays has likely seen close-up photographs of those distant bodies, courtesy of unmanned spacecraft propelled into space by earth-based scientists. Quite literally, a whole new universe of knowledge has opened up to those living in modern times.

A Desacralized Cosmos

All of which brings us to something a bit harder to explain— namely, how it isn't just the *amount* of knowledge we now have that's changed but the *quality of meaning we ascribe to it.* For the average man or woman in medieval times, the universe was suffused with mystery and superstition, with all major events happening through the intervention of hidden beings, angels, demons, and of course, God. If lightning were to hit the local cathedral in ancient times, it was unquestionably a sign from the Lord; or if disease broke out in the village it surely must have stemmed from a supernatural cause, whether from curses cast by others, punishment from God, or even from evil designs wrought by Satan and his minions. From one end to the other, the villager's earlier world was interwoven with the meanings and stories of Judeo-Christian mythology.

But for the average man or woman now, worldly phenomena are generally viewed as the expression of mechanical laws and "natural" processes. If the light of the Sun is blocked out by the Moon during an eclipse, it's not because of divine whim or supernatural agencies but physical cycles that can be predicted years or even centuries in advance. For many moderns, the world is more akin to a great machine, not altogether different from the local mill which drew water from the villager's nearby river in his or her times. Superstition and religion have been largely replaced now by the findings of science and its methodologies; humans didn't appear on the cosmic stage as players in a divinely-inspired drama but rather as biological entities in a vastly ancient process of evolution.

A New Sense of "Self"

In some ways, though, the most radical change that's occurred over the centuries involves our sense of *how we see ourselves as individuals.* To be sure, there are certain constants in human nature across the millennia, such as basic emotions like anger, lust, or the drive for power and attention. But there are also those ways in which we view our personalities very differently now from how we did in earlier times.

One of those stems from the development of modern psychology in the 19th and 20th centuries, especially the "depth psychological" theories of figures like Sigmund Freud and Carl Jung. Most of us take for granted now the existence of something called the "subconscious mind," which Freud originally described as a kind of subterranean realm of being that exerts profound influence over our everyday motivations and behaviors; yet such an idea would have seemed alien to our medieval counterpart. Indeed, the very notions of "psychology" or of an "inner life" are, for the most part, comparatively modern inventions. One finds fleeting glimpses of subtle or inner motivations in post-Medieval works of literature like *Hamlet,* but none at all in earlier versions of the original story Shakespeare actually based his play on. Try explaining what the subconscious is to our hapless villager and you'll probably find yourself falling back on problematic metaphors and word pictures, like saying it's similar to the way there is so much more going on inside that castle near his or her village than what was visible just on the outside. Like I said, problematic.

But another aspect of modern life that would surely surprise the villager centers around the extraordinary amount of *freedom* enjoyed by the average man or woman now. Generally, we now have the freedom to pick our marriage partner, our profession, religion, how we dress, where we live, and sometimes even our gender, surprisingly enough. We can become directly involved in government, if we so choose, whether by voting for our preferred candidate or running for office ourselves. In the villager's time, most of these were privileges enjoyed only by the wealthiest or most powerful, certainly not by commoners.

In turn, this all stems from a fundamental sea-change in the value we accord to ourselves as *individuals.* By way of contrast, what did it really mean to be an "individual" back in medieval times? While Christianity did harbor some individualistic elements in its teachings about how each person was created in "the image of God," and how the hairs on our heads were numbered, all this was largely overshadowed by the broader teaching of original sin, which said we could only be redeemed via the intervention of Jesus or an external church—and without those intermediaries, our individual soul was essentially worthless.

But as a result of various developments through the centuries, including the Renaissance, the Reformation, and the Enlightenment, the heavy-handed dogma of original sin began to erode and be replaced by a growing conviction in the *essential worth* of individuals. Part of this was political in origin, as proclaimed by liberal thinkers like John Locke and Immanuel

Kant, but it had a more metaphysical side, too, as influenced by Freemasonry and the reawakening of ancient Hermetic and Gnostic teachings. Together, these all combined to impart a sense that each person possessed a spark of divinity within, and was intrinsically worthy.

To some extent, that core idea has always been present, it's true, but that was reserved chiefly for initiates or "divine" rulers. Indeed, the suggestion that any *ordinary* person might be inherently divine was heretical enough to get many proponents burned at the stake in older times. But as a result of these subsequent developments, we've come to regard individuals not merely as subservient subjects of kings, popes, or God, but as unique and valuable beings, each with his or her own set of rights.

Brave New World

As I touched on at the start, every society within any historical era lives within its own "invisible landscape"—its own matrix of beliefs and assumptions which it takes for granted and which would probably seem unthinkable to citizens of other times and places. In one historical period it's acceptable to sacrifice fellow humans to a volcano in order to appease an angry god, while in another period it's not; in one era, comets and eclipses are interpreted as omens of doom, while in another they're not; in one period it's considered normal to treat women like possessions or as slaves, while in another it's not.

Likewise, our own moment in history has its own network of hidden assumptions about the world and our place in it, which shapes our values, actions and goals. We take it for granted that individuals enjoy certain rights, or that we can access vast amounts of information at the touch of a keyboard, and can fly across the planet at a moment's notice, and many other such wonders. Yet we rarely stop to consider how unusual these are in the broader context of history, let alone what truly mean.

So what accounts for the enormous *magnitude* of change we see shaping our world and society at this stage of history? Note, ours isn't "just another" historical era we've living in, comparable to any other, for the simple reason that ours is literally changing the face of our planet in unprecedented and perhaps even apocalyptic ways. *That's* new.

While sociologists, secular historians, and scientists certainly have their own theories about how this has all come about, astrologers point in a very different direction—namely, the doctrine of the Great Ages. As I've explained previously, these are the roughly 2100-year old periods associated with the precession of the equinoxes through the various constellations, each of which represents a fundamentally different paradigm, each of which possesses its own *zeitgeist* or "spirit of the age." Like tectonic plates shifting deep underfoot, these shifts bring about deep transformations in the archetypal gestalts that shape both the conscious and unconscious life of humanity.

At this moment, we're perched between the Piscean and Aquarian Ages, a transition that is clearly birthing an especially momentous time in history. The thought-experiment we've been exploring here helps illustrate the magnitude of this change in a number of ways—technologically, psychologically, spiritually. But notice that I've been careful not to place value judgments on these changes, as being either strictly "good" or "bad." That's because every major historical shift involves a trade-off of some sort, leading usually to *both* constructive and destructive outcomes.

For example, it's true that the average person now has access to a wealth of information about the world not available to those of earlier times. But we have to ask whether that expansion of knowledge has also brought with it a similarly expanded sense of *meaning*. As Jean Baudrillard said, "We live in a world where there is more and more information, and less and less meaning." True, we no longer see the merging of the Sun and Moon during an eclipse as being a dragon devouring the Sun; but in the process we've largely lost the sense that a phenomenon like this hold *any meaning at all.*

Likewise, we now possess capabilities that would have seemed superhuman to men and women of earlier times, which has resulted in a variety of newfound freedoms for many of us, with a multitude of new choices. But what kinds of "freedoms" are they, exactly, and at what cost? The average city-dweller is now almost completely dependent on electricity, an innovation which confers many gifts, no doubt. But what would happen if our modern-day power grid suddenly went down? Could we survive in our own time as long as the medieval villager could have in theirs, with their comparatively primitive tools and weapons? How much "power" would a modern individual today have if they were transported back to those earlier times and armed with the same means at their disposal as those inhabitants?

These are just some of the questions worth considering when trying to make sense of the changes transforming our world, with both its virtues and limitations. So whenever anyone asks me, "Will the Aquarian Age be good or bad?" I generally answer with a decisive, *"Yes!"*

I'll close with this. Suppose someone from *our* era could time-travel 1000 years into the future to view the conventions, experiences, and beliefs that will characterize *that* era. What would we learn about the hidden assumptions those future citizens hold about t*heir* time—and, in turn, about our own, when confronted by all those differences?

Hopefully, it's not being too idealistic to think that our species will even be *around* 1000 years from now. [1]

CHAPTER 36

ASTROLOGY AND THE THEORY
OF CORRESPONDENCES

*"I sense the world might be more dreamlike, metaphorical,
and poetic than we currently believe—but just as irrational as sympathetic magic when looked at in a typically
scientific way. I wouldn't be surprised if poetry—poetry
in the broadest sense, in the sense of a world filled with
metaphor, rhyme, and recurring patterns, shapes, and
designs—is how the world works."*

—David Byrne, *Bicycle Diaries*

Over the years I've had any number of friendly debates with
colleagues as to exactly how astrology *works*. During those
exchanges I've come across multiple theories which try to answer
that question, drawing on such wide-ranging concepts as geo-
magnetism, quantum non-locality, fractals, gravity, string theory,
sacred geometry, Jung's theory of "synchronicity," or perhaps some
subtle-but-as-yet-known energy of nature. Implicit in many of these
discussions, directly or indirectly, has been the allied query as to

just how far science can go towards either proving or explaining astrology.

My own thoughts about this are complex, since there are actually several issues at work here, rather than just one. But in a broad sense, I've come to believe understanding astrology's worldview requires a fundamentally different way of thinking about the world than what we employ when practicing science, reading a newspaper, or for that matter balancing our checkbooks.

Astrology involves a more symbolic and metaphoric mode of perceiving that "sees through" surfaces to uncover hidden dimensions of knowledge and connections not immediately apparent to the physical eye, and which trafficks in patterns of meaning rather than discrete bits of data. What follows are a few real-life examples which illustrate these nuances, and that I hope will stimulate further discussion into this complex and multi-leveled discipline.

The Many Faces of Venus in Capricorn

A woman came to me whose horoscope showed she was born with Venus in Capricorn. During our conversation she informed me that she'd been married twice over the course of her life—and both of those marriages took place on mountains. I found that fascinating, since mountains are of course associated with Capricorn, and Venus associated with love, so that juxtaposition of planet and sign seemed to find a perfect expression in her own marital experiences. (She had no real knowledge of astrology, by the way, so it was simply her love of high, scenic areas and scenic vistas that caused her to choose those locations for her nuptial vows, not any conscious preconceptions involving astrology.)

Needless to say, a manifestation like that would be perfectly understandable to any astrologer, because of the symbolism involved. But imagine trying to explain any of this to a hard-nosed scientist. What connection could possibly exist between a celestial pattern in the sky and romantic experiences on mountains down here on Earth? After all, it's one thing to claim there is a connection between the Moon and the tides, for example, since we can analyze how gravity works, measure the size of the Moon and the Earth, map out the distance between them, and so on, since that's all relatively understandable within a strictly mechanistic framework. But when you start talking about Venus up in a particular segment of the sky and someone down here on Earth getting married on mountains—what possible causal or mechanical relationship would explain something like *that*? And why *mountains*? Why not riverbanks, canyons, seashores, forests, or even alleyways?

But it gets even stranger than that. You see, it just so happened that my client had an identical twin, a brother, born several minutes after her, and who had the same basic Ascendant and Moon sign, and Venus in Capricorn. But that twin brother never got married on mountains, no. For him, Venus in Capricorn manifested through a profound *love of architecture*—yet another Capricorn symbol, in keeping with that sign's emphasis on structures. He designed buildings for a living, in fact, and did so with a beautiful eye for form and patterns.

I could multiply examples of other clients born with Venus in Capricorn who experienced that same planet/sign combination in still other ways—such as the artist who specialized in painting portraits of the elderly, or the woman who married a prominent politician, or even a client whose hobby was raising goats! Capricornian symbols, all. So aside from the question as to how there might be a tangible connection between Venus in Capricorn in the sky and someone getting married on mountains, there is the equally great mystery as to why there might be so *many different manifestations of that planet/sign combination in people's lives,* from mountains and architecture to the elderly and goats, and still others. What intrinsic connection could there possibly be among all these diverse forms, so seemingly different on their surface from one another?

The answer, esoterically, lies in a traditional concept referred to in previous chapters as the *theory of correspondences,* an ancient doctrine that suggests all phenomena are embraced in an invisible web of affinities. As such, phenomena that seem completely different on their surfaces may actually be linked, synchronistically, through a hidden network of "subterranean" resonances and affinities, based in turn upon a deeper ground of archetypal principles—whether you prefer to call those geometric principles, Numbers, planets, or something else entirely. These clients of mine with Venus in Capricorn reflected a connection with that celestial configuration not because that planet in that sign was somehow emanating "mountain-like," "architecture-like," or even "goat-like" (!) rays down to us on Earth, but because all these varied forms were cosmically linked through *subtle webs of meaning.*

Said a little differently, a person's horoscope reveals the essential archetypal principles at work in someone's life, but those essential principles can manifest through a wide range of forms and symbols, which are linked to one another by means of metaphor and analogy rather than any purely physical forces or dynamics.

Simple, eh? Well, maybe not. But that pretty much sums up the worldview of astrology, and it's dramatically different from the one which describes the world as seen through the eyes of conventional science.

Science Enters Through the Back Door

But there's an interesting twist to our story. During the early 1950s, French statistician Michel Gauquelin and his wife Francoise conducted a groundbreaking study into the workings of astrology. As a result of cataloguing literally thousands of birth horoscopes, they discovered that certain planetary patterns appeared with surprising consistency in the charts of prominent individuals in ways that correlated closely with basic astrological tenets. [1]

For example, among their findings was the discovery that a statistically significant number of prominent sports figures were born shortly after Mars either rose or culminated in the sky. On the other hand, Saturn tended to show up more conspicuously in the charts of scientists and physicians, while for actors and politicians Jupiter was more of a factor—and so on. While Gauquelin's research didn't support every facet of traditional astrological doctrine—nor was it designed to—it validated one of its most fundamental concepts, that there is a relationship between certain planetary positions at birth and certain professions. As John Anthony West used to say, that fact alone is enough to send the materialistic worldview crashing down like a house of cards, since it essentially validates the presence of *meaning* in our world.

Gauquelin's work is just one in a series of research projects over the decades which have attempted to apply the methodologies of science and statistics towards testing or validating astrology. Some of the other scientific models which have been applied towards this end are the quantum notion of "entanglement" [2], the principle of *fractals* [3], or even the mathematical concept of the *fibonacci series* [4]. But as I believe my earlier examples show, there will always be certain elements of astrology that lie just beyond the grasp of any purely materialistic approach, due to those factors of symbolism and "meaning" implicit in correspondence theory. In the end, it makes for an ironic situation, since science may actually wind up *proving* astrology works, insofar as showing something is really "there," without being able to fully explain *how* or *why* it does.

Let me explain what I mean by that. I mentioned how Michel Gauquelin's work revealed that Mars shows up prominently in the horoscopes of many sports champions. That is empirical, repeatable, and bears out a key facet of astrology. But it doesn't resolve the vexing question as to why *Mars* should specifically be the planet related to sports, and not Venus? Or the Moon? Or Saturn? Gauquelin's work is important in at least verifying that these odd connections do exist, but it doesn't actually bring us any closer toward understanding *why* they do.

Along a similar line, there are intriguing studies which show that certain celestial patterns involving the Sun are linked to the rise and fall of gold prices, and can be predicted in advance. [5] This, too, is empirical and demonstrable. But how do these findings explain why there would be a connection specifically between the Sun and *gold*—and not, say, with tin, copper, or lead?

As astrologers, we tend to take these many correspondences and rulerships for granted, but we shouldn't, because they hint at something truly profound about our discipline. Take just a moment to reflect, and it becomes clear that astrology incorporates hidden levels of meaning which link diverse phenomena throughout the world in deeply *symbolic* ways. As Ralph Waldo Emerson put it, "Secret analogies tie together the remotest parts of Nature, as the atmosphere of a summer morning is filled with innumerable gossamer threads running in every direction, revealed by the beams of the rising sun."

The Big Picture

To really understand this, I need to place it all into an even broader frame, so I'll finish with an example that raises more far-reaching questions about not just correspondence but astrology's broader workings in our world.

This one occurred to me while watching a news story on TV about a local resident who was sitting in the bleachers at a baseball game and became injured by a runaway foul ball. The story caught my attention because of a similar case from my own files involving a client who was also hit by a stray foul ball at a game, and who also sustained an injury to her face. Needless to say, when that client of mine first called to ask what was happening in her horoscope, I was just as intrigued as she was to find out. Not too surprisingly, I discovered that Uranus was closely squaring her Mars at the time—I say "not too surprisingly" because, as most astrologers know, that's a planetary combo commonly associated with unexpected accidents, especially ones involving the head (the part of the body ruled by Mars). To be sure, the symbolism of that ballpark incident fit perfectly for her, and succinctly illustrated the principle of correspondence in action.

But stop and think about that entire scenario for a moment. *Exactly at the point when the woman had an accident-prone aspect firing in her horoscope, a stray baseball hit by a complete stranger careened over from 70 feet away and hit her in the head.*

Yes, the symbolism fits perfectly, but what brought all those disparate factors together at that precise moment: the stranger at bat, the seemingly random foul ball, my client's face, and the overarching astrological configurations at the time? Somehow these all coalesced to give rise to that unique situation, with the intricacy of clockwork. Yet she herself had little control over (let alone conscious understanding of) how that all played out.

In cases like this, astrology no longer seems like just a matter of some mechanistic "force" emanating down from the skies to individuals, or of gravitational energies or quantum principles affecting people's lives, but of something much larger. Rather, we begin to see it involves *an organizing principle that extends throughout the entire environment, orchestrating phenomena and diverse people in meaningful ways which lie completely beyond the conscious control or influence of any one individual.* True, there are correspondences and abundant symbolic connections in our world. But what arranges and unifies them in the complex and interlocking ways we see them manifesting in our lives and throughout the entire world?

Perhaps you can see where I'm going with this. It's hard to avoid using weighty terms like "fate" or "destiny" or even "God" to explain the mysterious ways phenomena converge to fulfill the needs of a single horoscope and life, and all lives together. But what do terms like that really mean? One can always choose to fall back on words like "synchronicity," and I often do, but too often these terms are casually trotted out as if to explain the great mystery at hand when they merely slap a name onto it.

Examples like this strongly suggest the presence of a grand design encompassing our world within which our own destinies are embedded—*wheels within wheels,* as it were—all seemingly orchestrated by an overarching intelligence that coordinates events like a conductor directing a symphony orchestra, making it possible for diverse phenomena and individuals to coalesce in incredibly intricate and meaningful ways.

Seen through an astrological lens, the cosmos thus begins to look less like a dead machine and more like a vast *dream,* one that expresses itself in the language of symbolism, analogy, and correspondences rather than frozen, discrete "facts." In the end, it's not that science and astrology are at odds with one another so much as the fact conventional science is by itself ill-equipped to explain astrology's more symbolic and meaningful workings. As a result, the quantitative approach of science may indeed prove valuable in measuring or even validating some of astrology's key concepts, and open new doors to previously unknown techniques and concepts. [6] But to fully *explain* those principles and methods will require a deeper dive into the philosophical worldview which underlies our practice. By doing so we stand a better chance of grasping the rich depths which lie not only in the poetic heart of this ancient discipline, but within the cosmos itself. [7]

ENDNOTES

(All URLs were accessed in 2020.)

Chapter 2

1. Steven Johnson, *The Invention of Air: A Story of Science, Faith, Revolution, and The Birth of America.* Riverhead Books. 2009, p. 38.
2. Richard Tarnas, *Cosmos and Psyche: Intimations of a New World View.* Viking Books, 2006, p. 409.

Chapter 3

1. Ray Grasse, *The Waking Dream: Unlocking the Symbolic Language of Our Lives.* Quest Books, 1996, p. 196.
2. Ray Grasse, *Ibid,* p. 194-195.

Chapter 4

1. After mentioning to a class about how the 10th house (and MC) indicates qualities one is aspiring toward, someone in the audience once remarked, "I always thought the *11th house* was the part of the horoscope associated with aspirations, goals, and dreams?" In my work with clients over the years, I frankly

haven't found the 11th house to deal as much with aspirations or dreams as with friends and community.

2. The relationship between the Midheaven and the 1st house is similar to what exists between the Sun and the Moon in a horoscope, in terms of their respective concerns with "public" vs. "private." Consider my earlier example of the artist I knew born with Jupiter in Leo conjunct the MC but also with Saturn in Scorpio in his 1st house: he presented an outgoing, "sunny" disposition (his elevated Jupiter in Leo) but secretly grappled with darker issues or emotional wounds (his Saturn in Scorpio just below the horizon). In some ways, this is analogous to what we'd see in a person born with Jupiter conjunct the Sun but Saturn conjunct their Moon—the former suggesting a more outgoing and sunny public life, the latter pointing to a more uptight and "heavy" emotional nature.

3. These interesting entries from Wikipedia underscore both the constructive and destructive sides of McQueen's unique horoscope: "McQueen had an unusual reputation for demanding free items in bulk from studios when agreeing to do a film, such as electric razors, jeans, and other items. It was later discovered McQueen donated these things to the Boys Republic reformatory school, where he spent time in his teen years." Additionally, there's this: "In 1947, McQueen joined the United States Marine Corps and was promoted to private first class and assigned to an armored unit. Initially he reverted to his prior rebelliousness and was demoted to private seven times. He took an unauthorized absence by failing to return after a weekend pass expired, staying with a girlfriend for two weeks until the shore patrol caught him. He resisted arrest and spent 41 days in the brig. After this he resolved to focus his energies on self-improvement and embraced the Marines' discipline. He saved the lives of five other Marines during an Arctic exercise, pulling them from a tank before it broke through ice into the sea.

He was assigned to the honor guard, responsible for guarding then U.S. President Harry Truman's yacht." (One other curious detail from McQueen's life which nicely illustrates his Uranus in Aries on the Midheaven: his father was a stunt pilot for a barnstorming flying circus!)

Chapter 9

1. See my essay "Saturn, the Late Bloomer" in my book *Under a Sacred Sky: Essays on the Philosophy and Practice of Astrology* (Wessex Astrologer Ltd., 2015), where I explore this slow-developing side of Saturn in relation to the planets.
2. Robert L. O'Donnell, *Revolutionary: George Washington at War*, Random House, 2019, p. 24.

Chapter 13

1. This perspective on natal horoscopic patterns can also be applied to life-events triggered by transits and progressions, too. I remember talking years ago with my colleague Rosemary Clark about some difficult experiences a mutual friend I'll call "Louise" was undergoing during a tough Pluto transit. Among other things, Louise was contending with a dishonest and manipulative business partner who caused her untold problems. Feeling sorry for Louise, I spent several minutes complaining to Rosemary about that situation, choosing to lay the blame solely on Louise's business partner and suggesting Louise was just an innocent victim in the sordid drama. Pausing a bit, Rosemary interjected, "Well, let's not forget: it's Louise's Pluto, after all." That caught me off-guard, because it reminded me that it wouldn't really have happened to Louise if it wasn't somehow in her horoscope at the time. Here as well, this doesn't let the business partner off the hook for any bad ethical decisions, it simply points up how the world acts towards us in concert with our own horoscopes.

2. Cited in my book *Urban Mystic: Recollections of Goswami Kriyananda,* Inner Eye Press, 2018, p. 58.
3. Cited in my book *The Waking Dream: Unlocking the Symbolic Language of Our Lives,* Quest Books, 1996, p. 214.

Chapter 14

1. To give some idea of how extreme (and sometimes offbeat) the fascination for electricity became during the period around Uranus's discovery, consider this description from an article by Ruth Garde titled "Charged Bodies" about a curious sensation that drew attention the same year as Herschel's great find: "The 18th-century craze for electrical performance also provided fertile ground for more dubious practitioners, such as the renowned quack James Graham. Graham, a self-styled specialist in sexual health, opened his Temple of Hymen in Pall Mall in 1781. Its centerpiece was the Celestial Bed, which he claimed could help couples with marital and fertility problems. Its chief 'remedy' was based in static electricity: the bed was insulated by glass rod supports, which allowed it to become charged. 'According to Graham, the charged atmosphere was "calculated to give the necessary degree of strength and exertion to the nerves" and the users' charged bodies could ejaculate fluids more vigorously. Rental of the bed was an eye-watering £50 a night and was guaranteed to bless its users with progeny. For desperate couples this was no joke: here electricity was touted as a force that could heal and bring forth life.'" (Source: https://next.wellcomecollection.org/articles/charged-bodies)
2. Christopher Loring Knowles, "Chaos Magic vs The Robot Revolution" (http://secretsun.blogspot.com/2017/04/chaos-magic-vs-robot-revolution.html)
3. While the next return of Uranus to its discovery degree of 24°27" Gemini is technically slated to occur in early July 2031,

there are a number of other trigger points worth mentioning, in particular: The station point of Uranus in late September and early October of that year, at 27° Gemini, is close to that discovery degree (Uranus technically goes retrograde on October 3, but will remain in the same degree for weeks); Uranus contacts its discovery degree again during the first half of January 2032; Uranus will be stationary direct at 23°12" Gemini on March 1, 2032, but again, its influence will extend for weeks on either side; finally, Uranus moves forward to cross its discovery degree one last time during the last ten days of April 2032.

Chapter 15

1. I also believe that, despite obvious differences, there is more similarity between Saturn and Uranus than is generally acknowledged, in several ways. Consider how both bodies are "cool" and sometimes even cold in tone (e.g., individuals with Moon/Saturn or Moon/Uranus conjunctions are both notorious for being emotionally detached, or sometimes aloof); both Saturn and Uranus figure prominently in the horoscopes of scientists; both often display selfish tendencies; and both planets have their tyrannical side (though in the case of Uranus, it's camouflaged behind a more freedom-oriented façade; I've sometimes used the example of the computers in James Cameron's *Terminator* film series, where these technological servants of humanity wound up becoming our masters through the development of a truly intelligent A.I. network, called "Skynet").

Chapter 17

1. The debate over the value of mythic names assigned to planets has come up especially often in connection with Uranus. My friend and colleague Rick Tarnas has long suggested that the rebellious Greek titan Prometheus is in some ways more fitting to convey the rebellious essence of Uranus than the

tyrannical sky-god Ouranos. While I believe that holds an important truth, I don't think we can dispense with Ouranos entirely. I say that because the astrological Uranus strikes me as having both extremes of that rebel/tyrant polarity within it, as part of a two-fold dynamic. For instance, a Promethean rebel by his or her nature implies an oppressive power being railed against, while a tyrannical sky-god implies creatures who are subjugated by that power. Neither one of these truly exists in isolation, with that balance of power shifting from one extreme to the other, teeter-totter style. Uranus is like that, too, I've found, as if there is a Saturn core tucked within that Uranian exterior. As an imaginative example of this dynamic, consider my earlier example of the "Skynet" technology portrayed in James Cameron's *Terminator* films, where the technology transforms over time into a tyrannical "sky-god" all its own. Or look to how the Uranian energy manifested itself politically across the world shortly after its discovery in 1781: having begun with upstart rebels in countries like America and France, those same Promethean energies morphed into their virtual opposite, as with France's "Reign of Terror" and figures like Robespierre; or even the United States' eventual transformation from a beacon of freedom to an imperial military force hurling fire back down to Earth via drones and hi-tech bombers. In short, both the mythologies of Prometheus and Ouranos offer valuable keys towards understanding Uranus's powerful, complex symbolism, not just one or the other.

Chapter 18

1. Interestingly, Marshall Applewhite was born on May 17, 1931, just four days after another notorious cult leader, Jim Jones (born on May 13, 1931).

Chapter 20

1. See chapter 15 of my book *Under a Sacred Sky: Essays on the Philosophy and Practice of Astrology*, Wessex Astrologer Ltd. 2015.

Chapter 22

1. In addition to the tropical and sidereal zodiacal systems, a smaller number of astrologers employ a third system sometimes referred to as the "constellational zodiac," based more precisely on the constellations as they actually appear in the sky, unrestricted by artificial 30-degree divisions. For a good discussion of that approach, see *Quest for the Zodiac: The Cosmic Code Beyond Astrology*, by John Lash Lamb, Marion Institute, 2007.

2. Another example of the efficacy of the tropical zodiac can be illustrated through historic examples of planetary "ingresses"—those times when celestial bodies first enter a zodiacal sign. It's a staple of astrological doctrine that the movements of the slow-moving planets through the zodiac can exert a huge influence on shifting cultural trends. Over the years I've found that even looking to see what happens around the *first few days or weeks* of an ingress provides us with a sneak preview of what to expect during the subsequent passage of that planet through the sign, almost as if we're afforded "omens" of what is to come. Over the last couple of decades I've come across some interesting examples of that specifically using the tropical zodiac, of which the following strike me as especially noteworthy. (It's possible someone using the sidereal zodiac could come up with an equally impressive set of correlations, but I haven't seen that attempted yet.)

— In the years leading up to 2008, a growing number of tropical astrologers predicted that the imminent entry of Pluto into Capricorn could bring about a major shake-up in Wall Street and the global economy more generally, due to the turbulent impact of this planet on the sign associated with business and government. For me, that seemed a prime opportunity to test out the viability of the tropical zodiac, since the financial forecasts being proposed were so dramatic that it seemed to present a relatively clear-cut "before and after" case study. As it turned out, within weeks of Pluto's move into Capricorn in 2008, Wall Street went into a historic melt-down, leaving the global economy teetering on a financial precipice.

— On March 11, 2011, the planet Uranus was scheduled to move into the tropical sign of Aries, signaling a major transition which could impact society. I suspected that ingress could be especially important, since Uranus was starting to enter into a long-term relationship (square) with Pluto in Capricorn—suggesting the impending change could be extremely turbulent or even revolutionary. On the day before this ingress occurred, on March 10th, I spoke with an old friend, Tim Boyd (about to be president of the Theosophical Society in America, where I had worked previously as an editor) and mentioned this planetary shift to him. I specifically suggested that he watch the news carefully for any major "shake-ups" on the global front those next few days. As it so happened, that very next day, exactly as Uranus moved into fiery Aries, the Fukushima disaster occurred, with massive earthquake shaking Japan and triggering a tsunami that took the life of thousands, while causing a disastrous melt-down at the Haichi power plant. The destruction of the nuclear generator spread radiation across a wide region and continues to pose a serious risk for both humans and wildlife to this day.

— On May 15th, 2018, Uranus then entered the tropical sign Taurus. Because of the widely assumed associations of Taurus with the earth, many astrologers wondered whether we would start seeing some major earth changes taking place at the point of its entry into that sign. As it turned out, the week leading up to this shift saw major volcanic activity starting up in Hawaii, and on May 16th, the day after its entry into Taurus, there was a significant eruption of Mount Kilauea sending an ash plume 30,000 feet into the air. That wasn't the only Earth-related development occurring during that general period, however. Indonesia's Mount Merapi volcano began erupting in mid-May as well, sending plumes of smoke almost 4 miles into the air, and on May 29th there was a violent eruption of Guatemala's Fuego volcano, killing at least 62 people. On that same day, an earthquake of magnitude 5.5 also shook the Big Island of Hawaii, sending ash plumes from Mount Kilauea up to 8,000 feet. Indeed, this surge of volcanic activity led to New Scientist publishing an article (June 6, 2018) titled "Why Are So Many Volcanoes Erupting Around the World?"

— The planetoid Chiron is associated by many astrologers with issues of wounding and healing. This body shifted into tropical Pisces (the sign most associated with the ocean) on April 22nd of 2010. The Deepwater Horizon rig sank in 5000 ft. of water in the Gulf of Mexico that same day, causing incalculable damage to the Gulf and many of its creatures.

— On March 21ˢᵗ of 2020, Saturn moved into Aquarius, this happening almost precisely at a time when the theme of "social distancing," along with a widespread government crackdown on people congregating in groups, became prominent around the world due to the Covid-19 virus. This could hardly be a more perfect manifestation of Saturn, the planet of limitation, into Aquarius, the sign of groups and social interaction.

Chapter 23

1. My thanks to Lynn Hayes for her input about Pluto returns in the Roman Empire: https://www.astrodynamics.net/pluto-returns-roman-empire/
2. From a symbolic standpoint, it's worth noting that shortly after England's third Pluto return, Mary Shelley published her

famous work *Frankenstein,* a story ostensibly about the resurrec-tion of dead bodies—an overtly Plutonian theme.

3. https://www.history.com/topics/great-depression/dust-bowl

4. As I pointed out earlier, the third return of Pluto for England coincided precisely with the famed "madness of King George," when that country's imperial ruler literally drifted into insanity. While it's too early to say whether Donald Trump will still be president during the peak of the U.S. Pluto return (either way, we're within the general orb of that long-term cycle) it's hard to resist drawing parallels that period and this.

5. https://bigthink.com/politics-current-affairs/fdr-coup? rebelltitem=1#rebelltitem1

6. The popular TV series "Stranger Things" also offers another possible expression of America's Pluto return, with its narrative of dark subterranean forces growing out of control and threat-ening the lives of surface dwellers.

7. https://www.gilderlehrman.org/content/historical -context-mexican-americans-and-great-depression

8. The reckoning that Pluto is forcing Americans to take could prove to be even broader in scope than this. In a 2017 article for Rolling Stone magazine titled "The Madness of King Donald"—a piece that could just as easily been written as a commentary on the U.S. Pluto return—Matt Taibbi wrote about confronting America's long legacy of sins: " We Americans have some good qualities, too, don't get me wrong. But we're also a bloodthirsty Mr. Hyde nation that subsists on massacres and slave labor and leaves victims half-alive and crawling over deserts and jungles, while we sit stuffing ourselves on couches and blathering about our 'American exceptionalism.' We dumped 20 million gallons of toxic herbicide on Vietnam from the air, just to make the shooting easier without all those trees, an insane plan to win 'hearts and minds' that has left about a million still disabled

from defects and disease—including about 100,000 children, even decades later, little kids with misshapen heads, webbed hands and fused eyelids writhing on cots, our real American legacy, well out of view, of course... If you want to look in our rearview, its lynchings and race war and genocide all the way back, from Hispaniola to Jolo Island in the Philippines to Mendocino County, California, where we nearly wiped out the Yuki people once upon a time... This is who we've always been, a nation of madmen and sociopaths, for whom murder is a line item, kept hidden via a long list of semantic self-deceptions, from 'manifest destiny' to 'collateral damage.'... Now, the mask of respectability is gone, and we feel sorry for ourselves, because the sickness is showing."

https://www.rollingstone.com/politics/politics-features/the-madness-of-donald-trump-197853/ (Note: This lengthy passage from Matt Taibbi was not included in the original print version of my article in Mountain Astrologer magazine due to space limitations.)

Chapter 25

1. Occasionally one sees instances where this process of Scorpionic "tailspinning" plummets a person so profoundly into the depths that the experience translates into its exact opposite, culminating in the so-called "Phoenix effect," where they rise up from the ashes essentially transformed, in a way that the other signs generally don't experience quite so dramatically, due to their being comparatively more even-keeled in temperament.
2. William Blake, *Blake: Complete Writings*, edited by Geoffrey Keynes, Oxford University Press, 1966, 1969, p. 218.
3. Stephen Levine, *Guided Meditations, Explorations and Healings*, Anchor Publications, 1991, pp. 52-56.

4. Eugene T. Gendlin, *Focusing*, Bantam Books Inc., 1981. See also this author's later book on the same subject: *Focusing-Oriented Psychotherapy: A Manual of the Experiential*, Guilford Publications, 1996.

Chapter 26

1. Wonder Bright, "Why Should a Modern Astrologer Use Ancient Techniques?" https://starsofwonder.com/2018/01/why-should-a-modern-astrologer-use-ancient-techniques/ Taken out of context, this quote of hers might give the impression she's arguing for the superiority of ancient techniques over modern ones, but in fact she's simply articulating a particular perspective, and like myself, personally believes in a healthy cross-pollination of styles.

2. I would add here that modern astrology, in its purely psychological form, is actually far more "specific" than traditional systems when it comes to mapping out our *inner, emotional* lives. I've noticed an implicit assumption among a few traditionally-oriented astrologers that our inner world of experience is somehow less important than the outer, more tangible one, when in fact these are simply different spheres of everyday activity. On countless occasions I've had clients come to me who had little interest in their worldly fortunes as much as in the complex psychological dynamics they're experiencing at the time, especially under powerful Pluto, Neptune, or Saturn transits or progressions. In cases like these, the modern approach to astrology is considerably more detailed and specific when dealing with those subtleties of inner life as compared to traditional methods. In that context, traditional systems are considerably more "vague" when describing that inner terrain of psychological experience.

Chapter 27

1. Cited by astrologer Wade Caves, in personal communication with the author via social media.

Chapter 28

1. I've transcribed this comment from an online interview with Rob Hand's several years ago.
2. http://www.leelehman.com/pages/images/Dignity.pdf
3. https://rubedo.press/propaganda/2018/12/21/first-five-steps
4. For a more detailed explanation of Shelly Trimmer's philosophy of the chakras and astrology, see my book *An Infinity of Gods* (Inner Eye Press, 2019), specifically the chapter titled "The Three Channels."
5. As yet another simple example of the tight connection between zodiacal signs and the outer planets associated by modern astrologers with them, I've sometimes posed questions like these: (1) In terms of bodily symbolism, what zodiacal sign do you give rulership over the feet? Likewise, which planet do you believe governs the feet? (2) What zodiacal sign do you most associate with qualities of compassion for the underprivileged and society's outcasts? In turn, which planet do you associate with these same matters? (3) Which zodiacal sign do you most associate with factors of illusion or even deception? In turn, which planet do you most associate with illusion or deception? My point here is that the overwhelming majority of astrologers will, for each of these questions, answer with the zodiacal sign Pisces and the planet Neptune—rather than the more traditional planetary ruler, Jupiter. And if there is indeed such a close affinity between this sign and that planet, how could that not translate into practical, tangible resonances between those in real-world horoscopic interpretations?

Chapter 29

1. See chapter 1 of *Signs of the Times: Unlocking the Symbolic Language of World Events.*
2. My thanks to Laurence Hillman for suggesting this take on the film's story.
3. It may be that Melville's story was prophetic in another, even more far-reaching way. I recently came across a book titled *End of the Line* by Charles Clover, about the threat to our oceans and

food supply due to commercial overfishing. If things continue in the direction they've been heading, Clover argues, we're in serious danger of decimating our planet's marine life and upsetting nature's delicate ecological balance. That got me thinking. I've heard some astrologers suggest over the years that one telling indicator of the transition from the Piscean to the Aquarian Age will be humanity's wholesale shift away from its reliance on oil (Neptune). But after reading Clover's book, it struck me that an even more concerning symbol of the passing Piscean Age could well be the virtual death of the world's oceans (also Neptune). In light of that possibility, Melville's story of Ahab's attempts to kill the great White Whale could be a sobering omen for the coming Great Age in more ecological ways. (Note, too: in Melville's story, Ahab himself was the one who ultimately wound up being destroyed—not the whale or nature!)

4. Maria's story of leaving the Church behind is just one of two interlocking themes in *The Sound of Music* which illustrate the tug of war between the Piscean and Aquarian worldviews. In the movie, the von Trapp family finds itself increasingly pressured by the encroaching Nazi regime, and desperately struggles to break free from its oppressive influence. The Nazi Party was actually a *transitional symbol* or *hybrid* of two different Ages: at its core, it embodied the most intolerant and dogmatic instincts of the Piscean Age (remember, not only was Christianity the state religion of Nazi Germany but its chief icon was a twisted cross— clearly a climactic perversion of primal Piscean iconography), but its surface trappings were those of the emerging Aquarian era, including such factors as high technology, the power of mass media, and progressive attitudes towards health care (Nazi ideology warned of the dangers of tobacco, asbestos, and others toxins long before most other countries). By contrast, the von Trapp family represented the urge toward creative freedom, an impulse more purely aligned with the incoming Aquarius/Leo

axis. The Nazi party's efforts to squelch that freedom symbolized a desperate final push by members of the receding paradigm to subvert the potentials of the emerging new one. The movie's happy ending, with the family's escape out of Nazi-controlled territory, speaks to the hope of a final release from the suffocating grip of that bankrupt earlier worldview.

Chapter 30
1. *Lost Star of Myth and Time,* by Walter Cruttenden, St. Lynns Press, 2005.

Chapter 31
1. https://www.nytimes.com/2020/05/09/style/coronavirus-astrology-predictions.html
2. https://mountainastrologer.com/tma/donald-trump-and-the-saturn-pluto-conjunction/
3. Richard Tarnas, *Cosmos and Psyche: Intimations of a New World View.* Viking Books, 2006, p. 217.
4. http://www.andrebarbault.com/DOC/503.pdf
5. http://astrologynewsservice.com/news/astrologer-predicted-global-pandemic/
6. https://mountainastrologer.com/tma/reflections-on-coronavirus-and-the-saturn-pluto-conjunction/):

Chapter 32
1. Daniel Keyes, *The Minds of Billy Milligan,* New York: Bantam, 1981.
2. R. P. Kluft, "Treatment of Multiple Personality." Psychiatric Clinics of North America 7:9-29, 1984.
3. "Multiplicity and the Mind-Body Problem." *Investigations: Institute of Noetic Sciences Research Bulletin,* p. 19.
4. *Ibid.,* p. 20.
5. W. Brugh Joy, *Avalanche.* New York: Ballantine, 1990, pp. 61-62.

6. James Hillman, *ReVisioning Psychology*. New York: Harper and Row, 1977.
7. Ian Stevenson, *Xenoglossy: A Review and Report of a Case*. Charlottesville: University Press of Virginia, 1974.
8. Arthur Hastings, *With the Tongues of Men and Angels*. Fort Worth: Holt Rinehart and Winston, 1991, p. 163.
9. W. Brugh Joy, *Ibid.*, pp. 79-80.
10. "Multiplicity and the Mind-Body Problem," *Ibid.*, p. 5.

Chapter 33

1. My thanks to E. Alan Meece for first noting the Uranian connection between the first lunar landing in 1969 and Lindbergh's flight across the Atlantic in 1927.
2. The full written transcript of Armstrong's talk is available here: https://www.hq.nasa.gov/alsj/a11/A11CongressJOD.html

Chapter 35

1. My thanks for Lori Hoyt for her feedback on this essay.

Chapter 36

1. *Cosmic Influences on Human Behavior,* by Michel Gauquelin, ASI Press, 1978. See also http://www.astrology-and-science.com/g-hist2.htm
2. The quantum physical principle known as "entanglement" is based on something commonly referred to as *non-locality*. Simply put, this theory suggests that our conventional (or "local") notions of space and distance are actually illusions and everything is really connected at a deeper level beyond visible appearances. Manipulate a sub-atomic particle over on this side of the universe and it somehow seems to affect the behavior of a particular far away, instantaneously, in seeming defiance of the speed of light. Some have suggested this principle might help us understand the workings of astrology, because

of that element of "spooky action at a distance" and interconnectedness that it implies. If two particles widely separated in space can be instantaneously be connected, then perhaps this might also help explain astrology, and how humans might be connected to distant planets and stars—right? Well, not really. While that concept does illustrate one relatively small facet of astrology—namely, how distant phenomena can be connected to one another in non-causal ways—it does nothing at all to explain the more mysterious types of connections implied by astrology, specifically with the theory of correspondences. Correspondence theory takes that sense of connectedness one step further by incorporating tendrils of *meaning* which extend in many different directions—such as when someone born with Venus in Capricorn is drawn toward getting married specifically on *mountains,* or cause their twin brother to become involved with architecture, or compel another client to become involved with raising goats. These are relationships of a very different sort than those which simply involve particles instantaneously connected through space.

3. A fractal is any geometric form which involves patterns of self-similarity across different scales, similar to the way the fringes of snowflakes mirror the overall shapes of those snowflakes. It's definitely true that fractals do mirror certain aspects of traditional correspondence theory, as expressed by the Hermetic axiom "As above, so below" (something I pointed out in *The Waking Dream*), while also resonating well with certain other facets of astrology (e.g., the day-for-a-year method of progressions mentioned earlier, in which a movement of a planet several days past birth mirrors the influence of that planet an equal number of years moving forward into their life). Indeed, the *horoscope itself* seems to be "fractal-like" in the way a person's life reflects the patterns of the entire cosmos but in miniature. But here as well, there are dimensions of meaning involved which

would completely elude any purely materialistic understanding of fractals. Just try explaining to a skeptically-minded scientist how fractalized principles like these somehow translate into a person's real-world experiences. For instance, suppose that 30 days after that scientist was born, his/her progressed Venus moved forward to conjunct their natal 7th house cusp, and that's exactly when they got married. Astrologically, that's straightforward, and definitely fractal-like. But the scientist would be baffled as to what mechanism could possibly link those mathematical measurements specifically with *someone getting married*! Here as well, the strictly scientific approach can't explain the symbolic manifestations which arise out of those abstract principles and processes.

4. Skeptics often claim that the zodiac's twelve-fold structure is largely arbitrary and not inherent in the world itself. (After all, why not divvy the sky up into eight zodiacal signs? Or fourteen?) Astrologer Russell Ohlhausen argues there is indeed a good reason for this twelve-fold patterning based on something known as the Fibonacci number sequence. (See https://cosmicintelligenceagency.com/fibonaccizodiac/) It's a brilliant conception, although here as well, one would be hard-pressed to explain why or how that numerical basis specifically translates into the myriad experiences and tangible symbols of actual human life. For example, even if you could show that the zodiacal sign Gemini likely arises out of a specific numerical pattern or sequencing, how would that explain why the Geminian segment of the zodiac should relate specifically to matters like communication and thinking, and not to such concerns as home, mother, and nurturing (experiences normally associated with Cancer)? In short, even this theory of Ohlhausen's requires a symbolic component above and beyond pure mathematics and geometry to explain its real-world manifestations, which is a component science is unable to fully account for.

5. See *www.astrosoftware.com/goldpriceforecast.htm;* also *http://astrologynewsservice.com/news/astrological-study-on-gold-prices-hits-the-mother-load/*

6. For more information about cutting-edge research into the application of scientific methods to astrology, see the work of David Cochrane, whose videos on YouTube are an invaluable resource for astrologers at every level of expertise: www.youtube.com/channel/UCD0hTApPdhw4ImbIGxzyO7g).

7. For a discussion of the deeper role of symbolism, metaphor, and sacred geometry in astrology, see also my essay *The Songs of Dismembered Gods: Exploring the Archetypal Roots of Astrology,* adapted from chapter 11 of my book *The Waking Dream* for The Mountain Astrologer (February, 2011), and featured online on the Astrodienst site here: https://www.astro.com/astrology/tma_article181029_e.htm

ABOUT THE AUTHOR

Ray Grasse is an internationally-recognized astrologer and writer, and author of several books including *Under a Sacred Sky, An Infinity of Gods, Urban Mystic,* and *Signs of the Times.* His first book, *The Waking Dream,* was called "a masterpiece" by Colin Wilson. He worked on the editorial staffs of Quest Books and The Quest Magazine for 10 years, and has been associate editor of The Mountain Astrologer magazine for 20 years. He received a degree in filmmaking from the Art Institute of Chicago under Stan Brakhage, and studied extensively under teachers in both the Kriya Yoga and Zen traditions. He currently lives in the American Midwest. Hs websites are www.raygrasse.com and www.raygrassephotography.com

Printed in Great Britain
by Amazon